RESEARCH HIGHLIGHTS IN SOCIAL WORK 38

Transition and Change in the Lives
of People with Intellectual Disabilities

Research Highlights in Social Work series

This topical series examines areas of particular interest to those in social and community work and related fields. Each book draws together different aspects of the subject, highlighting relevant research and drawing out implications for policy and practice. The project is under the general direction of Professor Joyce Lishman, Head of the School of Applied Social Studies at the Robert Gordon University.

Also in the series

Growing Up with Disability
Edited by Carol Robinson and Kirsten Stalker
ISBN 1 85302 568 2
Research Highlights in Social Work 34

Social Work
Disabled People and Disabling Environments
Edited by Michael Oliver
ISBN 1 85302 178 4
Research Highlights in Social Work 21

Social Care and Housing
Edited by Ian Shaw, Susan Thomas and David Clapham
ISBN 1 85302 437 6
Research Highlights in Social Work 32

Effective Ways of Working with Children and their Families
Edited by Malcolm Hill
ISBN 1 85302 619 0
Research Highlights in Social Work 35

The Changing Role of Social Care
Edited by Bob Hudson
ISBN 1 85302 752 9 pb
Research Highlights in Social Work 37

Adult Day Services and Social Inclusion
Better Days
Edited by Chris Clark
ISBN 1 85302 887 8
Research Highlights in Social Work 39

Dementia
Challenges and New Directions
Edited by Susan Hunter
ISBN 1 85302 312 4
Research Highlights in Social Work 31

Mental Health and Social Work
Edited by Marion Ulas and Anne Connor
ISBN 1 85302 302 7
Research Highlights in Social Work 28

RESEARCH HIGHLIGHTS IN SOCIAL WORK 38

Transition and Change in the Lives of People with Intellectual Disabilities

Edited by David May

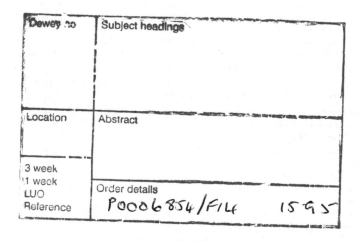

Dewey no	Subject headings	
Location	Abstract	
3 week 1 week LUO Reference	Order details P0006854/FILE	1595

Jessica Kingsley Publishers
London and Philadelphia

Research Highlights in Social Work 38

First published in the United Kingdom in 2000 by
Jessica Kingsley Publishers Ltd
116 Pentonville Road
London N1 9JB, England
and
325 Chestnut Street
Philadelphia, PA 19106, USA
www.jkp.com
Copyright © 2001 Robert Gordon University, Research Highlights Advisory Group,
School of Applied Social Studies

Library of Congress Cataloging in Publication Data
A CIP catalog record for this book is available from the Library of Congress

British Library Cataloguing in Publication Data
A CIP catalogue record for this book is available from the British Library

ISBN 1 85302 863 0

Printed and Bound in Great Britain by
Athenaeum Press, Gateshead, Tyne and Wear

Contents

CHAPTER I

Editorial

David May

In what was the first systematic statement of the principle of normalization, the essential elements of a 'normal life' for people with intellectual disabilities were outlined. They included:

> The opportunity to undergo the normal developmental experiences of the life cycle: infanthood, with security and the respective steps of early childhood development; school age, with exploration and the increase of skills and experience; adolescence, with development towards adult life and options. As it is normal for a child to live at home, it is normal for adults to move away from home and establish independence and new relationships. Like everybody else, retarded people [sic] should experience the coming of adulthood and maturity through marked changes in the settings and circumstances of their lives. (Nirje 1980, p.33)

When first written, in 1969, this must have struck many as an impossible – even absurd – ambition (although such ideas had been informing Scandinavian policy on intellectual disability for the best part of a decade). People with intellectual disabilities – 'the mentally retarded' – were viewed as one-dimensional people, in some way not fully human, whose identity and being were subsumed within their disability. Their fate then was either to remain at home, to live out often significantly foreshortened lives as 'eternal children' under the care and tutelage of parents, or to be confined to institutions where unvarying routine, denial of individuality and separation from the wider world afforded only the most attenuated existence. Either way they were generally excluded from those experiences which for most of us define our lives – starting school, getting a job, leaving home, marrying, having children, retiring from work, and all the other less momentous but necessary stages in between. This was not out of any malign intent, but simply because such a prospect was literally unthinkable, inconsistent with their 'unfortunate' status.

Times have changed. In 1988 I edited, along with the late Gordon Horobin, an earlier volume (16) in the Research Highlights series entitled *Living with Mental Handicap: Transitions in the Lives of People with Mental Handicaps.* The book, as its subtitle suggests, was loosely organized around the concept of the life stage. The purpose was to call attention to the parallels between our own lives and those of people with intellectual disabilities, to consider shared concerns and experiences, but also what still remained to be done in order to make Nirje's vision a reality. Increased life expectancy, which meant that many more people – even those with severe disabilities – were surviving well into adulthood, suggested that this was not only an appropriate but perhaps necessary way to examine the growing complexity of their lives; but even then it was hardly a novel idea. Ten years earlier the Jay committee, insisting on the right of people with intellectual disabilities to 'as normal a lifestyle as possible', had recognized that needs would inevitably change over the life course and that services must reflect and respond to those changes (Jay 1979). At much the same time the King's Fund (1980) produced its An Ordinary Life programme for developing community-based services and integrating people with intellectual disabilities into the mainstream of society. The language of normalization now dominated the discourse of policy makers and service providers and we were learning to think about people with intellectual disabilities in ways that emphasized their common humanity rather than their differences.

Murray Simpson (Chapter 6), however, plausibly argues that for all its influence on the thinking of campaigners for better services, normalization would have had little practical effect in the absence of a policy of community care: 'an ordinary life' is incompatible with an organization of care that has the long-term hospital at its heart. Almost two decades before our book appeared and some years before the ideas of normalization had begun to spread across the Atlantic, the UK government, in common with governments throughout the western world, had formally committed itself to specific targets for the reduction of the long-stay hospital population and the development of alternative residential and day services.

Even in terms of the limited objectives it set for shifting the balance of care from institutions to the community, progress was disappointingly slow. Any resultant success was achieved largely by restricting admissions rather than (until latterly, at least) through any systematic attempt to return existing hospital residents to the community, where facilities for their reception were, in any event, undeveloped and incoherent. Certainly many examples of good practice could be found that pointed the way forward (Cambridge *et al.* 1994), but the pace of change across the UK was at best uneven. To take Scotland, for example, which admittedly had always shown a greater fondness for institutional solutions than other parts of the UK (Hunter and Wistow 1987), a survey carried out in the mid-1980s found that three-quarters of all adults with intellectual disabilities living outside of the family home, including one-half of the 'most able' group, and almost all those who were 'exceedingly physically dependent', non-mobile, doubly incontinent or presented with challenging behaviour, were still in long-stay hospital (Baker and Urquhart 1987). While community residential provision more than doubled in that decade, by the end it still provided little more than one-third of all residential places. Not until 1995 did the number of community places first exceed those in the hospital sector. Moreover, a policy that was defined in terms of the location of care rather than quality of life and whose success was measured in bed numbers, did not necessarily bring any great change to the daily lives or public image of people with intellectual disabilities: all too often institutional forms, and the segregation from the wider society that accompanied them, were simply transferred to the community. Sir Roy Griffiths's conclusion on more than 30 years of debate and activity was that 'in few areas can the gap between political rhetoric and policy on the one hand or between policy and reality in the field on the other hand have been so great' (Griffiths 1988, para.1–9).

This then was the situation at the time that *Living with Mental Handicap* (Horobin and May 1988) appeared. The publication in that same year of the Griffiths report (Griffiths 1988) – 'the most significant statement about community care since the Seebohm report on the future of personal social services in 1968' (Hunter and Judge 1988) – followed a year later by the government's response, *Caring for People* (HMSO 1989) and legislation in the form of the NHS and Community Care Act 1990, marked a turning point in the evolution of community care policy and official attitudes to the place of people with intellectual disabilities in society. The equivocation that had surrounded the role of the institution appeared to have been resolved and community care was unambiguously defined in terms of 'a normal life'. The key question was no longer: '*Should* people with learning difficulties be included in our communities?', nor '*Can* they be?', but '*How* is it best achieved?' (Thomas 1990, p.131). The government's answer – a government, one hardly needs reminding, which was intent upon reducing public expenditure, rolling back the state and promoting private enterprise – was to propose 'a mixed economy' of care offering 'choice, flexibility, innovation and competition'. The language of consumerism was invoked in a way that seemed to promise a shift in the balance of power away from professionally dominated and inherently conservative bureaucracies towards service users. While much of this may be dismissed as self-serving rhetoric, the extent to which it represented a break with the past should not be underestimated.

When, therefore, the editorial board of Research Highlights first raised the possibility of reissuing *Living with Mental Handicap* in some form, it was clear that a simple second edition would not do; too much had happened in the meantime – to the kinds of lives which people with intellectual disabilities were now experiencing, as well as the social and political context in which they were living out those lives – for minor revisions to the text to suffice. All the chapters presented here are new and only two of the contributors to the earlier volume remain. Chapters on adolescence, adulthood, marriage and parenting are included, in addition to chapters that take a fresh look at topics previously explored – the early years, schooling and school leaving and old age. This more articulated version of the life course that appears in *Transition and Change* is a measure of the distance that people with intellectual disabilities have travelled in the last 13 years towards the realization of 'a normal life', as well as reflecting the not inconsiderable increase in research activity on matters pertaining to ageing and the life course in that same period.

But we should beware of becoming too self-congratulatory. For all the obvious progress of the last decade or so, compared with the wider population the lives of people with intellectual disabilities remain for the most part circumscribed and impoverished. They continue to be denied roles and to be excluded from areas of life to which most of us expect access as of right: marriage and parenting are the obvious examples (although changes are afoot here, see May and Simpson, Chapter 7), as well as employment. For many young people with intellectual disabilities adolescence is more of an end state than a period of transition (see Shepperdson, Chapter 4), and certainly their prospects on leaving school appear quite different from their non-disabled peers (see May, Chapter 5). Other life stages are experienced in such qualitatively different ways that when they are applied to people with intellectual disabilities it seems an almost metaphorical use. Exactly what do we mean when we talk of someone who may never have had a single day's paid employment in his or her adult life as having 'retired'?

Intellectual disability is not, however, a homogeneous category. As Walsh reminds us in Chapter 8, the experience of it is mediated through other equally powerful social variables, such as class and ethnicity, as well as age and gender, and perhaps most powerfully of all, disability (its nature and severity); a point which largely for reasons of space we are perhaps guilty of not sufficiently attending to. Much of the progress of recent years – in terms of access to further education, independent living, supported employment, the right to marry and have children – has been confined to the more able part of the population, those whose intellectual disability is at the very least contestable. In the study of a cohort of people with intellectual disabilities at middle age, all of whom had entered adult services on leaving school in the late 1960s, more than one in three of those with IQs of less than 50 were, almost 30 years later, still living at home and attending day centres and a further quarter were in long-stay hospital (May and Hogg 2000). What characterizes their lives is not so much change as its absence.

Intellectual disability, of course, presses not only on those with it, but also on their families and carers. Their concerns and the demands on them also change as, with their disabled offspring, they progress through the life course. We include three chapters that focus on family carers. Robinson (Chapter 2) deals with the early, pre-school years. Here the comparison with Seed's chapter in the earlier volume suggests that the situation is improving, if perhaps too slowly. Sometimes it may seem as if families are in danger of being overwhelmed by too much advice and offers of help. As Robinson points out, a more coherent child-centred policy for disabled children might make more effective use of the help that is available. Some things, however, never seem to change. Given the regular airing of the problem over the years and the fact that we know how matters should be handled, it is particularly disappointing to learn that when informing parents of their child's disabilities, doctors are still too often getting it wrong.

In Chapter 4 on adolescence, Shepperdson draws attention to the critical role of parents in assisting or, more often, impeding the transition to adulthood. Drawing on her own work in South Wales, she describes how parents of disabled children, in their natural concern to protect the child from harm or hurt, exercise a degree of surveillance and control that keeps them apart from their peers and confines many of them to a state of protracted adolescence. She also notes – and it is a point taken up by Grant in Chapter 10 on older carers – that the restrictions imposed by caring often weigh more heavily on parents as both they and their intellectually disabled son or daughter grow older. This is not because their situation had changed in any material respect, but rather because this – what Grant refers to as 'perpetual parenting' – was not what they had bargained for. Yet, as Grant is also at pains to point out, caring brings its own rewards and quiet satisfactions – feelings of responsibilities discharged and a job well done.

Many social workers (and others), imbued with the enthusiasm of recent converts, have too often been inclined to regard families as the enemies of change rather than as potential partners in the process. Certainly, it must seem puzzling, and not a little frustrating, to find families leading the opposition to the closure of a long-stay hospital or protesting against plans to restructure an adult training centre. Yet viewed from the perspective of hard-pressed parents, the promotion of independence and 'an ordinary life' can in practice look very much like a denial of their own experience and a threat to hardwon services. For older carers, especially, whose memories of public indifference and neglect remain undimmed, such moves, however much couched in fashionable rhetoric, are likely to be viewed with suspicion. The failure to address their concerns or even on occasion to consult them at all is, as Brown, Orlowska and Mansell (1996) argue, located in the ambiguity that surrounds the identity of the social worker's client; an ambiguity that ironically arises in part from a greater readiness to accept the person with disabilities as a person in his/her own right.

It is tempting to believe that the way ahead is now clear; that we have turned away from the errors of the past; that the correct policies are in place and all we now need, some fine tuning apart, is the political will (and of course the necessary resources). Such complacency should be resisted. The past, particularly in relation to intellectual disability, is littered with such illusions. As the drive towards community care was being renewed in the 1990s, questions were even then being raised about the direction in which this was taking us; not so much the goal of an inclusive society in which people with intellectual disabilities would participate as active citizens, with all the rights and responsibilities that that entails, but rather just what in practice that might mean and how it was to be achieved. Integration is not inclusion, and dispersal to the community does not necessarily put an end to segregation and isolation, or enhance quality of life. On the contrary, it can inhibit the development of a collective identity and encourage self-blame: 'If services are individualised, problems are personalised. If vulnerable people are dispersed from one another neither they, nor people working on their behalf, are able to see common threads or patterns' (Brown and Smith 1992a, p.153). Normalization (or at least certain versions of it), which for the last quarter century has provided the radicalizing force driving service reform and a set of organizing principles around which all could unite, is now itself attracting criticism for its conformist tendencies, cultural conservatism, moral authoritarianism and failure to address the needs of carers or acknowledge the realities of power in an inherently unequal world (Brown and Smith 1992b). Empowerment and self-determination are the new watchwords (Ramcharan *et al.* 1997) and we are urged to move away from what Thomson (Chapter 3) calls a 'deficit model of adjustment' that locates the problem in individual shortcomings in favour of an approach which requires that we (society) change to accommodate a range of disabilities in acknowledgement of the fact that there are many varieties of a 'normal' life, all equally valid.

Acknowledgements

Once again I wish to record here my thanks to the Editorial Board of Research Highlights, and especially its chair, Joyce Lishman, and her deputy, Alex Robertson, for advice and support throughout which was much appreciated (as well as much needed), and to Anne Forbes, who prepared the material for publication with her usual skill, efficiency and patience.

References

Baker, N. and Urquhart, J. (1987) *The Balance of Care for Adults with a Mental Handicap in Scotland.* Edinburgh: ISD Publications.

Brown, H. and Smith, H. (1992a) 'Assertion, not assimilation: A feminist perspective on the normalisation principle.' In H. Brown and H. Smith (eds) *Normalisation: A Reader for the Nineties.* London: Routledge, pp.149–171.

Brown, H. and Smith, H. (eds) (1992b) *Normalisation: A Reader for the Nineties.* London: Routledge.

Brown, H., Orlowska, D. and Mansell, J. (1996) 'From complaining to campaigning.' In J. Mansell and K. Ericcson (eds) *Deinstitutionalization and Community Living: Intellectual Disability Services in Britain, Scandanavia and the USA.* London: Chapman & Hall.

Cambridge, P., Hayes, L. and Knapp, M. (1994) *Care in the Community: Five Years On.* Aldershot: Ashgate.

Griffiths, R. (1988) *Community Care: Agenda for Action.* London: HMSO.

HMSO (1989) *Caring for People: Community Care in the Next Decade and Beyond.* Cm 849. London: HMSO.

Horobin, G. and May, D. (eds) (1988) *Living with Mental Handicap: Transitions in the Lives of People with Mental Handicap.* London: Jessica Kingsley Publishers.

Hunter, D.J. and Judge, K. (1988) *Griffiths and Community Care: Meeting the Challenge.* London: King's Fund.

Hunter, D.J. and Wistow, G. (1987) *Community Care in Britain: Variations on a Theme.* London: King's Fund.

Jay, P. (1979) *Report of the Committee of Enquiry into Mental Handicap Nursing and Care.* Cm 7468. London: HMSO.

King's Fund (1980) *An Ordinary Life: Comprehensive Locally-Based Residential Services for Mentally Handicapped People.* London: King's Fund Centre.

May, D. and Hogg, J. (2000). 'Continuity and change in the use of residential services by adults with intellectual disability: The Aberdeen Cohort at mid-life.' *Journal of Intellectual Disability Research 44,* 1, 68–80.

Nirje, B. (1980) 'The normalization principle.' In R.J. Flynn and K.E. Nitsch (eds) *Normalization, Social Integration, and Community Services.* Baltimore: University Park Press, pp.31–49.

Ramcharan, P., Roberts, G., Grant, G. and Borland, J. (eds) (1997) *Empowerment in Everyday Life: Learning Disabilities.* London: Jessica Kingsley Publishers.

Thomas, D. (1990) 'Concluding comments.' In T. Booth *Better Lives: Changing Services for People with Learning Difficulties.* Sheffield: Joint Unit for Social Services Research, pp.131–133.

CHAPTER 2

Transition and Change in the Lives of Families with a Young Disabled Child

The Early Years

Carol Robinson

The last 25 years have seen significant changes in the lives of disabled children and their families. Perhaps the single most important change has been de-institutionalization. No longer are severely disabled children sent off to long-stay hospitals, and today 98 per cent of disabled children are estimated to be living at home in the community. The OPCS (Office of Population Censuses and Surveys) has estimated that within the UK there are 360,000 disabled children under the age of 16 years (Meltzer, Smyth and Robus 1989). However, the definition of *disabled children* used in the OPCS surveys was broad and encompassed a wide range of childhood impairments. It includes children with mild physical or sensory impairments as well as those with severe intellectual disabilities or multiple impairment. As a result of better neo-natal and paediatric care, the number of children with more complex and severe impairments has increased in both the UK and the USA (Alberman, Nicholson and Wald 1992; Glendinning *et al* 1999; Hochstadt and Yost 1991).

This chapter reviews the research dealing with families who are raising a disabled child and seeks to spell out its implications for practitioners. The focus is on the early years of childhood – up to age 5. In this period there are three major adjustments required of parents: first, to the knowledge of their child's disability; second, like any parents, to the changes in lifestyle that the new arrival inevitably brings; third, to the challenges that arise when the child moves on from the security of the home to the less protective environment of the school. These all make heavy demands on parents. They may create tensions and cause distress. As such they deserve particular attention from social workers and others working with families with a disabled child. These adjustments, along with other issues faced by such families, are here dealt with chronologically. The chapter is divided into the following subsections:

- Finding out about the child's impairment.
- Adjusting to a new way of life.
- Early intervention and support.
- Playgroups and nurseries.
- Statements of educational need.
- Taking a break.

Under each of these headings, the existing legal framework will be discussed in the context of any proposed changes to the current organization of services. In addition, any specific issues that affect families from minority ethnic groups, children with complex health needs or challenging behaviours will be highlighted.

Finding out about the child's impairment and the process of disclosure

Unless parents are told soon after the birth that their child has an impairment, they may well suspect that there is something unusual about their child's development (Cunningham and Sloper 1977). A number of studies have indicated that parents often feel they were not taken seriously when they first voiced their concerns (Hall 1997; Quine and Pahl 1986; McKay and Hensey 1990). But even where parents learn of their child's disability from a doctor, the research evidence is that in many cases this is not well handled (Cunningham, Morgan and McCuken 1984; Spastics Society 1992, 1994; Wikler, Wasow and Hatfield 1981).

Cunningham (1994) analysed over 30 studies in which dissatisfaction was expressed by parents about the way information was disclosed to them at the point of diagnosis. He argues that these dissatisfactions fall into three broad categories:

- *The manner in which the information was conveyed:* the person was too cold, unsympathetic or insensitive.

- *Problems with the information:* including a general lack of information or guidance and the giving of a negative, inaccurate, misleading or contradictory account.

- *Organizational aspects:* such as delays, difficulty obtaining help, poor co-ordination and a lack of privacy and time.

Obtaining information and support from professionals at this critical time can be even more problematic for families who do not use English as their first language (Shah 1997). For some families who experience difficulty understanding verbal information, translated written material could be extremely helpful, but is generally in short supply. Baxter *et al.* (1990) also point to the shortage of appropriate counselling for minority ethnic groups. It is still rare for resources to be allocated so that families can receive counselling and support from someone who has knowledge, skills and the same ethnic background. To date, insufficient attention has been paid to this issue by both researchers and practitioners.

Spain and Wigley (1975) and Jacobs (1977) found that there was widespread reluctance among doctors to admit that they might not have handled well the task of telling parents about their child's diagnosis. Many believed that there was no good way to tell bad news and attributed any criticisms made by parents to resentment about the diagnosis. Cunningham *et al.* (1984) have dispelled this notion through a small controlled experiment in which parents heard the diagnosis in an 'ideal' manner from a consultant paediatrician and a specialist health visitor. All those receiving this 'ideal' service were satisfied with the way in which they had been told, whereas only 25 per cent of the control group expressed satisfaction. A number of other relevant research studies (Cunningham and Davies 1985; Cunningham and Sloper 1977; Sloper and

Turner 1993) indicate that a set of guidelines for good practice can be achieved. These all rest on the principle that the parents and child should be respected and briefly, are as follows:

- Parents should be told as soon as possible when impairment is suspected or diagnosed (Nursey, Rhode and Farmer 1991).

- Parents should have with them someone they trust.

- They should be told in private.

- The baby or child should be present.

- They should be given sufficient time.

- There should be two professionals involved, one of whom will have some continuing involvement with the family.

- A second interview should be held within 48 hours so that parents can ask follow-up questions.

- Accessible written information should be given.

- Parents should be given privacy immediately after each meeting.

- Parents should be given accurate information about the diagnosis and the possible implications for their child's progress.

- Clear information should be provided about what assistance can be given to both child and family.

- Parents should be given the opportunity to meet another family that has a child with a similar condition.

- It is helpful to offer to tell other family members the diagnosis and to meet them to answer any questions.

- Convey to parents that their feelings, while unique to them, are natural and commonly experienced.

If good practice such as this is to become routine in hospitals, then the issue of disclosure must itself be given greater priority. Resources, in particular, need to be committed to ensure that all relevant staff are sensitive to the issue and trained in the practices. Moreover, for good practice to be maintained it must be monitored and reviewed. This is only likely to be achieved if someone is given specific responsibility for this aspect of practice. Several attempts have been made to improve practice around disclosure including the development of packs, videos (King's Fund 1987) and specific initiatives such as Scope's 1994 'Right from the Start' campaign. However, change appears to be slow (Cunningham 1994).

Adjusting to a new way of life

The arrival of a newborn child means that life for the couple 'is never the same again'. All babies need high levels of care and the dynamic of the partnership is inevitably altered by the presence of a highly dependent third person. However, the specific needs which many disabled children have may mean that once the child is discharged from hospital life becomes exceptionally demanding. Beresford (1995), Glendinning *et al.* (1999) and Robinson and Jackson (1999) have identified a long list of additional tasks that parents of severely disabled children face simply in order to keep their children alive. These included the administration of medication, tube feeding, suction and physiotherapy on a daily basis. The likelihood of such medical interventions being needed was greater among children under than over 2 years of age, although approximately 2 per cent were found to be dependent on at least one piece of medical equipment beyond this age (Beresford 1995). The constant round of physical care tasks and the stress associated with some of the unfamiliar and more technical aspects of these children's care is liable to put a strain on family life. Siblings may also receive less attention than the disabled child, or take on the role of caregivers (Townsley and Robinson 2000).

Disabled children are more likely to experience social, communication and behavioural difficulties than other children (Pahl and Quine 1984). Difficulties associated with communication are likely to be frustrating for the child and parent alike and may be associated with such behaviours as aggression, absconding or self-harm (Clarke-Kehoe and Harris 1992). Although these problems tend to increase in terms of frequency and intensity as children become older (Harris 1993), they may manifest themselves in the early years and will need careful management if the difficulties are to be kept in check. Whether parents have positive strategies to deal with such behaviours or not, they will inevitably find that they need to be even more vigilant than they would be for any young child (Snook and Nally 1996).

There is also ample evidence of the additional costs associated with rearing a disabled child (Baldwin 1985; Buckle 1984; Kagan, Lewis and Heaton 1998). At the same time, the earnings potential of families with disabled children is likely to be curtailed because the demands of caring reduce the options for paid work outside the home (NCH 1993; Thomas *et al.* 1994). In addition, we now know that, contrary to the earlier contention that disability affects all sections of society in equal measure, disabled children are more often found in larger and poorer families (Gordon, Parker and Loughran 1996).

The presence of a disabled child has also been linked to higher rates of breakdown in parental partnerships and a higher incidence of single parent-hood (Baldwin and Carlisle 1994; Lawton 1998). Moreover, the evidence suggests that the risk of breakdown increases with the severity of the child's impairment (Baldwin and Carlisle 1994) and the presence of a second disabled child (Lawton 1998). Beresford (1995), for example, found that over a quarter of her large sample of families caring for a severely disabled child were headed by lone parents.

Recent research has also identified a link between family size and the presence of disabled children. Robinson (1999) in two separate studies analys-ing the family composition of severely disabled children with complex health needs, found that over half the children in each study came from families with three or more dependent children. This was higher than in the population in general where only 31 per cent of families have three or more dependent children (Office of National Statistics 1999). Lawton (1998) also found a strong linear relationship between the number of children in a family and the presence of more than one disabled child. Given the economic disadvantages already presented, it is easy to see that children with the greatest need for undi-vided parental time and additional resources are least likely to receive them.

At the same time as parents are adjusting to their disabled child, they are also likely to be adjusting to the attentions of professionals from a variety of agencies. While there is evidence that families appreciate support and practical help, many families find it stressful relating to a range of people from several different agencies (Beresford 1994; McConnachie 1997). Moreover, families may receive conflicting advice if several professionals are involved (Townsley and Robinson 2000). Research has consistently supported the idea of a keyworker to provide a single point of contact and to co-ordinate the activities of the multiplicity of professionals who are often involved (Beresford 1995; Glendinning 1986). However, such schemes are rarely implemented. Further research is being conducted to establish how such a service can best be organized (Mukherjee *et al.* forthcoming).

There are problems associated with interagency working at all levels (Audit Commission 1994; Baxter *et al.* 1990; Sloper and Turner 1992; Townsley and Robinson 2000). A lack of co-ordinated planning and service development leaves many families poorly supported. Children with complex health needs or challenging behaviours, while more likely to be in contact with health professionals than other disabled children, are rarely well served by existing provision. This is partly because there have been shifts in definitions of what constitutes health and social care, with tasks previously considered to be definitely within the health domain now being considered as social care. The argument goes something along these lines: 'if parents can do it, then so can non-parent carers who do not have medical or nursing qualifications'. Unfortunately, such liberal approaches to health care delivery have been introduced of necessity, but at a time when there is greater awareness of the insurance and liability issues which face people working in social care settings. Indeed, some local authorities have produced policies that restrict the involvement of their staff and, sometimes, foster carers in anything that is defined as nursing care. The effect of such policies can be disastrous since they may leave some children without any service, either because health agencies do not provide one or because children are placed in unsuitable settings (Robinson and Jackson 1999; Townsley and Robinson 2000).

The government has recognized the need to develop strategies to encourage more effective interagency working and in August 1998 produced a discussion paper entitled *Partnership in Action*. In this document there are three key proposals that have the potential to improve service delivery to disabled children who need support from a variety of agencies. These can be summarized as follows:

- Pooled budgets between health and social services.

- Lead commissioners from one authority who could transfer funds and delegate functions to the other to take responsibility for commissioning both health and social care.

- Integrated provision that would allow NHS trust providers to provide social care services and social services departments to provide a limited range of community health care services.

Subsequently, the White Paper *Modernising Social Services* (DoH 1998) sought to overcome some of the problems related to the delivery of services to children in need, including disabled children. Problems identified in the document included poor assessment practices, poor quality provision, inconsistent and inappropriate care and inadequate safeguards. The particular difficulties that families with disabled children often experience in obtaining a service were also noted. The White Paper proposed that services should take a holistic view of children's needs and stressed the need to plan in this way at a strategic level by making planning a council-wide function so that education and social services departments work together. In addition, the reforms were intended to emphasize a consistent approach so that all services work to the same objectives and priorities.

The Quality Protects initiative was also launched in 1998 to try and tackle existing problems with social services provision. This initiative presented a number of key objectives, including some from the National Priorities Guidance for Health and Social Services. The programme, designed to run over a three-year period, carried with it an additional £375 million. It also incorporated a specific sub-objective to establish more short-term (respite) placements with a consistent . This was paralleled by developments for carers under the Carers' National Strategy (DoH 1999), which placed emphasis on the entitlement to have a break for carers of people of all ages. A further £140 million was made available for the development of such services between 1999 and 2002. Unfortunately, this money was initially conceived as being primarily for the development of support services to carers of adults, although the carers' strategy was intended to apply to carers of disabled children as well. The Carers (Recognition and Services) Act 1995 gave carers, including those caring for children, the right to have an assessment of their own needs. However, recent evidence indicates that social workers rarely perceive the act as relevant to parent carers of people with intellectual disabilities, particularly if the family has a young disabled child (Williams and Robinson 2000). Hence, carers' needs are unlikely to be given separate attention unless there is a significant reorientation in current social work practices.

Early intervention and support

Early intervention is generally understood as an umbrella term used to describe programmes of education or therapy designed to accelerate the development of children with disabilities in the pre-school years (Jones 1998). During the past three decades there has been a rapid expansion in the range of early intervention programmes for disabled infants and toddlers in the UK and elsewhere (Carpenter 1997). Indeed, the law in the UK supports early intervention if a child is unlikely to achieve a reasonable standard of health or development, or health and development could be impaired without access to services, or the child is disabled (Children Act 1989, Children (Scotland) Act 1995 and Children (Northern Ireland) Order 1995). Mitchell and Brown (1991) argue that early intervention programmes have arisen because of a number of factors:

- The growing awareness of the importance of experiences in the early years for future development, especially for children who have impairments or are otherwise vulnerable.

- The need for parents who have continuing responsibility for their child at home to obtain regular support and advice, particularly in relation to promoting the child's development prior to starting school.

- An increased recognition of the rights of disabled children to have equal opportunities to develop their potential.

Interventions for under-twos tend to be home based and include pre-school learning programmes such as Portage. These may start soon after the child has been identified as having special needs. However, home-based interventions may operate in tandem with centre based programmes. Carpenter (1997) noted the following features of effective interventions:

- Service delivery that was *family-focused* in which parents (and siblings as appropriate) were seen as service deliverers who made an invaluable contribution. The context for service delivery was balanced between the home and community based settings according to what was most convenient and comfortable for the family.

- *Parents and professionals were mutually valued* and accorded each other respect. The common aim was to provide an unbroken circle of support for the child.

- *A shared agenda and goals* with an open and frank exchange of information, with parents having choices about approaches and goals.

- *Emphasis on collaborative working,* in which programme implementation was seen as a joint venture.

- *Effective ongoing evaluation* so that adjustments were made as needed in line with the child's and family's best interests. This required adaptability and resourcefulness among professionals.

While there is evidence that many parents appreciate and feel supported by the provision of services which explicitly attempt to aid the child's development (Cameron 1997; Hall 1997; Read 1996), others have levelled specific criticisms at many existing programmes of early intervention. These can be summarized as follows:

- A concern that they are premised on a negative concept of disability which seeks to make the child more 'normal' or socially acceptable (Middleton 1996; Oliver 1993; Wills 1994).

- Doubts about their long term effectiveness (Buckle 1994; Carpenter 1997).

- Programmes are too narrow and fail to take account of the family's circumstances. They may be too rigid or unrealistic, especially if the family is headed by a lone parent, is economically disadvantaged, isolated or comes from a different ethnic background to the programme organizer (Jones 1998; Russell 1997).

- Parent–child and other family relationships can be adversely affected because the programme emphasizes the need for parental involvement with the disabled child (Fitton 1994; Guralnick 1991; Johnson and Crowder 1994).

- The child and family may become stigmatized and segregated because the intervention marks them out as different. This is particularly so if the intervention is entirely home based (Shakespeare and Watson 1998; Vincent *et al.* 1996).

- It is the parents, rather than the child, who have rights (Jones 1998; Middleton 1996).

Thus, it can be argued that even if Carpenter's complete list of good practice points has been incorporated into an early intervention service, two basic issues remain unresolved. First, even if a spirit of partnership is present, early intervention programmes may nonetheless be premised on negative concepts of disability (Wills 1994). Second, interventions may give only the parents, not the children, rights. Jones (1998), in seeking to find a positive way forward, argues that for interventions to be truly effective the child needs to be seen foremost as a person with rights. She therefore recommends that interventions should incorporate combined, flexible packages of care from education, social services and health authorities which emphasize inclusion and seek to challenge underlying values and beliefs about disability. These will inevitably rely on the provision of resources to make inclusion possible. In the next section, we consider how far playgroups and other community-based pre-school services are likely to be available.

Playgroups and nurseries

Current playgroup and nursery provision for disabled children is patchy, both in the number of actual places available and the level of inclusivity offered. In some areas nursery education may be available in ordinary nursery schools with extra support provided so that the child can participate as fully as possible. In other areas, nursery places are provided through social services or health in either integrated or specialist units. Nursery classes paid for by the local education authority (LEA) may also be provided in special units attached to ordinary schools. Sometimes these are with a paid teacher and voluntary helpers. In addition, independent providers have been found willing to offer places to children with impairments and special needs, but training and support are necessary if such placements are to be sustainable (Cameron and Statham 1997). Statham (1996) examined early years provision in Wales under the 1989 Children Act (implemented 1991) and reported that a scheme (Special Needs Referral Scheme) designed to find places in local playgroups for children with intellectual disabilities had worked well. This scheme, sponsored by the Welsh Office and local social services departments, provided playgroups with extra helpers and special equipment as needed and supported parents and staff. The biggest problem was that the demand for places exceeded the number available. There is an argument for increasing resources to allow such developments to expand.

At present, pre-school provision is beset by a number of problems:

- poor co-ordination between agencies
- poor communication strategies so that both parents and professionals lack information about the range of options available
- lack of access to mainstream provision often as a result of inadequate resources to make inclusion possible.

When the 1989 Children Act was introduced it required local education authorities and social services departments to carry out a joint review of services available for children under the age of 8 every three years. Since 1998, each area has had to establish an early years development partnership or forum in which providers of early years services are represented. The early years forum was expected to consult parents about existing provision and incorporate their views into a development plan. This in turn was required to show that appropriate provision had been made for children with special needs. It is too early to comment on the impact of these new plans as a means of increasing inclusive educational opportunities in the pre-school years. However, the government has two other related aims that are likely to affect all young children, including disabled children. First, there is the explicit policy of assisting parents who wish to work through the development of wider childcare provision (National Childcare Strategy 1998). Second, there is the proposal to improve educational standards and increase support to families by making available educational places for all children aged 4 years and over whose parents wish to take them up.

In addition, a £452 million Sure Start initiative (DfEE 1997b) has been established to provide integrated health and education programmes for families and toddlers in disadvantaged areas. Although none of these government initiatives is particularly targeted at families with disabled children, the needs of this group are acknowledged in each case. A growth in provision generally may ease some of the current access problems, provided resources are made available to allow additional support to be established as needed. Although the recent Early Years Access Initiative (DfEE 1998a) goes some way towards meeting this need for resources since it carries funding for making public educational buildings more accessible, the money is not currently available to provide specialist resources or training in early educational settings.

Statements of educational need

One of the processes which families in the UK with a young disabled child will face is that of 'statementing' or assessment of educational need. Under the 1993 Education Act and the consolidating 1996 Education Act, disabled children have a statutory right to an assessment of their educational needs and to have those needs met from the age of 2 years. All disabled children should be assessed to identify whether they have any special educational needs and, if so, what these are. Most children with severe impairments will be identified early. Health trusts and district health authorities are under a duty to bring children under the age of 5 to the attention of the LEA if they believe they may have special educational needs. An estimated 20 per cent of children nationally are thought to have special educational needs, but not all of them will require special provision (of any type) to be made for them and so will not require a statement of need to be prepared (DfEE 1994). Currently, within the UK, there are wide variations between LEAs in making statements of educational needs, with less than 2 per cent of pupils having statements in some areas compared with over 4 per cent in others (DfEE 1997a).

Many parents see the obtaining of a written statement of need as important in itself since it provides a lever by which they can obtain the services their child needs. However, parents may not agree with the statement that is produced or, more particularly, with the decision about where their child should be educated. It is recognized that opportunities to attend a mainstream school are variable across the country (DfEE 1998a). If they feel strongly and the LEA is fixed in its view of what is needed, parents may decide to appeal to the Special Educational Needs tribunal. Parents should be given a named person, independent of the LEA, who can provide information and advice about their child's educational needs. This person could also encourage parental involvement in the assessment process. However, a named person is not always provided and some families find assistance through special education support groups. Under the proposed revised Code of Practice for the Identification and Assessment of Special Educational Needs, there will be a statutory requirement to provide independent parental supporters who can be either individuals or groups (Mallett, personal communication). Currently, it seems that the assessment and identification of special educational needs can be a stressful experience for families, especially if they do not have access to informed and helpful support (Middleton 1992).

Taking a break

Research has consistently shown that families value having a break from the normal routine of caring. However, parents only appreciate short-term (respite) care if it is of high quality and offers children a positive experience (Beresford 1995; Robinson and Jackson 1999; Robinson and Stalker 1989). The range of possible options for obtaining a short break varies across the UK, but typically the following types of services are available:

1.   Family-based schemes (known as both Shared Care or Family Link schemes) where the child goes to stay with another family or individual.

2.   Sitting services that offer evening or day time cover.

3.   Residential homes that specialize in short-term care.

4.   Care attendant schemes where the person goes into the child's home and can provide personal care.

Other services available for older children include befriending services and play schemes. For children under 5, certain types of existing short break services may be less than satisfactory. For example, residential care in which the child is separated from his or her parents and where familiar routines may be disrupted can be very unsettling (Oswin 1984). In recent years some local authorities have restricted the use of residential provision to children over the age of 5 and, in some cases, to children over 10. This would not be problematic for families if alternative services were always available to provide for young children, but this is not always the case – especially if the child has specific needs which cannot easily be accommodated within foster care settings (Robinson and Jackson 1999; Townsley and Robinson 2000).

Although family based services are generally well liked because of their informality and potential to reduce social isolation, for the last decade there have been waiting lists for these services (Beckford and Robinson 1993; Orlik, Robinson and Russell 1990; Prewett 1999; Robinson and Stalker 1989, 1991). Certain groups are consistently over-represented on these waiting lists: in particular, children who present challenging behaviours and those who have high levels of dependency. Boys are also over-represented, especially those who are over the age of 10 years.

In recent years, concern has been expressed about providing short breaks to children who have complex health needs, not only because of the knowledge that is needed to provide good care but also because of anxiety about litigation if something goes wrong. This is a particular issue if the person providing the care is not a parent and is not a registered nurse. Such concerns have led some local authorities to introduce restrictive policies that prohibit placements with any non-parent carer who is either an employee of the authority or an agent of it. This includes residential care staff and foster carers (Townsley and Robinson 1997). Fortunately, many authorities have yet to develop any specific policy around the care of children with complex health needs and as a consequence children in these areas continue to receive the services they need. If however restrictive policies are in place, the options for families to obtain a break are likely to be very limited. Some families may not receive a service at all and some children may experience unsatisfactory placements in hospital wards and nursing homes. Lack of appropriate provision for children with very high levels of need has also prompted demand for short-term care in children's hospices (Robinson and Jackson 1999).

In-home support with a trained sitter or personal carer is likely to be helpful to families with young children. These services are well liked when the person coming into the home is known to the family. However, where that person keeps changing, parents are less happy, particularly if they feel compelled to provide instruction in essential procedures and forewarning of all possible eventualities on each occasion a new 'helper' appears (Townsley and Robinson 2000). Several problems emerge when overnight care is required. Families do not necessarily benefit from this as much as they might where:

- their accommodation is limited, bedrooms are shared and they have to fit in an additional person

- sitters are not totally confident

- if the child is likely to awaken (Beresford 1995).

Overall, parents want more breaks than are currently available through social services, even though the majority have modest requirements (Robinson, forthcoming; Robinson and Stalker 1990). This is because budgets for short-term care are often restricted and schemes are not in a strong position to command more owing to their low profile within social services departments (Prewett 1999).

If parents of young children are to benefit from breaks which are intended to enable them to spend time together as a 'normal' family and recharge their batteries, they need to be offered a range of options so that they can select the one which best suits their child and family. At present, most authorities have a limited portfolio of services and there is little evidence of planning tailored to individual needs. Consequently, what is provided simply fails to perform the preventive function that it could.

Conclusions

Research into the early years of children with disabilities suggests that they and their families face a number of difficulties at this time:

- unsatisfactory experiences over diagnosis and its communication to parents

- involvement with a multiplicity of professions, support that is unco-ordinated and lacks the presence of a significant and consistent keyworker

- an absence of information about services and financial entitlements, especially where the family is from a minority ethnic group (Chamba *et al.* 1999)

- segregated and specialist interventions in the pre-school years, especially in cases where the child has profound and multiple impairments

- financial disadvantage resulting from the greater costs associated with the child's care and the reduced opportunities for paid employment and promotions that their caring responsibilities bring

- the fight to obtain the type of education which they, the parents, want for their child

- difficulties in obtaining short-term breaks, especially where the child presents with challenging behaviour, has complex health needs or comes from a minority ethnic group.

Recent Social Services Inspectorate reports refer to virtually all these difficulties and point to the lack of coherent child-centred policies for disabled children (SSI 1998a, 1998b). Indeed, it is all too easy to make the early years in the lives of families with a disabled child sound grim, but research also indicates a positive outlook and remarkable coping mechanisms among many families of severely disabled children (Beresford 1994). Moreover, in the current political climate there at least appears to be a greater willingness to make the radical changes to existing social policies that are required to provide a more coherent and consistent support service to families of disabled children. It remains to be seen whether this will yield any consistent improvement in the support that these families receive.

References

Alberman, E., Nicholson, A. and Wald, K. (1992) *Severe Learning Disability in Young Children: Likely Future Trends.* London: Wolfson Centre, Institute of Preventive Medicine.

Audit Commission (1994) *Seen But Not Heard: Co-ordinating Community Child Health and Social Services for Children in Need.* London: HMSO.

Baldwin, S. (1985) *The Costs of Caring.* London: Routledge and Kegan Paul.

Baldwin, S. and Carlisle, J. (1994) *Social Support for Disabled Children and Their Families: A Review of the Literature.* Edinburgh: HMSO.

Baxter, C., Poonia, K., Ward, L. and Nadirshaw, Z. (1990) *Double Discrimination: Issues and Services for People with Learning Difficulties from Black and Ethnic Minority Communities.* London: King's Fund.

Beckford, V. and Robinson, C. (1993) *Consolidation or Change? A Second Survey of Family Based Respite Care Services in the UK.* Bristol: Shared Care UK.

Beresford, B. (1994) *Positively Parents: Caring for a Severely Disabled Child.* London: HMSO.

Beresford, B. (1995) *Expert Opinions. A National Survey of Parents Caring for a Severely Disabled Child.* Bristol: Policy Press.

Buckle, J. (1984) 'The massive costs of raising a mentally handicapped child.' *Dig Around,* 13 March.

Cameron, R. (1997) 'Early interventions for young children with developmental delay: The Portage approach.' *Child: Care Health and Development 23,* 1, 11–27.

Cameron, R. and Statham, J. (1997) 'Sponsored places: The use of independent day care services to support children in need.' *British Journal of Social Work 27,* 85–100.

Carpenter, B. (1997) 'Finding the family: Early intervention and the families of children with special educational needs.' In B. Carpenter (ed) *Emerging Trends in Family Support and Early Intervention.* London: David Fulton Publishers.

Chamba, R., Ahmed, W., Hirst, M., Lawton, D. and Beresford, B. (1999) *On the Edge: Minority Ethnic Families Caring for a Severely Disabled Child.* Bristol: Policy Press.

Clarke-Kehoe, A. and Harris, P. (1992) '...It's the way that you say it.' *Community Care,* 6 July.

Cunningham, C. (1994) 'Telling parents their child has a disability.' In P. and H. Mittler (eds) *Innovations in Family Support for People with Learning Difficulties.* Chorley: Lisieux Hall Publications.

Cunningham, C.C. and Davies, H. (1985) *Working with Parents: Frameworks for Collaboration.* Milton Keynes: Open University Press.

Cunningham, C.C. and Sloper, P. (1977) 'Parents of Down's Syndrome babies: Their early needs.' *Child: Care Health and Development 3*, 325–347.

Cunningham, C.C., Morgan, P. and McCuken, R.B. (1984) 'Down's Syndrome: Is dissatisfaction with disclosure of diagnosis inevitable?' *Developmental Medicine and Child Neurology 26*, 33–39.

Department for Education and Employment (DfEE) (1994) *Code of Practice on the Identification and Assessment of Special Educational Needs.* London: HMSO.

Department for Education and Employment (DfEE) (1997a) *Excellence for All Children. Meeting Special Educational Needs.* Green Paper. London: The Stationery Office.

Department for Education and Employment (DfEE) (1997b) *Sure Start Programme.* London: The Stationery Office.

Department for Education and Employment (DfEE) (1998a) *Meeting Special Educational Needs. A Programme of Action.* Suffolk: DfEE Publications Centre.

Department for Education and Employment (DfEE) (1998b) *Meeting the Childcare Challenge. A National Strategy for Childcare.* London: The Stationery Office.

Department of Health (DoH) (1998) *Modernising Social Services. Promoting Independence, Improving Protection and Raising Standards.* White Paper, Cm 4169. London: The Stationery Office.

Department of Health (DoH) (1999) *The Carers' National Strategy.* London: The Stationery Office.

Fitton, P. (1994) *Listen to Me: Communicating the Needs of People with Profound Intellectual and Multiple Disabilities.* London: Jessica Kingsley Publishers.

Glendinning, C. (1986) *A Single Door: Social Work with Families of Disabled Children.* London: Routledge and Kegan Paul.

Glendinning, C., Kirk, S. with Guiffrida, A. and Lawton, D. (1999) *The Community Based Care of Technology Dependent Children in the UK: Definitions, Numbers and Costs.* Report commissioned by the Department of Health. Manchester: National Centre for Primary Care Research and Development, Manchester University.

Gordon, D., Parker, R. and Loughran, F. (1996) *Children with Disabilities in Private Households: A Re-analysis of the OPCS Investigation.* Bristol: School for Policy Studies, University of Bristol.

Guralnick, M.J. (1991) 'The next decade of research on the effectiveness of early intervention.' *Exceptional Children 58*, 2, 174–183.

Hall, D. (1997) 'Child development teams: Are they fulfilling their purpose?' *Child: Care, Health and Development 19*, 209–220.

Harris, P. (1993) *The Nature and Extent of Aggressive Behaviour amongst People with Learning Difficulties (Mental Handicap) in a Single Health District.* Bristol: Norah Fry Research Centre, University of Bristol.

Hochstadt, N.J. and Yost, D.M. (1991) *The Medically Complex Child. The Transition to Home Care.* Philadelphia: Harwood Academic Publishers.

Home Office (1998a) *Supporting Families. A Consultation Document.* London: The Stationery Office.

Home Office (1998b) *Meeting the Child Care Challenge – A Framework and Consultation Document.* Cm 3959. London: The Stationery Office.

Jacobs, J. (1977) 'Improving communications between health service professionals and parents of handicapped children: A case study.' *British Journal of Mental Subnormality 23*, 54–60.

Johnson, C. and Crowder, J. (1994) *Autism: From Tragedy to Triumph.* Boston MA: Branden Publishers.

Jones, C. (1998) 'Early intervention: the eternal triangle? Issues relating to parents, professionals and children.' In C. Robinson and K. Stalker (eds) *Growing Up With Disability.* London: Jessica Kingsley Publishers.

Kagan, C., Lewis, S. and Heaton, P. (1998) *Caring to Work: Accounts of Working Parents of Disabled Children.* London: Family Policy Studies Centre.

King's Fund (1987) *Shared Concern* (video and booklet). London: King's Fund.

Lawton, D. (1998) *Complex Numbers: Families with more than One Disabled Child.* Social Policy Report 8. York: University of York.

McConnachie, H. (1997) 'The organisation of child disability services.' *Child: Care, Health and Development 23*, 1, 3–9.

McKay, M. and Hensay, O. (1990) 'From the other side: Parents' views of their early contacts with health professionals.' *Child: Care, Health and Development 16*, 373–381.

Meltzer, H., Smyth, M. and Robus, N. (1989) *OPCS Surveys of Disability in Great Britain, Report 6: Disabled Children: Services, Transport and Education.* London: HMSO.

Middleton, L. (1992) *Children First.* Birmingham: Venture Press.

Middleton, L. (1996) *Making a Difference: Social Work with Disabled Children.* Birmingham: Venture Press.

Mitchell, D. and Brown, R.I. (1991) *Early Intervention Studies for Young Children with Special Needs.* London: Chapman and Hall.

Mukherjee, S., Beresford, B. and Sloper, P. (1999) *Unlocking Keyworking.* Bristol: Policy Press.

NCH Action for Children (1993) *NCH Factfile.* London: NCH Action for Children.

Nursey, A.D., Rhode, J.R. and Farmer, R.D.T. (1991) 'Ways in telling new parents about their child and his or her mental handicap: A comparison of doctors' and parents' views.' *Journal of Mental Deficiency Research 35*, 48–57.

Office of National Statistics (1999) *Social Trends 29.* London: The Stationery Office.

Oliver, M. (1993) 'Conductive education: if it wasn't so sad it would be funny.' In J. Swain, V. Finkelstein, S. French and M. Oliver (eds) *Disabling Barriers – Enabling Environments.* London: Sage.

Orlik, C., Robinson, C. and Russell, O. (1990) *A Survey of Family Based Respite Care Schemes in the UK.* Bristol: Norah Fry Research Centre, University of Bristol.

Oswin, M. (1984) *They Keep Going Away: A Critical Study of Short Term Residential Care Services for Children who are Mentally Handicapped.* London: King's Fund Centre.

Pahl, J. and Quine, L. (1984) *Families with Mentally Handicapped Children: A Study of Stress and of Service Response.* University of Kent. Health Services, Health Services Research Unit.

Prewett, E. (1999) *Short Term Break – Long Term Benefit.* Sheffield: Joint Unit for Social Services Research, University of Sheffield.

Quine, L. and Pahl, J. (1986) 'First diagnosis of severe mental handicap: Characteristics of unsatisfactory encounters between doctors and parents.' *Social Science and Medicine 22*, 53–62.

Read, J. (1996) *A Different Outlook: Service Users' Perspectives on Conductive Education.* Birmingham: Foundation for Conductive Education.

Robinson, C. (1999) 'Access to short-term care services for families caring for a disabled child with complex health needs.' Unpublished paper. Bristol: Norah Fry Research Centre, University of Bristol.

Robinson, C. (forthcoming) 'Short breaks for families caring for a severely disabled child with complex health needs.' *Child and Family Social Work*, forthcoming.

Robinson, C. and Jackson, P. (1999) *Children's Hospices. A Lifeline for Families?* London: National Children's Bureau.

Robinson, C. and Stalker, K. (1989) *Time for a Break. Respite Care: A Study of Providers, Consumers and Patterns of Use.* An interim report to the Department of Health. Bristol: Norah Fry Research Centre, University of Bristol.

Robinson, C. and Stalker, K. (1990) *Respite Care – The Consumer's View.* Second interim report to the Department of Health. Bristol: Norah Fry Research Centre, University of Bristol.

Robinson, C. and Stalker, K. (1991) *You're on the Waiting List. Families Waiting for Respite Care.* Fourth interim report to the Department of Health. Bristol: Norah Fry Research Centre, University of Bristol.

Russell, P. (1997) 'Foreword.' In B. Carpenter (ed) *Emerging Trends in Family Support and Early Intervention.* London: David Fulton Publishers.

Shah, R. (1997) *The Silent Minority: Children with Disabilities in Asian Families,* 2nd edn. London: National Children's Bureau.

Shakespeare, T. and Watson, N. (1998) 'Theoretical perspectives on research with disabled children.' In C. Robinson and K. Stalker (eds) *Growing Up With Disability.* London: Jessica Kingsley Publishers.

Sloper, P. and Turner, S. (1992) 'Service needs of families of children with severe physical disability.' *Child: Care, Health and Development 18*, 259–282.

Sloper, P. and Turner, S. (1993) 'Risk and resistance factors in the adaptation of parents of children with severe physical disability.' *Journal of Child Psychology and Psychiatry 34*, 167–188.

Snook, J. and Nally, B. (1996) 'Family stress and how to cope with it.' In *Autism on the Agenda: A Collection of Papers from the National Autistic Society Conference, May 1994.* London: National Autistic Society Conference.

Social Services Inspectorate (SSI) (1998a) *Disabled Children: Directions for their Future Care.* Wetherby: Department of Health (CI (98) 12).

Social Services Inspectorate (SSI) (1998b) *Removing Barriers for Disabled Children: Inspection of Services to Disabled Children and their Families.* Wetherby: Department of Health (CI (98) 12).

Spain, B. and Wigley, G. (1975) *Right from the Start.* London: Mencap.

Spastics Society (1992) *A Hard Act to Follow.* London: Spastics Society.

Spastics Society (1994) *Right from the Start.* London: Spastics Society.

Statham, J. (1996) *Young Children in Wales: An Evaluation of the Implementation of the Children Act 1989 on Day Care Services.* London: Thomas Coram Research Unit.

Thomas, M., Goddard, E., Hickman, M. and Hunter, P. (1994) *General Household Survey.* London: HMSO.

Townsley, R. and Robinson, C. (1997) *On Line Support. Effective Support Services to Disabled Children Who are Tube Fed.* Interim report to the NHS Executive. Bristol: Norah Fry Research Centre, University of Bristol.

Townsley, R. and Robinson, C. (2000) *Food for Thought? Effective Support for Families Caring for a Child who is Tube Fed.* Bristol: Norah Fry Research Centre, University of Bristol.

Vincent, C., Evans, J., Lunt, I. and Young, P. (1996) 'Professionals under pressure: The administration of special education in a changing context.' *British Educational Research Journal 22,* 4.

Wikler, L., Wasow, M. and Hatfield, E. (1981) 'Chronic sorrow revisited.' *American Journal of Orthopaedic Psychiatry 51,* 63–70.

Williams, V. and Robinson, C. (2000) *In Their Own Right? The Impact of the Carers Act 1995 on People with Learning Disabilities and their Carers.* Bristol: Policy Press.

Wills, R. (1994) 'It's time to stop.' In K. Ballard (ed) *Disability, Family Whanau and Society.* Palmerston North, New Zealand: Dunmore Press.

CHAPTER 3

Individuals with Learning Difficulties in the School Context

George O.B. Thomson

Introduction

In this chapter we shall consider the situation of children and young people with learning disabilities within the context of formal school education. First, we shall briefly consider the nature of changes in thinking and practice about provision for special educational needs, drawing attention to the nature of changing paradigms, the dominance of professional groupings and the conflict which the author sees existing in relevant education and child care legislation. The chapter will next consider the changing nature of assessment of special educational needs and concludes with a critical examination of the debate on the inclusion of children with learning disabilities into mainstream contexts.

Shifting paradigms

There can be no doubt that over the past 25 years education systems across the globe have shown an unprecedented level of concern for the education of children with special educational needs. One approach has been to translate this concern into developing policies; making provision; and ensuring that resources are devoted to this sector. While some educational systems find it difficult to commit financial resources to education, nevertheless there are present strong humanistic traditions. This international consensus has become expressed formally in a number of charters and instruments issued on behalf of the

United Nations. The significant themes in contemporary special education are well known and understood and include:

- provision of education for all children irrespective of the severity of any disability
- the need to provide compensatory education of a high quality
- the desirability that such services be provided within the regular school system.

This latter theme raises the twin issues of the integration of children with disabilities as an educational goal and as a technical solution to the problems of instruction and management which they might pose. It is this last point which continues to be controversial and we shall return to it later in the chapter. However, the eventual integration of children with disabilities into the mainstream of school and society has become a social imperative which few educationists would dispute; although many might question the appropriateness of some of the approaches used. 'Integration', 'inclusion' and 'mainstreaming' are accepted and widely used terms in the educational lexicon. They are terms which are frequently used interchangeably, sometimes adding a degree of conceptual opacity to the 'debate'. Integration can be discussed only in the general context of change in special education and the need for this has been approached in a number of ways.

A typical approach has been to affirm general principles, carry out research and fact finding into needs, embark upon the process of organizing services and training staff and, finally, to introduce legislation which can realistically ensure that such principles are followed and that individual needs are met. Perhaps the best known example of this lies in the passing of Public Law 94–142 (Education of all Handicapped Children Act 1977) in the USA. This set national standards for the education of all children with disabilities. The act was the outcome of many pressures by parents, professionals, disabled persons and the general community. Significant among these was the conviction that only through firm legal provision could the necessary changes be implemented and maintained. The issue of 'integration' is perceived then as an equity issue, a point stressed by Kirp (1982), among others – who interpret the deployment of legislation to promote integration as an extension of the argument that civil rights be secured for all individuals, be they marginalized from the mainstream of society by virtue of ethnic origin, socio-economic factors or disability. Italy, Denmark and the UK, among others, quickly followed by enacting legislation to ensure the move away from segregated provision.

Within the UK context, the principal catalyst for change in thinking and practice was the publication of the Warnock Report (DES 1978) as it became known. In November 1973 the then Secretary of State for Education and Science, the Rt Hon Margaret Thatcher, announced the appointment of a committee of enquiry under the chairmanship of Mrs Mary Warnock 'to review educational provision in England, Scotland and Wales for children and young people handicapped by disabilities of body or mind ... and to make recommendations'. The Committee's report, *Special Educational Needs* (DES 1978), was delivered in March 1978, almost simultaneously with the publication of the Scottish Education Department's HMI Report on *The Education of Pupils with Learning Difficulties* (SED 1978). Both publications gave rise to resultant legislation in 1981 which amended The Education (Scotland) Act 1980. This legislation introduced the legal requirement that children with special educational needs required these needs to be identified, assessed, and so 'recorded' in a Record of Needs. This document required the relevant education authority to state the measures proposed by the authority to meet the needs of the child and also to incorporate the views and wishes of the parent(s)/guardian(s) and the young person him/herself if s/he was over 14 years of age.

In the parallel legislation for England and Wales the document is called a 'Statement of Needs' with 'statemented child' being the descriptive phrase used. The Scottish terminology is used in this chapter. In essence the legislative requirements are the same in both systems.

The emergence of consultative documents leading to proposals for legislation does not, of course, imply consensus. Some professionals (for example, Thomson, Ward and Gow 1988) hold the view that educational legislation of the type referred to above at best can reflect the more advanced form of current practice; is founded upon principles and expectations which may have only a limited currency; and may lead to the growth of bureaucracies and interest groups and thence to destructive litigation. In the event, the very existence of the legislation may not guarantee the delivery of targeted services.

Among other things, the Warnock Report was the product of a growing awareness and debate within a range of professionals delivering support services to children, their families and schools, that traditional models were inadequate and inappropriate. From a concern about the negative aspects of labelling, there emerged the abandonment of categories of handicap. From an awareness of the inadequacies of a category-based approach to assessment, there developed the focus on a needs-based approach to assessment which emphasized a 'continuum of needs' – crude and unidimensional though this has proved to be. From a growing political agenda of accountability, there developed a sensitivity to the role of parents and the place of organizations, especially schools, in supporting children with special educational needs.

Hailed as a landmark of its kind and influential in determining the patterns of working by educational psychologists, the report and its related legislation have come in for criticism over the intervening years, not least by its chairman. Writing in *The Observer* in October 1992, Mary Warnock delivered herself of the following damning indictment: 'The main fault of the report on special education ... which lay behind the 1981 Act, was its naïveté. Indeed, it now appears naïve to the point of idiocy.'

At this time of writing, the Warnock models of practice are seen to be inadequate and inappropriate in the context of a more interactionist and interprofessional mode of service delivery. The legislative requirement that children whose special educational needs 'require regular review' should have these needs 'recorded' has been the object of continued critical comment from those professional groups most closely concerned with the procedures. The paradigm of needs-based assessment along a unidimensional continuum of special educational needs has moved away from that position towards one which stresses multidimensionality. The Warnock concept of 'parents as partners' would seem to have been replaced by 'parents as adversaries', as the growing number of appeals against decisions of education authorities would appear to testify. The essentially simplistic and descriptive notions of 'integrated provision' contained in the Warnock Report have been superseded by a much more sophisticated argument concerned with 'inclusive education' – a theme to which we shall return.

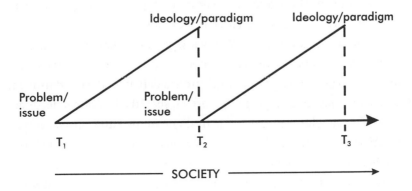

Figure 3.1 Paradigm evolution according to Söder (1998)

Two points are worth making as we contemplate the somewhat confused landscape of 'special educational needs'. First, it is important to remember that the Warnock Report was a product of a particular time and a prevailing orthodoxy. The emergence and domination of particular orthodoxies – or paradigms – at particular points in time is itself a fascinating enquiry. One Swedish commentator, Söder (1998), has observed that such paradigms usually lag behind society's own thinking as it develops. At any one point in time, a theme or problem is identified. In turn, perspectives develop and evolve into an 'ideology or paradigm' which holds sway. Meantime, society has moved, and other issues develop such that dominant modes of thinking can sometimes be distant from social realities. This is best illustrated by Figure 3.1. An example might be the manner in which debates attendant on integrated versus segregated provision for children with learning difficulties and/or disabilities raged throughout the 1980s. The orthodoxy which developed held the view that 'integration' was a social or moral imperative. Meantime, society, in the form of parents and carers, holds to a more ambivalent and less polarized point of view. We can think of the Warnock Report in a similar manner. Over the period since 1978, the paradigm of needs-based assessment along a unidimensional-dimensional continuum of special educational needs had become the prevailing practice. Yet 'society', in the form of professional opinion, practice and attitudes, had moved away from that position. In essence then, from our perspective at the turn of the millenium, we should not be too condemnatory of a report whose genesis lay in thinking and practice of at least a quarter-century ago.

It could be argued that the 'post-Warnock legislation' derives from at least two major theoretical perspectives. At a general level, there is that perspective which indicates a major paradigmatic shift – from a deficit model of adjustment towards a system model of change. In the former, special educational needs are seen to derive from a within-individual pathology; in the latter, special educational needs derive from the difficulties encountered by the individual in interacting with her or his environment. Hence it is the system which is required to adapt and accommodate to the individual. For some time now, this view has been represented widely in the educational psychology literature of which Apter (1982) and Campion (1985) would be illustrative examples.

At a more particular level, Kirp's (1982) comparative analysis of British and US special education highlights a significant difference in the philosophical approaches to provision for special educational needs in both countries. Here, the distinctions between legislation for Scotland as compared with that for England and Wales are irrelevant. In Kirp's view, a range of policy options are available when an educational system seeks to provide for special educational needs. In the USA 'legislation' is the preferred option. Concepts such as civil and individual rights and due processes of law dominate. In Kirp's view, these reflect a cultural tradition of individualism by which the USA is stereotyped. In contrast, UK practice is dominated by what Kirp calls 'professionalization', wherein strategically placed or dominant professional groups control or act as 'gatekeepers' to procedures, processes, resources and so on.

A much more important point remains however. There is a range of somewhat bewildering, confusing and sometimes contradictory legislation, the cumulative effect of which would seem to be hindering rather than helping to support individuals experiencing special educational needs, by diverting professionals away from their principal task of delivering such support. For example, the existing Education (Scotland) Act 1980 as amended, together with its supporting circulars, reflects in its various sections an outmoded model of psychological practice. It implies a deficit model of adjustment; it stresses an individual casework orientation to practice and ignores the importance of contexts as determinants of behaviour. The existing act takes a narrowly prescriptive view of 'children with special educational needs'. In contrast, the Children (Scotland) Act 1995 offers a much more inclusive definition of the needs of children. The effect is that two parallel pieces of legislation, aimed at improving and increasing the delivery of services to children, are potentially in conflict. A further example of seemingly contradictory legislation with consequent knock-on effects is that of the Self Governing Schools etc (Scotland) Act 1989. Here, the rights of parents to request placement of their children in schools outwith Scotland and even outwith the UK, seems to be in marked contrast with the more narrowly interpreted 'rights' in circulars supporting the 1980 Act. Perhaps the time has come to focus thinking on a new consolidated Education Act which would bring together a more coherent and systematic framework from which to launch education into the twenty-first century. Such an act should take account of changed models of practice. The legislation should reflect a more dynamic view of 'special needs' and the support systems required to circumvent handicap.

At the time of writing, the Scottish Parliament has been established with fully devolved powers except for foreign, defence and macro-economic policies. A new bill is to be laid before the Scottish Parliament early in the year 2000 seeking to redress some of the anomalies and confusions which presently exist.

Assessing 'special educational needs'

The Record (or 'Statement') of Special Educational Needs is a legal document prescribing the circumstances under which such a record may be drawn up; describing the nature of a child's needs; how these should be met and involving the parents in the whole process. Contentiously, there are parts of the Record which are exempted from parental appeal. While parents can appeal against the placement recommendations contained in the document, they are denied any right of appeal against an education authority's failure to deliver or put into place the measures proposed in the Record to meet the child's needs. This continues to create tension between parents on the one hand and education authorities on the other. The effects of the legislation on provision for special educational needs have been evaluated by the writer and his colleagues (Riddell, Thomson and Dyer 1992; Thomson, Riddell and Dyer 1989, 1990). In brief, they reported that the then twelve existing education authorities differed considerably in the development of their policies to implement the legislation; inconsistencies existed both across and within education authorities in terms of the criteria used in determining which pupils should have their needs 'recorded' and that integration of such pupils into the mainstream occurred in only a few authorities and there it was restricted to those pupils experiencing sensory and/or physical disabilities.

Since the Thomson *et al.* research was conducted, subsequent reorganization of local authorities in Scotland has dispensed with the two-tier system of 12 regional authorities with subordinate district councils in favour of 32 all purpose-authorities. It is the writer's belief that this has exacerbated the situation reported by him and his colleagues in their 1989 to 1992 reports.

The UK experience is one in which educational psychologists find themselves occupying a bureaucratic role sometimes at odds with their professional identity. Nevertheless, the practice of educational psychology certainly testifies to the shifting paradigm referred to earlier in which issues such as consultancy work with 'front line' professionals in the delivery of services is the preferred mode of working. Reference has been made earlier to the statutory requirement to 'record' children with special educational needs. This has proved to be a somewhat problematic area of educational provision, exacerbated by the variability of practice across the country in the administration of the procedures. Also the unidimensionality of the 'continuum of needs' is seen to be restrictive. Current thinking suggests the need to shift more towards a multiaxial approach in which account has to be taken of types of educational support available to a school and the levels of educational needs of a given pupil. There is a widely held consensus view on these points, though terminology may differ from commentator to commentator. For example, Center (1987), working in the Australian context, proposed a model for delivering special education services embracing eight levels of service delivery. Mitchell and Ryba (1994) in New

Zealand, echoing this view, described a more parsimonious model. In Scotland, Cross *et al.* 1994) argued for an approach to recording special educational needs which took account of dimensions of needs and provision.

Drawing upon data gathered in the context of research on incidence levels as well as taking account of current literature on the issue, the author argues that thinking about support for pupils with special needs involves consideration of at least six distinct aspects, each of equal importance. Also, instead of thinking about 'special educational needs' it is perhaps more relevant to consider 'a pupil's educational support needs'. This term is used deliberately to move the emphasis away from the within-child model of a pathology towards a systems-based approach which stresses the extent to which the context has to adjust or change. The six strands conceptualized are indicated below:

- the physical environment
- the nature of the curriculum and how it is delivered
- the level of pupil support needs
- access to specialized resources
- access to specialized support agents or agencies
- the mode of communication.

Further, it is possible to grade the level of 'need' on each of these variables along a four-point continuum. Drawing upon research evidence, Thomson, Stewart and Ward (1995) described a multiaxial approach to the assessment of educational support needs.

A 6 × 4 matrix was proposed, with cell descriptors providing an operational basis on which decisions may be taken regarding the support for a pupil with educational support needs. This may be taken as a relevant illustration from the Scottish context on how thinking and practice has developed on the issue of delivering services to pupils with such needs. The matrix also has the potential as an 'audit tool' for any educational context where pressures are such that criteria require to be established by which scarce resources might be optimally deployed to support pupils with educational support needs.

The 'inclusion' debate

Earlier in this chapter, reference was made to the significant themes which dominate provision of support for children with significant educational support needs. Among them was the desirability that such support be provided within the regular school system. The integration of such individuals is seen as an equity issue which few educationalists would dispute. However, the debate is somewhat obscured by a tendency for protagonists to adopt polemical rather than empirical stances.

There can be no doubt, however, as to the almost universal advocacy for the inclusion of children with special needs within the mainstream of educational provision. One of the most significant statements on this theme is the Salamanca Statement (UNESCO 1994). The city of Salamanca in Spain is synonymous with inclusive education since it is in this city that the World Conference on 'Special Needs Education: Access and Quality' was held in June 1994. The driving force for inclusive education was realized in the resolution, known as the Salamanca Statement. Endorsed by 92 countries and 25 international organizations, the message was clear and unambiguous:

> We, the delegates of the World Conference on Special Needs Education … hereby affirm our commitment to Education for All, recognising the necessity and urgency of providing education for children, youth and adults with special education needs within the regular education system, and further hereby endorse the Framework of Action on Special Needs Education, that governments and organisations may be guided by the spirit of its provisions and recommendations. (UNESCO 1994, p.9)

This then was the catalyst for the movement towards greater inclusion of individuals with special educational needs into the mainstream system.

The problem with polarized constructs such as 'integration' and 'segregation' is that neither is sharply defined. Frequently 'integration' really means 're-integration' of a pupil after a period of segregation or, alternatively, as a strategy to avoid separation from the mainstream. The implicit assumption is that the educational programme followed by a particular child is the same for the rest of his or her peers, albeit modified in terms of content and pace. Stressing access to the curriculum denies the reality that for some pupils this might be wholly unrealistic, as Jordan and Powell (1992) make clear in an account of an autistic pupil and his 'problems' in accessing an appropriate curriculum. The danger is that 'integration' is seen as 'mainstreaming' of pupils in terms of curricular access. As a consequence of decategorization of handicap, access to the curriculum experienced by children in normal class contexts is taken as the hallmark of 'integration'. Söder (1989) has challenged this idea and argued for an *appropriate* education for individuals with special educational needs which seeks to ensure their access to a curriculum which is developed along the principles of personal growth and development. In essence, his argument is that 'education' will vary in proportion to the variability of individual needs. This is much closer to the notion of 'inclusion' of children into learning environments as a matter of equity.

The policy analysis literature examining the efficacy of legislation in promoting integration practices suggests that what is important in the effective implementation of policies supporting the integration of pupils with special educational needs are three important variables:

- high quality professional preparation of teachers at pre- and in-service levels to equip and update them in meeting the needs of a diverse classroom population

- support and commitment from educational administrators

- high quality support services at the classroom level of both material and manpower.

Representative of this view is the work reported by Vitello (1991) in Italy and Jull (1989) followed by Walton, Rosenqvist and Sandling (1991) in Scandinavia. It would appear then that legislation to promote integration practices has, at best, an enabling or permitting function. By itself it cannot ensure application; that requires the commitment and willingness of individuals strategically placed to enact the mandate. What then of the success or otherwise of the goal of integration of pupils with special educational needs into a truly inclusive educational environment?

The concept of inclusive education takes various forms and rests on a range of assumptions. At the broadest level, it may be defined as the process of educating children and young people with special educational needs in settings where they have the maximum association, consistent with their interests, with other children and young people of the same age. The starting point for inclusive education is that all children with special educational needs should have access to and receive an education. This requires a recognition that, without exception, all children are capable of being educated and that all children have a right to an appropriate education. This is the philosophy of the Salamanca Statement (UNESCO 1994). However, it may be useful to pay heed to a South African commentator. Naicker (1996, p.3) regards inclusive education as: 'a theoretical and philosophical construction. In order to operationalise that conceptual definition one has to give it a practical dimension. The practical dimension will vary from context to context.'

Thus the actual form inclusive education takes will depend on human resources, the state of development of the education system related to education training, physical facilities, fiscal resources, the extent to which the concept has been debated and the value attached to human dignity. Thus how one defines inclusive education will depend to a large extent on the resources in one's context. In this regard, Naicker's views are consistent with this writer's views (see Thomson 1996) that the voluminous research activity on this issue is fundamentally flawed by asking the wrong research questions. Irrespective of the social or moral imperative argument, it can be argued that the issue of where a pupil with special educational needs should be educated should always be subordinate to how that child's needs are identified and met.

In arriving at decisions regarding an individual pupil's needs, at least four variables must be considered:

- the functional and adaptive characteristics of the child
- the extent of the resource needs of the child which ensue
- the level of services available to the child and his/her parents or carers
- the views and wishes of the parents and carers.

In this way, decisions may be taken on the basis of a full understanding of the particular needs of individuals leading to the provision of an appropriate person-centred curriculum which allows that individual to be included into the mainstream of society. The emphasis is turned away from questions of how to fit an individual child into a mainstream system towards those which address the fundamental point – how can systems be adapted and changed to accommodate a range of difference. Hence the paradigm shift referred to earlier in this chapter of the move from a deficit model of adjustment towards a systems model of change.

Naicker (1996), Lomofsky *et al.* (1998) and this writer (Thomson 1996) share a common belief in the need for radical pragmatism where practical dimensions differ from context to context but within an overall belief system where the concept of inclusive education has been debated and where the value placed on human dignity is paramount. This may be criticized as merely high-flown rhetoric but must be the premise from which the inclusion movement starts. The practicalities are important as Naicker (1996) has stressed.

An interesting and relevant commentary on this way of thinking has been offered by Tomlinson (1997). The context within which he was writing was that of chairman of a UK government enquiry into the post-school education of those with learning difficulties and/or disabilities. Despite the narrow focus of his paper, his argument resonates with the themes and issues on which this chapter has focused. Tomlinson (1997) talks about 'inclusive learning' rather than 'teaching'. The distinction is more than semantic since what he puts forward is a theory of learning which places the responsibility for providing appropriate education with the teachers, managers and the system (ultimately society) rather than making the individual learner 'the problem' – the one with a deficit. The theme of the paper is encapsulated in the view that: 'a good education system is not merely about offering access to what is available, but also the making of what needs to be available accessible: the moulding of opportunity' (Tomlinson 1997, p.184).

Tomlinson (1997) describes a matching process at three levels: between the teacher and the learner; between the school and the learner; and between the system as a whole and the learner. The outcome of this matching may differ from context to context and in this regard he makes an emphatic statement:

[The] concept of inclusiveness is not synonymous with integration. It is a larger and prior concept. The first step is to determine the best possible learning environment, given the individual student and learning task. For those with learning difficulty the resulting educational environment will often be in an integrated setting and increasingly so as the skills of teachers and capacities of the system grow. Sometimes it will be a mixture of the integrated and the discrete. And sometimes ... it will be discrete provision. No apology is necessary for the paradox ... that ... the concept of inclusive learning is not necessarily coincident with total integration ... into the mainstream. (Tomlinson 1997, pp.192–193)

As Naicker (1996) has argued, in the transitional context which is South Africa, so too does Tomlinson (1997) in the developed system which is the UK; namely, full inclusion implies a very well resourced education system if it is to do justice to all learners. Inclusion as an aim should be retained and worked towards. In the progression towards this goal, it may very well be the case that full realization of the goal may require a medium to long term strategy. The implications for an education system are that 'inclusive education' could take various forms and may differ from area to area depending on infrastructure, personnel, teacher training and other factors.

What Naicker (1996) and Tomlinson (1997) are arguing is that inclusion is a theoretical construct. What is required is the need to give it meaning practically by understanding thoroughly the contexts in which education systems reside relating to finance, teacher capacity and training. Above all there is a need to recognize what it is that those professionals involved in supporting pupils with educational support needs have to offer the mainstream. Support for pupils with such needs in segregated settings has been underpinned by a paradigm that focused on a within individual pathology of deficit. Inclusive education, on the other hand, takes seriously the critical interrogation of pedagogical practices and moves away from the deficit model of adjustment.

While many educational systems are moving towards accepting the philosophy of inclusive education, there are major obstacles to its implementation. These include such factors as large classes, negative attitudes to disability, examination-oriented education systems, a lack of support services, rigid teaching methods, assessment dominated by medical model, a lack of parent involvement, and a lack of clear national policies. What then are the essential components for the successful inclusive education of children with special educational needs? The overriding assumption is that the success of inclusive education depends upon it being viewed as part of a system which extends from the classroom to broader society. Its success depends on what goes on day to day, minute by minute in classrooms and playgrounds. It depends on teachers and headteachers who, in turn, depend on the leadership of educational administrators at national and local levels. Ultimately, it depends on the vision of legislators to pass the necessary laws and provide the appropriate resources.

In summary then, it is clear that while most countries are moving towards accepting the philosophy of inclusive education, there are many obstacles still to be overcome. For inclusive education to advance, several paradigm shifts are required. There are perhaps three which merit attention. First, there is the need to reconceptualize disability and effect that paradigm shift referred to earlier, namely from a deficit model of adjustment to a systems model of change. The point here is the need to recognize the importance of the interactions between individuals and their various environments. Associated with this is the need to shift away from categories of disabilities to descriptions of the educational support needs of the learners. This is the point of the multiaxial audit tool referred to earlier.

A second paradigm shift relates to pedagogy. Here the shift is from prescriptive teaching to interactive teaching; from undifferentiated, whole class approaches to a mix of whole class and small group teaching; from an emphasis on competition towards a balance between competition and co-operation.

Finally, there has to be a shift in the role of assessment; away from assessment being used to determine or describe individuals' position in a range of classificatory systems towards a view of assessment which provides an account of what it is a learner knows, can do or has experienced; to be less dominated by an examination system and more conscious of the holistic needs of the learner. For these paradigm shift to occur and allow for the development of truly inclusive educational systems, priority should be given to the following:

- developing clear and consistent national policies on inclusion

- providing advice and guidance to schools

- ensuring high quality pre- and in-service teacher education.

Conclusion

This chapter has attempted to provide an overview of current thinking about the education of individuals with learning difficulties in the school context. It began by examining the paradigm shift which has occurred in thinking about children with special educational needs by moving away from a within-individual model towards one which stresses the importance of the contexts in which individuals learn. The focus then moved to an examination of the role which legislation plays in bringing about effective provision for individuals with significant learning difficulties. In this, attention was drawn to what the writer perceived as inherently contradictory legislation promoting and safeguarding children's interests. Consideration was then given to the changing nature of assessment of special educational needs. In this, a multiaxial approach developed by the author was described. It was argued that this was more in keeping with the interactionist perspective which presently characterizes the delivery of services to individuals with significant needs. The chapter concluded with a critical examination of the concept of 'inclusive education'.

One hallmark of any liberal society is the manner and extent to which it caters for the needs of all its citizens. Issues of social equality are superordinate to those of efficiency. The adoption of market-led economic theory in developed economies is widespread. The extension of such an ideology has become evident in many areas of social policy – in health, social work and not least in education. Concepts such as accountability, devolved management of resources, efficiency and value for money have become the familiar jargon of our times. In the field of provision for those with significant educational support needs, the major issue confronting any society is how it responds to the needs of those marginalized – socially, educationally, occupationally and economically – by virtue of their disabilities. Such individuals present specific, sometimes complex, needs. While individual or collective responses are to be encouraged, it must remain the central, moral obligation of society to distribute resources in a manner which will enable dependent individuals to grow, develop and lead fulfilling lives. No less is expected of a nation's education service.

References

Apter, S. (1982) *Troubled Children/Troubled Systems.* London: Pergamon Press.

Campion, J. (1985) *The Child in Context.* London: Methuen.

Center, Y. (1987) 'Integration – historical perspectives.' In J. Ward *et al. (eds) Educating Children with Special Educational Needs in Regular Classrooms: An Australian Perspective.* North Ryde: Macquarie University Press.

Children (Scotland) Act 1995 (1995) Edinburgh: HMSO.

Cross, J., Abraham, C., Kirkaldy, B. and Smith, E. (1994) 'The dimensions used in records of needs.' Final Report to the Scottish Office Education Department. Mimeograph: University of Dundee.

Department of Education and Science (DES) (1978) *Special Educational Needs (Warnock Report).* Cm. 7212. London: HMSO.

Education (Scotland) Act 1980 (1980) Edinburgh: HMSO.

Education (Scotland) Act 1981 (1981) Edinburgh: HMSO.

Jordan, R.R. and Powell, S.D. (1992) 'Stop the reforms – Calvin wants to get off!' *Disability, Handicap and Society* 7, 1, 85–88.

Jull, K.D. (1989) 'Some causes and unique features of special education in the Nordic countries.' *International Journal of Special Education 4,* 85–96.

Kirp, D. (1982) 'Professionalisation as policy choice in British special education in comparative perspective.' *World Politics 34,* 2, 134–174.

Lomofsky, L., Thomson, G.O.B., Gouws, A. and Englebrecht, L. (1998) 'New paradigms in provision for special educational needs: South Africa and Scotland in comparative perspective.' In W. Morrow and K. King (eds) *Vision and Reality: Changing Education and Training in South Africa.* Cape Town: University of Cape Town Press.

Mitchell, D. and Ryba, K. (1994) *Students with Education Support Needs.* Report to the New Zealand Ministry of Education. Hamilton: Waikato University Press.

Naicker, S. (1996) 'The challenge of inclusive education.' Unpublished paper delivered at Department of National Education, February 1996. South Africa: National Curriculum Committee.

Riddell, S., Thomson, G.O.B. and Dyer, M. (1992) 'A key informant approach to the study of local policy making in the field of special educational needs.' *European Journal of Special Needs Education 7,* 1, 47–62.

Scottish Education Department (SED) (1978) *The Education of Pupils with Learning Difficulties.* Edinburgh: HMSO.

Söder, M. (1989) 'Disability as a social construct: The labelling approach revisited.' *European Journal of Special Needs Education 4,* 2, 117–129.

Söder, M. (1998) 'Research paradigms in special education.' Unpublished seminar paper delivered under the Northern Scholars Scheme. Edinburgh: University of Edinburgh.

Thomson, G.O.B. (1996) 'Incorporating children with learning disabilities in the normal school system.' In S. Nakou and S. Pantelakis (eds) *The Child in the World of Tomorrow: The Next Generation.* Oxford: Elsevier Science, pp.198–211.

Thomson, G.O.B., Riddell, S. and Dyer, S. (1989) 'Policy, professionals and parents.' Mimeograph. Edinburgh: University of Edinburgh.

Thomson, G.O.B., Riddell, S. and Dyer, S. (1990) 'Parents, professionals and social welfare models: The implementation of the Education (Scotland) Act 1981.' *European Journal of Special Needs Education 5*, 2, 96–110.

Thomson, G.O.B., Stewart, M.E. and Ward, K. (1995) 'Criteria for opening records of needs.' Mimeograph. Edinburgh: University of Edinburgh.

Thomson, G.O.B., Ward, J. and Gow, L. (1988) 'The education of children with special needs: A cross-cultural perspective.' *European Journal of Special Needs Education 3*, 3, 125–137.

Tomlinson, J. (1997) 'Inclusive learning: The Report of the Committee of Enquiry into the Post School Education of those with Learning Difficulties and/or Disabilities, in England, 1996.' *European Journal of Special Needs Education 12*, 3, 184–196.

UNESCO (1994) *The Salamanca Statement and Framework for Action on Special Needs Education.* Paris: UNESCO.

US Department of Education (1977) *Public Law 94–142 the Education of all Handicapped Children Act.* Washington DC: USGPO.

Vitello, S. (1991) 'Integration of handicapped students in the United States and Italy: A comparison.' *International Journal of Special Education 6*, 2, 213–222.

Walton, W.T., Rosenqvist, J. and Sandling, J. (1991) 'A comparison study of special education in the public school system in Denmark, Sweden and the United States.' *International Journal of Special Education 6*, 3, 403–416.

CHAPTER 4

Negotiating Adolescence

Billie Shepperdson

Adolescence is normally regarded as a turning point for young people, signifying the onset of physical maturity and, in terms of status and identity, their passage from childhood to adulthood. In this transitional period childish behaviour and activities are replaced by a period of experimentation which, it is expected, will eventually lead to the adoption of adult lifestyles. This chapter asks how far people with intellectual disabilities are able to use this transitional time to experiment and generally to adopt a lifestyle that is comparable with that of their ordinary peers. A wider question is how far adolescence for people with learning disabilities is merely a transitional or interim period, a gateway to an autonomous adulthood or whether, in social terms, it is a period which is prolonged well into the ages when adult life is usually taken for granted.

The adolescent years

As Conger and Galambos (1996) outline, early psychological theories which suggest that adolescence is biologically determined, that it is a unique and distinct developmental stage, and that it is invariably characterized by emotional upheavals have all been questioned. Nowadays, the importance of environment, as well as biology, in shaping behaviour is given greater stress. Longitudinal studies emphasize the persistence into adolescence of personality traits which have first been observed in childhood, so casting doubt on the notion of adolescence as a distinct phase, in favour of it being a time of more gradual and continuous development. Similarly, objective measurement of the emotional states of adolescents imply that emotional turmoil – and especially the emphasis on negative emotions – is not inevitable.

There is more general agreement in the social and political sphere about adolescence. The crucial task for the adolescent is to move from the protected life of a child to the autonomous and independent life of an adult, one who is in control of his own life and makes his own decisions. Adolescence is the bridging period between these two stages of dependence on the one hand and complete autonomy on the other. Viewed from this non-biological perspective, individuals are unlikely to be at the same stage exactly at the same time. The age at which adolescence starts and ends cannot be clearly defined, although most regard the teenage years as the time of ordinary adolescence.

In contrast to the literature on adolescence and ordinary youngsters, there is little which is directly comparable for teenagers with intellectual disabilities. Most ordinary accounts of adolescents make little mention of intellectual disability. For example, a recent discussion of teenagers for social workers (Coleman 1999) noted the particular vulnerability of disabled youngsters but did not spell out their unique problems, or suggest solutions. Similarly, there is no separate discussion of adolescence in some standard works on intellectual disability (e.g. Fraser, MacGillivray and Green 1991). Nevertheless, the literature on intellectual disability does contain a great deal of discussion on issues which are commonly regarded as matters concerning adolescents – notably, independence and autonomy. However, for those with intellectual disabilities, the chronological age at which these outcomes are achieved can vary greatly and, for some, the struggle towards them may begin in adolescence but, arguably, can last well beyond the chronological age at which most people achieve them. This perhaps helps to explain the reluctance of authors to link age and behaviour too closely.

Work by Baker (1991) gives some indication of why the achievement of independence may be delayed in people with intellectual disability. He argues that independence and separation from parents is essentially the result of initiatives from young people themselves. Children begin to make up their own minds on certain issues and, in doing this, reject certain aspects of their parents. He suggests that this rejection and subsequent conflict is fundamental if parents and children are both to begin to recognize their separate identities and so allow the child to move towards becoming an independent adult. Unfortunately, it is just this sort of personal assertiveness which is difficult for some young people with intellectual disabilities. Nor are they helped by living lives which are relatively isolated from their peers who could set an example in this sphere. Without the initiatives of parents, who may be keen to avoid conflict, there is the danger of some children with intellectual disabilities remaining in a state of childlike dependence forever. Taylor (1997) nicely illustrates the two-way nature of the development of independence from a parental perspective:

> 'My reality is that I am hesitant to allow him to follow the natural progression towards self-reliance. It is a hesitancy born of fear and love. It is sometimes deliberate and sometimes unconscious but always well-intentioned. Who in the world wants her child to fail, to get hurt, even to stumble. The expectation on the part of my child is also a factor. On one recent morning my son was up before me. I soon discovered him sitting at the kitchen table, ravenous, waiting for me to get his breakfast. He is fully capable of getting a cup and bowl from the dishwasher, milk and juice from the refrigerator and cereal from the closet. But his expectation is that Mum is supposed to do it.' (Taylor 1997, p.13)

Thomson, Ward and Wishart (1995) explore similar themes. They discuss the achievement of adulthood and associated independence in terms of obtaining employment and living away from parents. They also explore the personal attributes which mark out those who move successfully along the path from child to adult and emphasize the attainment of social competence, the ability to undertake complicated social interactions and the ability to adopt family and societal roles. Given that employment and independent living can be arranged for people, regardless of their own efforts, it is the personal attributes which are paramount – but more difficult to achieve.

A further related consideration is implicit in the literature and crucially important for youngsters with learning disabilities. Adolescence is the time when experimentation usually accelerates for ordinary youngsters. It is arguable that to become competent, to be able to make choices and to manage risk successfully, exposure to suitable life experiences is required; those which allow for the opportunity to make choices and experiment and practical (albeit controlled) exposure to potential hazards (e.g. Field, Hoffman and Posch 1997).

This chapter will explore in greater detail some of these issues of competence, parental perceptions, self-image and lifestyles which allow for learning. Social competence of young people is clearly important if they are to work towards independence and it will also influence how they are regarded in their parents' eyes. Both aspects – their own achievements and the perceptions of their parents – will influence how young people feel about themselves (Jenkins 1989). Finally, because of the need to be given the opportunity to learn, the lifestyles of young people and the chance they have for ordinary experimentation and risk taking will be discussed in comparison with the situation for ordinary youngsters. The account will also include comparable information on people with intellectual disabilities who are in their mid-twenties. This is to illustrate further the delayed development of autonomy and independence in people with intellectual disabilities which characterizes their teenage years and which can still be a feature into their twenties.

The account uses material from a series of studies of two cohorts of people with Down's syndrome who were brought up with their families in South Wales. The cohorts were not selected by service use but by place and date of birth. Down's syndrome people form about one-third of the population of people with moderate and severe intellectual disabilities. It is the largest single syndrome associated with such intellectual disabilities (Craft 1979; McGrother *et al.* 1996). The syndrome includes people who are mildly and severely disabled (Carr 1988) and, because of this wide range in their abilities, people with Down's syndrome are good representatives of the total population with intellectual disabilities.

The original cohort, 53 people with Down's syndrome, were born in South Wales in the years 1964 to 1966. Carers were interviewed and the cohort's language and social competence skills were tested at three stages: infant school age (1970s), the mid-teens (1980s) and the mid-twenties (1990s). A second cohort of 26 people with Down's syndrome, also from South Wales (the comparative cohort) who were born between 1973 and 1975, were studied in the same way. They and their families were seen twice: at infant school age (1980s) and in their mid-teens (1990s). Certain changes to families and services that had occurred in the intervening years meant that this cohort was particularly privileged compared with those in the original one. Services had improved

(Welsh Office 1983) and changes in fertility meant that the youngsters enjoyed a family life more like that of their non-disabled peers: parents were younger and they were less often the youngest in the family. They were also from higher social class backgrounds (Shepperdson 1985). From these cohort studies it is possible to compare teenagers living in the 1980s with those in the 1990s. It is also possible to see how far the original cohort teenagers were continuing further along the path to adulthood in their mid-twenties, or were still pursuing lives more like adolescents (Shepperdson 1988, 1992, 1993).

The social competence and self-care skills of teenagers

Most of the research suggests that young people with intellectual disabilities often need help in very fundamental areas of everyday life. The examples which follow relate mainly to young people with Down's syndrome, although such youngsters – for whatever reason – do better than others with similar abilities who do not have the syndrome (Carr 1995). The account therefore errs on the side of optimism.

In three basic areas – dressing, toilet training and bathing – although improvements from childhood are made, it seems that high proportions of teenagers continue to require assistance. In the South Wales studies only one-half of the comparative cohort were able to dress themselves in their teenage years, up from one-quarter at infant school age. While three-quarters could now go to the lavatory unaided, their numbers had not substantially increased since childhood, although they now no longer required close supervision. Half the teenagers could bath themselves (Shepperdson 1994). This compares with Carr's 21 year olds, about two-thirds of whom could dress, were toilet trained, and able to bath themselves (Carr 1995). Although Buckley and Sacks (1987) found higher proportions of teenagers competent in these areas, their information was collected by questionnaire, not interview.

However, looking after one's self is more than the mere performance of physical acts of self-care, and parents are acutely aware of this. For example, carers of almost all adults on the Leicestershire Register of people with intellectual disabilities reported that people still presented a safety problem in adulthood (McGrother *et al.* 1996). Crucially, parents were unsure how far their young people were aware of risk and how far they could be trusted to react sufficiently flexibly to avoid danger. The tension between risk taking and the opportunity to learn is clear.

In the South Wales studies, 15 per cent of comparative teenagers were never left alone in the house and, of those who were, over half were left alone for less than 15 minutes. Over a third were never allowed outside the house alone and, of those who were, few had much freedom. The following quotations show the problems for parents as they struggled to balance the need to protect with the need (and wish) to widen youngsters' experiences, the variations in approaches they adopted, and the barriers to learning that arose from their decisions:

> 'If I go and hang the clothes on the line she comes looking. "Where's Mammy?" I wouldn't go next door. I keep the door locked – she'd let anybody in.'

> 'If he's home from school he doesn't want to go out and I will leave him watching a video for 15 or 20 minutes while I go to the village. "Don't answer the door or telephone," I say. It took us a long time to do it but it's an essential thing to do, to start off. I wouldn't dream of going as far as town.'

> 'It's two or three minutes to my mother's. I ring to say she's coming. She keeps to the path, she hasn't a lot of road sense.'

> 'He's not [out] at all. He has a tendency to run away. He used to have a bike but as soon as he could ride it, he'd be off. He was lost one day – the police and all his brother's friends were out.' [When was that?] 'About five years ago.' [Has he improved?] 'I don't know. I haven't given him the opportunity. He outgrew the bike and I wouldn't let him have a new one. You have to be cruel to be kind. I couldn't handle another bike.' [The teenager's father would have allowed this.]

As far as self-care overall is concerned, only 46 per cent of comparative teenagers were independent in six of seven very basic self-care tasks (eating, dressing, toilet training, bathing, shaving/menstruation, staying in alone, going out alone) and less than a third could perform all seven tasks.

These statistics paint a fairly depressing picture of the potential for independence of teenagers. This would be misleading on four counts. First, these averages conceal an enormous range in levels of independence.

Second, the data show that new generations of teenagers – those who had the benefit of enhanced services – were more likely than those of a decade earlier to master personal care skills. Significantly more were able to dress themselves and were competent in at least six of the seven basic self-care tasks. More were also toilet trained and could bath themselves.

Third, they were acquiring these skills at an earlier age. On dressing and toilet training they were already doing better than the adults in the original cohort. On safety issues, too, more were left alone for brief periods (85 per cent of *teenagers* in the comparative cohort compared with 69 per cent of *adults* in the original cohort) and more went out alone (65 per cent compared with 52 per cent). While 38 per cent of adults in the original cohort were skilled in at least six of the seven self-care tasks, 46 per cent of the teenagers in the comparative cohort had already reached this level.

Fourth, information concerning the original cohort, as adults in their twenties, shows that their self-care abilities had continued to improve. The evidence therefore supports the notion of an extended learning period and an extended adolescence, as far as personal care is concerned. Only a quarter could dress themselves at teenage, but by their twenties a third could do this. Again, just over a quarter could bath at teenage, but two-thirds were able to do this a decade later. Over a third stayed at home by themselves at teenage, but this had doubled to two-thirds by the twenties – and almost a fifth of the whole cohort could be left for over half a day. The numbers allowed out quite freely had more than doubled, to 19 per cent. Slight gains only were made on toilet training.

What we do not know is whether the favoured environment of the comparative cohort meant they simply achieved their potential sooner, or whether there are still more gains to be made as they reach their twenties. Nor do we know how far those in their twenties will continue to improve yet further as they get older.

Parental expectations of their adolescents

How parents perceive their children influences youngsters' self-image. Parental perceptions are influenced by their day-to-day life with their youngster. This section describes adolescence from the point of view of carers.

McGrother *et al.* (1996) examined the amount of daily help needed by adults with intellectual disabilities in Leicestershire, but from the perspective of carers. Two-thirds of carers provided personal care for their adult, 80 per cent took them out, 60 per cent kept them company and provided occupation and 90 per cent gave practical domestic help. Todd and Shearn (1996) also spelled out the enormous variety of tasks involved in looking after someone with intellectual disabilities. The amount of care needed inevitably influences parental expectations about adulthood for their youngsters.

While most recognize adolescence as an important stage for young people, it is a turning point for parents too. Until this time, parents could regard their own situation as similar to that of others bringing up children. Even though the child could be associating with children of a younger chronological age ('his friends are all younger and the age gap is increasing', South Wales studies) their own family roles were broadly those of other parents with dependent children, and so understandable to themselves and to others. On the brink of adulthood, this changes:

> 'It's not so much when they're young – it's as they get older you notice the difference.' (South Wales studies)

> 'We did not feel as isolated and embarrassed then [when they were children] as we do now they are adults.' (MacLachlin *et al.* 1989)

It was at this point, too, that some parents began to resent their own restricted lives. Even though they were no more tied than they had been before, crucially their own expectations about what life should be like had changed:

> 'Maybe a little bit [resentful] now, yes. Now and again I feel bitter – I'd like to go out because we're very fond of dancing – I'd like to go to dances and you know you can't go. But now we've got a sort of – a different life. We've just accepted it.' (Shepperdson 1988, p.79)

Even though there are male carers (Parker 1990) the burden often falls disproportionately on women, and some felt disadvantaged (McGrother *et al.* 1996; Todd *et al.* 1993):

> '[My husband's] life has been his own. My life is not my own and that's the only way I can put it.'

'Obviously it's different for other family members, but less than for me. I want to do more. Something for me now.' (South Wales studies)

Adolescence heralded another difficulty for carers. Until this time the needs of their offspring had been similar to those of all children – readily understood and more or less easy to meet. As the 'child' grew up, uncertainties crept in and there was no ready precedent for meeting the needs of young people who had such severe limitations in their levels of independence (Zetlin and Turner 1985):

'There's no one to show her how a teenager should behave.' (South Wales studies)

Some resolved the issue of providing a social life by involving the teenager in their own activities, but parents could not pretend that this was reproducing a normal teenage life, or a normal life for themselves. Parents became trapped in a role which some did not want and they could not, in the nature of things, have the satisfaction of performing well.

The role of expectations in parental adjustment to their prolonged period of parenting is clear. Using the South Wales studies, it is possible to illustrate how parental satisfaction and expectations have changed from the 1980s to 1990s. In objective terms, the comparative youngsters were less dependent than the original cohort had been as teenagers, and there were more services to help. Furthermore, parental lifestyles were not substantially different for the parents of the two cohorts and yet, subjectively, the comparative carers took a more pessimistic view than the original cohort carers had done at the same stage about the degree of handicap of their youngsters and of the difficulties attached to caring for them. Fewer regarded their teenager's disability as slight and fewer considered caring had become easier (Shepperdson 1993). They were also more likely than the older generation of mothers to stress the loss of their own choices in life.

Along with higher expectations for themselves, the comparative carers also had higher expectations for their children. They were more likely to recognize the possibility of future improvements in their abilities: they had greater ambitions about what their children would do when they left school and significantly fewer were destined for the Adult Training Centre – at first, at least

(Shepperdson 1995a). Parents were also more ready to consider future residential care for their teenagers – not as a last resort, but as a positive option – although they were probably helped in this by the greater variety of options becoming available in Wales. However, the majority of parents in both cohorts, at all study stages, still considered that their teenagers would need some support – in varying degrees – for the rest of their lives.

These dilemmas led to the use of ambiguous language by parents in the comparative cohort concerning their teenagers:

'She's reached an awkward stage – neither child or grown up. She's like a 5- or 6-year-old. She would talk to anyone. You couldn't leave her.'

'Though she's 16, she is not even like a 12-year-old. I have a 12-year-old niece, she's full of herself. There's a large difference.'

'It's harder now he's a young man. Naturally he isn't as old as he is and you wouldn't leave an 8- or 9-year-old alone. He's very much between the other two children' [7 and 13 years old]. (South Wales studies)

These dilemmas remained for mothers of the original cohort, who were well into their twenties: 'Forever a child.' 'She's like a teenager, with teenage problems.' 'I say, "You're 25, you must act like a little lady!".' The ambivalence of parents about the maturity of their young people is all too apparent, but how do young people with intellectual disabilities regard themselves? This is perhaps crucial because it suggests how assertive they will be in adopting the lifestyle they themselves think is appropriate.

The self-image of young people with intellectual disabilities

The self-confidence that comes from having a positive self-image is crucial for realizing potential (see Zigler and Hodapp 1986) and is probably necessary if teenagers are to be assertive about their future status. Unfortunately, an intellectual disability is frequently associated with stigma (Harris 1995) and acquiring a positive self-image in these circumstances can be difficult.

According to parents, the South Wales teenagers in the comparative cohort emphazised their own growing maturity:

'He has to go to bed himself – he's a man he tells you.'

'He says, "I'm a man – I'm grown up". This is a problem because he thinks he can do more than he can.'

'"I'm a lady now, Mam" – you mustn't call her a kid or a child.' (South Wales studies)

Nevertheless, over half the parents spoke of youngsters being conscious that they differed from others and, for example, described them standing on the edge of groups of ordinary teenagers, unable to participate and being highly aware of this. Over a third of teenagers recognized a common identity with others who had Down's syndrome and would comment 'someone like me'. A few vehemently denied a handicapped identity. In some ways a higher ability level could actually increase the frustrations of the young person if they were very aware of the discrepancy between their chronological age and their abilities and freedoms, and their aspirations and achievements. One mother spoke of her daughter's painful awareness that her own cookery efforts fell well behind those of her sister.

Other studies had similar findings. Davies and Jenkins (1995) interviewed young people aged 18 to 26 years. Many (42 per cent) had little understanding of the term 'mental handicap' at all, but 30 per cent did understand, but did not apply it to themselves. The remainder had some comprehension of the term and applied it to themselves to a varying extent.

Cunningham, Glenn and Fitzpatrick (in draft) in a wider study of the self-concept of people with Down's syndrome and their transition into adulthood, focused on the role parents play in developing the understanding of young people about disability. The average chronological age of the 78 youngsters in their sample was 19 years 11 months. Using Verbal Mental Age (VMA) as an index for cognitive ability, they found that the youngsters' abilities to formulate social categories followed the same developmental model as for ordinary children. So, it was only when the young people had a VMA over 5.2 years that they became aware of Down's syndrome and disability and then began to understand some of the implications of these categories. On the basis of their research, the authors urge parents to be open and proactive with their youngsters on disability issues, bearing in mind their level of understanding, and to continue to give appropriate information as their offspring mature.

Lifestyle risk and experimentation

The section on social competence and independence touched on the issues of choice and risk. It is during adolescence that ordinary children begin to be given important choices and learn how to cope with risk. This section discusses how far youngsters with intellectual disabilities are encouraged to learn these important lessons. Manthorpe *et al.* (1997, p.70) regard risk as the 'barometer of care' and how it is managed the keystone of ordinary living. It is reasonable to ask how people are to learn to make decisions and handle risk if they have no chance to practise.It is especially important for people with intellectual disabilities who usually need more practice than others to master skills, not less. Heyman and Huckle (1993) confirm the significance of such opportunities during upbringing and found that adults were more likely to reach their potential in daily living skills if they had been brought up in 'risk-tolerant' families. However, Conway (1998) suggests that breaking away from families and behaving independently is harder for adolescents with disabilities than it is for others.

In the South Wales studies, even in quite small matters, most teenagers were – for many reasons – not making decisions for themselves. Parents, in theory, were keen to encourage decision making, but when choices led to even modestly risky behaviour (for example, wearing an unsuitable garment), they often felt it legitimate to intervene. The lifestyles of the teenagers encompassed a wide range in behaviour, but there was usually one common factor: lifestyles were watched and, to a large extent, controlled by parents. Even where independence was encouraged, this was set up or 'allowed' by parents and then monitored to ensure risk-free safety. The choices which were made by parents were no doubt ones that many parents would like to encourage – designed, as they were, to add up to a 'nice', 'moderate', 'safe', 'clean', 'healthy' lifestyle. But, however admirable, these choices are not representative of the range of options open to most teenagers. Most ordinary teenagers incorporate experiment into their growing up, whether parents want this or not.

As we know, ordinary teenagers can be assertive about their own opinions and independence, are close to friends, and sometimes indulge in potentially harmful activities – some drink to excess, some take drugs, smoke and engage in sexual relationships. How far are young people with intellectual disabilities able to make the same choices – including risky ones – as other teenagers? The examples which follow illustrate the extent of parental, rather than teenage, choice.

Everyday choices

The disability movement has firmly refuted any suggestion that needing practical assistance with self-care tasks is a barrier to being an independent and autonomous individual, but the need for other forms of assistance may be more of a threat.

To illustrate these problems at their most basic level, while up to two-thirds of teenagers in both cohorts in South Wales had some input into choosing which clothes to wear in the morning, only half were fully responsible in this sphere, and this proportion had hardly changed by the time the original cohort had reached their twenties.

Similarly, with buying clothes, few teenagers in either cohort were given a completely free hand. Few mothers said 'I give him the money and he goes', although some were trying to encourage choice, 'It's up to you, it's your money'. Again the proportion in charge of their own wardrobes had hardly increased by the time the original cohort had reached their twenties.

There was similar parental control over finance. While just under half of both cohorts were given pocket money as teenagers, the amounts were usually small. By their twenties the situation had not really changed for the original cohort and only a quarter had a regular and fixed amount every week (Shepperdson 1994).

Choice of friends

Friendships are very important to most young people. Balding (1998) found that about half of his sample of 14- to 15-year-olds had met a friend the evening before they completed his questionnaire. In contrast, several studies suggest that youngsters with intellectual disabilities are isolated. Richardson, Koller and Katz (1994), Carr (1995) and Grant (1993) found their social networks were severely restricted. Even if they were integrated into various activities, they could still find themselves socially isolated. Heyman and Huckle (1993) noted that most of the adults attending the adult training centre wanted to see more of their colleagues at home, but this was often not recognized by informal carers.

Given the limited freedom of the youngsters, contact with friends at home is usually dependent on arrangements made by two sets of parents. In fact, less than a third of the South Wales teenagers in the comparative cohort had friends they ever met at home (never mind on a regular basis). This was also the case for the earlier, original cohort, and by their twenties even fewer (less than a sixth) had friends they saw at home. The trajectory was not towards expanded contacts, but rather the reverse. This does not mean the youngsters were social isolates. The later generation of teenagers, especially, engaged in a variety of activities, both for 'special' groups (e.g. Gateway clubs) and for the general public (e.g. rugby clubs, youth clubs). Nevertheless, close, one-to-one, equal and spontaneous relationships were uncommon for both cohorts (Shepperdson 1992, 1993).

It is a sad reflection of the esteem in which disabled people are held that, while most people choose people like themselves for friends (Allan 1989), the most valued friends for people with intellectual disabilities are those without disabilities, with clear implications here for self-esteem (Chappell 1994).

Choices in sexual activity

Adolescence is usually associated with the beginning of romantic/sexual relationships with the opposite sex and a time for sexual experimentation. Balding (1998) reports that only about a sixth of 14- to 15-year-olds had never had a friend of the opposite sex, although over half did not have a current one. Once more, people with intellectual disabilities differ from their peers.

Heyman and Huckle (1995), in their work on the management of risk for people with intellectual disabilities, found that sexual relationships were perceived by parents to be a potentially dangerous hazard, to be avoided, not risked. While many parents might agree with this for any youngsters, the confined and controlled lives led by young people with intellectual disabilities – watched when they stay in, go out, seek (or are exposed to) information, and with few peer contacts to broaden horizons – make it possible for parents of these teenagers to reduce risks to ones they choose and are happy with.

This was apparent in the South Wales studies (Shepperdson 1995b). Comparing the two cohorts, it was possible to detect more permissive parental attitudes to sexual relationships emerging. However, these were rarely translated into action and there were many barriers to sexual experiences and experimentation. In practical terms, opportunities for such activities were limited. Parents usually knew about the activities of their teenagers, and blossoming relationships or sexual encounters were rarely encouraged. Further, sex education was not always given, even though at teenage many parents recognized the necessity for it. For the original cohort it seemed, in the eyes of parents, that this need had declined by the time the youngsters reached their twenties. Somehow the time had passed, the difficult years had been negotiated, it had not been found necessary for their own particular son and daughter and, in the absence of any crisis, parents certainly did not want to provoke an interest in matters which could not be indulged. 'The less he knows the better, we don't go looking for trouble.' (Shepperdson 1995b, p.342)

Parents were asked about the state of sexual knowledge of their youngsters. Sadly, the state of education being as it was, youngsters knew more about events that they were unlikely to encounter – pregnancy and birth – than they did about more likely situations – sexual intercourse. Moreover, while many parents discouraged sexual experimentation and despite their protection, some of the young people had had experience of the less desirable aspects of sexual experience, such as rape, incest, sexual abuse, seduction and unwanted pregnancy.

Even with permissive parents, it cannot be over-emphasized that their expectations of sexual activity were within a very narrow and respectable range: the importance of loving, longstanding relationships was stressed and more deviant activities never discussed, except as something to be avoided. Parents were rarely in favour of parenthood.

This account is of the majority. On a happier note, some parents gave their teenagers excellent education and encouraged relationships. Marriage was on the agenda for two of Carr's 21-year-olds, and at least one of the young women in the South Wales original cohort. However, no area better illustrates Baker's point about children needing to grasp adult life, if it is to be achieved, than in the field of sexual experience. Parents remarked that if their teenagers insisted on sexual partners, or 'if their happiness depended on it', they would accept it. However, since teenagers knew little officially of sexual matters, had few opportunities to gather information, were protected from practical experiences and lacked skills of negotiation and assertiveness, even if they overcame these other barriers, parents were unlikely to be tested on this point.

Choices concerning alcohol

Balding (1998) found that 71 per cent of 14- to 15-year-olds had drunk some form of alcohol in the past week. Over half sometimes drank without their parents' knowledge. Evidence suggests that people with even mild intellectual disabilities know little about alcohol and are vulnerable to social pressure to drink – so they know less but may need to know more. They are able to benefit from alcohol education programmes (McCusker *et al.* 1993). Lawrensen, Lindsay and Walker (1995) found that fewer people with intellectual disabilities reported drinking than in the general population, and they drank less, but two-thirds were unaware of potential dangers and none knew what those dangers were.

In the South Wales studies, 62 per cent of the comparative teenagers drank alcohol. Drinking was often limited to 'sips' or 'at Christmas'. The words 'we do limit it' were used frequently by parents, and even for those over age: 'It's got to be in moderation'. As with so many activities, drinking was closely monitored and, for example, friends of parents who bought drinks for the teenagers were asked to let the parents know.

Unfortunately, alcohol was not discussed with all parents of the original cohort at teenage, but at 24 to 27 years, 78 per cent of the men did drink some alcohol and so did 70 per cent of the women. Two of the men drank as much as four pints at a sitting, but this was unusual and drinks were often diluted or more of a token. Some of the women were given 'sips' only. In one exceptional instance, a young woman raided her parents' drinks cupboard while they were out and got thoroughly drunk. For most of the time though, as with so much else, the keynote was parental awareness, watchfulness and control.

Choices concerning smoking

Balding (1998) found that a third of 14- to 15-year-olds had smoked in the last seven days. No one in the South Wales cohorts was known to smoke. By adulthood, 12 per cent of the men had 'tried' a cigarette or 'had a puff'. One woman had been offered a cigarette and three had smoked in the past. This may reflect the higher abilities, and so opportunities, of these young women.

> 'She'd been trying them and buying them – she hid it from us. [We only knew because] she said, "I've given that up now".'

> 'She hasn't wanted to. I'm glad because I couldn't stop her – I'd have to accept it, or given up myself.'

Conclusion

There are usually more similarities than differences between children with intellectual disabilities and their non-disabled peers (Byrne, Cunningham and Sloper 1988), but adolescence marks the onset of an increasing divergence. Parents of young people with intellectual disabilities have a particularly difficult task because, unlike other parents, they are in a position to control their offsprings' lives and thus protect them from making mistakes. Their natural fears, combined with a lack of assertiveness on the part of the youngsters themselves, may well result in these young people remaining stuck at the transitional stage between child and adult – adolescents in lifestyle long beyond the chronological age at which it would seem reasonable.

Professionals should recognize that the learning period and growth of independence and autonomy may be considerably extended for people with intellectual disabilities. They should reassure parents that development will continue into the twenties and even beyond, and ensure that appropriate opportunities are provided to encourage maximum potential. The model of ordinary adolescence may indicate the stage at which progress will occur, but not necessarily the chronological age. Parents should be helped to negotiate the difficult path between allowing independence, learning about risk and offering only that protection which is appropriate. As for all youngsters, emotional upsets or 'mistakes' should not lead necessarily to increased protection, but rather be regarded as part of growing up.

Modern attitudes mean that nowadays independence is more often encouraged for youngsters. Parents too are more likely to recognize their own right to lay aside caring duties. Furthermore, it has been suggested that new generations of youngsters may be achieving greater levels of competence in self-care, making independence a more realistic option. These changes – in attitudes, parental wishes and in the youngsters themselves – may result in opportunities which will encourage the development of adult maturity. However, while service providers pay lip service to such developments, until the service support necessary to achieve these aims – such as advocacy and independent living options – becomes universally available, many people with intellectual disabilities will be denied the chance to use the adolescent years for the development of the skills which they will need in adult life.

References

Allan, G. (1989) *Friendship: Developing a Sociological Perspective*. Hemel Hempstead: Harvester Wheatsheaf.

Baker, P. (1991) 'Parents – problems and perspectives.' In W.L. Fraser, R.C. MacGillvray and A.M. Green *Hallas' Caring for People with Mental Handicaps*, 8th edn. Oxford: Butterworth Heinemann.

Balding, J. (1998) *Young People in 1997*. Exeter: University of Exeter, Schools Health Education Unit.

Buckley, S. and Sacks, B. (1987) *The Adolescent with Down's Syndrome*. Portsmouth: Portsmouth Polytechnic.

Byrne, E.A., Cunningham, C.C. and Sloper, P. (1988) *Families and their Children with Down's Syndrome: One Feature in Common*. London: Routledge.

Carr, K. (1988) 'Six weeks to 21-years-old: a longitudinal study of children with Down's syndrome and their families.' *Journal of Child Psychology and Psychiatry 29*, 407–431.

Carr, J. (1995) *Down's Syndrome. Children Growing Up*. Cambridge: Cambridge University Press.

Chappell, L.L. (1994) 'A question of friendship – community care and the relationships of people with learning difficulties.' *Disability and Society 9*, 4, 419–434.

Coleman, J. (1999) 'The trouble with teenagers.' *Community Care*, 7 – 13 October.

Conger, J.J. and Galambos, N.L. (1996) *Adolescence and Youth*. 5th edn. New York: Longman.

Conway, S.P. (1998) 'Transition from paediatric to adult-orientated care for adolescents with cystic fibrosis.' *Disability and Rehabilitation 20*, 6–7, 209–216.

Craft, M. (1979) 'Chromosomal anomalies.' In M. Craft (ed) *Tredgold's Mental Retardation*. London: Ballière and Tindall.

Cunningham, C.C., Glenn, S. and Fitzpatrick, H. (in draft) 'Parents telling their offspring about Down's Syndrome and disability.' Liverpool: School of Health, John Moores University.

Davies, C.A. and Jenkins, R. (1995) 'She has different fits to me: how people with learning difficulties see themselves.' *Disability and Society 12*, 1, 95–109.

Field, S., Hoffman, A. and Posch, M. (1997) 'Self determination during adolescence – a developmental perspective.' *Remedial and Special Education 8*, 5, 285–293.

Fraser, W.L., MacGillvray, R.C. and Green, A.M. (1991) *Hallas' Caring for People with Mental Handicaps*, 8th edn. Oxford: Butterworth Heinemann.

Grant, G. (1993) 'Support networks and transitions over two years among adults with a mental handicap.' *Mental Handicap Research 6*, 36–55.

Harris, P. (1995) 'Who am I? Concepts of disability and their implications for people with learning disabilities.' *Disability and Society 10*, 3, 341–351.

Heyman, B. and Huckle, S. (1993) 'Not worth the risk – attitudes of adults with learning difficulties and their informal and formal carers to the hazards of everyday life.' *Social Sciences and Medicine 37*, 12, 1557–1564.

Heyman, B. and Huckle, S. (1995) 'Sexuality as a perceived hazard in the lives of adults with learning difficulties.' *Disability and Society 10*, 2, 139–155.

Jenkins, R. (1989) 'Barriers to adulthood: Long-term unemployment and mental handicap compared.' In A. Brechin and J. Walmsley (eds) *Making Connections*. London: Hodder and Stoughton.

Lawrenson, H., Lindsay, W.R. and Walker, P. (1995) 'The pattern of alcohol consumption within a sample of mentally handicapped people in Tayside.' *Mental Handicap Research 8*, 1, 54–59.

McCusker, C.G., Clare, I.C.H., Cullen, C. and Reep, J. (1993) 'Alcohol-related knowledge and attitudes in people with a mild learning disability – the effects of a sensible drinking group.' *Journal of Community and Applied Social Psychology 3*, 1, 29–40.

McGrother, C.W., Hauck, A., Baumik, S., Thorp, C. and Taub, N. (1996) 'Community care for adults with learning disability and their carers: Needs and outcomes from the Leicestershire Register.' *Journal of Intellectual Disability Research 40*, 2, 183–190.

MacLachlin, M., Dennis, P., Lang, H., Charnock, S. and Osman, J. (1989) 'Do the professionals understand? Mothers' views of families' service needs.' In A. Brechin and J. Walmsley *Making Connections*. London: Hodder and Stoughton.

Manthorpe, J. and Walsh, M. with Alaszewski, A. and Harrison, L. (1997) 'Issues of risk practice and welfare in learning disability services.' *Disability and Society 121*, 69–82.

Parker, G. (1990) 'With due care and attention. A review of research on informal care.' Occasional paper no. 2. London: Family Policy Studies Centre.

Richardson, S.A., Koller, H. and Katz, M. (1994) 'Leisure activities of young adults not receiving mental handicap services who were in a special school for mental handicap as children.' *Journal of Intellectual Disability Research 38*, 163–175.

Shepperdson, B. (1985) 'Changes in the characteristics of families with Down's syndrome children.' *Epidemiology and Community Health 39*, 4, 320–324.

Shepperdson, B. (1988) *Growing up with Down's Syndrome*. London: Cassell.

Shepperdson, B. (1992) *Longitudinal Study of a Cohort of People with Down's Syndrome.* Report for ESRC. Swansea: University College of Wales.

Shepperdson, B. (1993) *A Longitudinal and Comparative Study of Teenagers with Down's Syndrome.* Report for Leverhulme Trust. Swansea: University College of Wales.

Shepperdson, B. (1994) 'A comparison of the development of independence in two cohorts of young people with Down's syndrome.' *Down's Syndrome: Research and Practice 2*, 1, 11–18.

Shepperdson, B. (1995a) 'Changes in options for school leavers with Down's syndrome.' *Care in Place 2*, 1, 22–28.

Shepperdson, B. (1995b) 'The control of sexuality in young people with Down's syndrome.' *Children: Care, Health and Development 21*, 5, 333–349.

Taylor, C. (1997) 'Learned helplessness.' *Down's Syndrome Association Newsletter 86.*

Thomson, G.O.B., Ward, K.M. and Wishart, J.G. (1995) 'The transition to adulthood for children with Down's syndrome.' *Disability and Society 10*, 3, 325–340.

Todd, J., Shearn, J., Beyer, S. and Felce, D. (1993) 'Careers in caring – the changing situation of parents caring for an offspring with learning difficulties.' *Irish Journal of Psychology 14*, 1, 130–153.

Todd, S. and Shearn, J. (1996) 'Struggles with time, the careers of parents with adult sons and daughters with learning disabilities.' *Disability and Society 11*, 3, 379–401.

Welsh Office (1983) *All Wales Strategy for the Development of Services for Mentally Handicapped People.* Cardiff: Welsh Office.

Zetlin, A.G. and Turner, J.L. (1985) 'Transition from adolescence to adulthood: Perspectives of mentally retarded individuals and their families.' *American Journal of Mental Deficiency 89*, 6, 570–579.

Zigler, E. and Hodapp, R.M. (1986) *Understanding Mental Retardation.* Cambridge: Cambridge University Press.

CHAPTER 5

Becoming Adult

School leaving, Jobs and the Transition to Adult Life[1]

David May

> Work makes you feel you are normal, like everyone else, and gives
> you self-respect.
>
> (Disabled adolescent, quoted in CERI 1983)

In the normal course of events most children progress naturally and with little ceremony, if not always smoothly, to full adult membership of society. There comes a time – its precise occurrence varies – when everyone, families included, begins to think of them as fully mature, independent and responsible citizens. Adulthood is an emergent status realized through the gradual acquisition of certain rights, privileges and responsibilities. Many of these are mundane, even trivial: the right to purchase cigarettes, consume alcohol, drive a car. Others are of greater moment, touching as they do on our status as participating members of society: the right to vote, fight for our country, enter into legal contracts, marry.

For young people with an intellectual disability, as Shepperdson argues in Chapter 4, such a natural progression cannot be taken for granted. To the extent that a sustainable claim to adulthood involves a degree of independence and

---

[1]   This is an extensively revised version of the chapter that appeared in Research Highlights 16 *Living with Mental Handicap*, G. Horobin and D. May (eds), Jessica Kingsley Publishers, 1988, under the title: 'From handicapped to normal: Problems and prospects in the transition from school to adult life.'

control over one's life which is so often denied people with intellectual disabilities, adulthood is for them an inherently problematic concept, at best imperfectly realized and for some postponed indefinitely.

While not wishing to discount the importance of family in the construction of adult identities (see again Shepperdson, Chapter 4) the difficulty that young people with intellectual disabilities experience has in good measure arisen from their exclusion from the jobs market. In our contemporary society work serves both materialist and symbolic functions. As Hockey and James (1993) note, '[it] does not simply provide the means of earning a living' (although one should not discount the importance of financial rewards, not least in allowing one to get out from under parental control); 'it is a significant source of cultural meanings, shaping the structure of the individual's daily life and social encounters and providing a sense of self and social identity' (p.136). Denied access to work, young people, it has been argued, remain 'trapped in a state of suspended animation' (Willis 1984) or 'no man's land' (Coffield, Borrill and Marshall 1986) – no longer children, but not yet adults.

While it may not be possible to state precisely when the child becomes the (wo)man, the beginnings of the process (at least in its social manifestations) are much easier to locate. School leaving – the termination of the years of compulsory education – remains, even in our less age-conscious society, one of life's decisive turning points. The kind of future we can look forward to, indeed the kind of person we will become, are very often effectively determined at this time. Beyond the severely practical problems entailed in finding a job or, more ambitiously, choosing a career, the event itself is invested with considerable symbolic significance. As historians of childhood from Aries (1973) onwards have argued, it is the schoolroom above all other institutions that has both defined, and confined the modern child, shaping the experiences to which s/he is exposed and, by extension, the qualities with which s/he is endowed (May and Strong 1980). While leaving school may not bring immediate elevation to adult status, it does clearly signal the end of childhood.

For those children who are labelled as intellectually disabled the significance of leaving school is even more far reaching. Since their presence in the special class or unit formally proclaims their disability as well as their childhood, leaving school promises release from both (Cheston 1994). What is involved at this time, although all too frequently obscured by the urgency of the need for appropriate post-school placements, is a reassessment of identity and status. Therein lies the significance of the sharp decline in prevalence rates in the years immediately following school leaving, which for much of the past century has been such an enduring feature of the epidemiology of intellectual disabilities (Richardson and Koller 1985). Around this time more than a half of all children ever classified as intellectually disabled would regularly disappear from administrative purview. Absorbed into the general labour force by the demand of the industrialized economies for cheap, unskilled workers, they ceased for all practical purposes to be 'intellectually disabled'. But in recent years all this has changed; the old economic order has given way to a much more uncertain environment. Unemployment has risen significantly and few young people now move easily into work on leaving school, with implications not only for the transition from child to adult, but more specifically for the kind of adulthood to which people with intellectual disabilities might aspire.

School leaving and the experience of work: the research evidence

Concern with the vocational adjustment of people with an intellectual disability has a long history and has generated a considerable body of research (see Goldstein 1964 for a comprehensive review of earlier work). Its range in both time and space presents problems of comparability (May and Hughes 1988). I propose in this chapter to focus on just five studies dealing with the experience of intellectually disabled school leavers in the labour market in one region of the UK. Taken together they provide a unique record of the changing fortunes of this group over the past 50 years.

Ferguson and Kerr's (1955, 1958) surveys of separate male and female cohorts leaving Glasgow's special schools in the late 1940s (median IQ = 65) provide data for a time when, in their words, only 'the lazy, the fed-up and the eccentric' failed to find work: 88 per cent of the young men and 79 per cent of the young women in their samples were in open employment by their mid-twenties. Moreover, two-thirds of the boys had been continuously employed over the two-year period covered by the survey, the great majority in the same job. 'It was not at all uncommon,' they report, 'to find illiterate men holding relatively well-paid jobs over long periods, even where the level of general intelligence was very low, though, in general, the lower the intelligence, the poorer the job' (Ferguson and Kerr 1958, p.36).

Similarly with the females: only 11 per cent had been continuously unemployed since leaving school, while 27 per cent had been in the same job for the whole period, and 61 per cent had held no more than two jobs in that time. Unlike the boys, for whom unemployment was inversely related to IQ, no such obvious relationship was apparent in the the girls' case, apart from the fact that few with an IQ of less than 50 were able to find work at all.

All but a handful of both sexes were confined to unskilled or semi-skilled work: the boys mainly as labourers in factories and shipyards, the girls as machinists, packers, bottlers and washers in bonded warehouses, with some in domestic service. Nevertheless, the authors conclude:

> [The] final impression left by the performance of these lads since they left school is, as with the corresponding group of girls, one of amazement that they have been so successful in holding jobs, even in their middle twenties, when the mad scramble for juvenile labour has largely passed. With meagre educational equipment, usually without the advantage of a pushing parent, and often with all the handicaps of an indifferent home, the great majority have contrived to keep in steady work. (Ferguson and Kerr 1958, p.38)

The second study (Jackson 1968) was carried out more than a decade later in Edinburgh. This involved a three-year follow-up over the period 1959 to 1962 of 188 'educable mentally retarded' (EMR) pupils (105 males: mean IQ = 64 and 83 females: mean IQ = 58) from five special schools serving the city. No point-specific employment rates are given, but 52 per cent of males and 58 per cent of females experienced less than six months unemployment in that period, while 17 per cent of males and 20 per cent of females were either considered unemployable or did not find jobs. Job turnover was higher than for the Ferguson and Kerr samples (mean number of jobs held: males 4.6, females 3.5). The males were especially likely (27 per cent of all jobs held) to be employed as delivery boys for bakeries, laundaries or dairies, while almost half of the jobs held by females involved semi-skilled work in food and drink manufacturing.

There was a positive relationship between IQ and successful adjustment to employment (as measured by the time out of work and the number of jobs held). Those considered unemployable or who had withdrawn from the labour market had significantly lower IQs than those remaining in open employment.

The work by Richardson and his associates in Aberdeen is part of a much more ambitious programme of research into the causes and consequences of intellectual disability (Richardson and Koller 1996). They followed a cohort of young people, born between 1951 and 1955, from school leaving, in the late 1960s, up to age 22. With one exception, all those with severe intellectual disabilities entered adult services on leaving school. They therefore report separately on the job histories of 154 (89 males and 65 females) all with IQs of 50 or more (mean IQ = 65) (Richardson, Koller and Katz 1988).

In employment terms little seems to have changed since Ferguson and Kerr's time, with almost all young people leaving school for work. Four-fifths of Richardson's sample with 'mild mental retardation' (82 per cent of males and 77 per cent of females) moved from school into jobs. Six years later, at age 22, male employment had fallen slightly, to 74 per cent, but for the women it had declined dramatically to only 28 per cent, although a further 29 per cent were now full-time housewives. Employment levels for young people with intellectual disabilities of both sexes were lower than for a comparison group of non-disabled young people.

By age 22, 18 per cent of males and 29 per cent of females in the study group had withdrawn from the labour market and were receiving services for people with intellectual disabilities. They were by and large those with the lowest IQs (a mean of 60 compared with 67 for those in work), although 20 per cent of those with jobs at the end of the period had IQs of less than 60.

Compared with their non-disabled peers, the young people in the Aberdeen cohort with intellectual disabilities had 'lower levels of job skills, were paid less for the same level of job skill, less often had jobs requiring interpersonal skills, less often took part-time jobs, less often became apprentices and for those who entered apprenticeships less often completed the apprenticeships' (Richardson *et al.* 1988, p.489). However there was no significant difference for either sex on job turnover. On the three principal measures of success in the labour market used by Richardson *et al.* – total amount of unemployment experienced, job turnover and time out of the labour market – 42 per cent of those with mild intellectual disabilities, both male and female, had records that were the equal of their non-disabled comparisons.

While unemployment remained low in the immediate post-war period, it began to rise, imperceptibly at first, from the late 1960s. A survey carried out for the Warnock committee in the mid-1970s (Walker 1982) which revealed that less than half of 'handicapped' school leavers were now able to find work, surely sounded a warning. But it was the recession of 1979 to 1981, with its traumatizing effects on British manufacturing industry, that radically transformed the situation. Data from the Scottish School Leavers project show that in 1983 the proportion of young people generally moving into full-time jobs on school leaving had fallen to 42 per cent, down from 72 per cent in the late 1970s. By 1987 it had fallen further, to 26 per cent. Those leaving without any formal qualifications were even less likely to find work (Furlong 1990).

The study by May and Hughes (1986) in Tayside coincided with the sudden onset of the recession and graphically illustrates its impact on young people with intellectual disabilities. Over an 18-month period they followed 100+ young people leaving schools and units for pupils with special educational needs in the region during the academic session 1980 to 1981, nearly two-thirds of whom (N = 63) were pupils with mild to moderate intellectual disabilities.

Only three – all males – moved directly into a job, in two cases obtained through family connections. In all, 9 of the 63 (4 males (13%) and 5 females (16%)) held jobs in the study period, but for most it was a short-lived experience, in one case for less than a full day. At the end of the period there were still just three people (again all males) in employment, only one of whom had held on to the same job for the whole period. More than half (52%) were unemployed, including eight who had been continuously so since leaving school. A further 16 per cent had dropped out of the job market altogether and were attending day centres for people with intellectual disabilities.

'Success' in the job market correlated with IQ. All of those attending schools or units for severe intellectual disability (all with IQs of less than 51) moved into adult services. The mean IQ of those who found work, however briefly, was 75 compared with 60 for those from schools or units for children with mild to moderate intellectual disabilities entering day centres. Somewhat ironically, the most able 25 per cent (mean IQ = 78), all of whom continued to press their claims to employment, experienced significantly more 'unoccupied' time (i.e. time when they were neither employed, in training, nor receiving services) than those with lower IQs.

The final study I wish to consider here was carried out in the late 1980s by a group of researchers at Edinburgh and Stirling universities. It differs from the others examined in two important respects. First, it employs a national, Scotland-wide sample. Second, it is not limited to young people with intellectual disabilities, but includes all those with a 'record of needs', reflecting the changes to the organization and structure of special needs education consequent upon the 1980–81 Education (Scotland) Acts (see Thomson, Chapter 3). The full sample consists of 618 pupils with special educational needs (SEN) who attained statutory school-leaving age in the academic session 1986–87. Little information is provided on school background, but it is noted (Ward, Thomson and Riddell 1994) that only 7 per cent had experienced mainstream schooling. Data collection occurred at three separate stages: school leaving, in 1990 at age 19-plus, and in 1993 at age 22-plus. There was a high attrition rate (in excess of 22%) and in the paper by Thomson and Ward (1995), which contains the most detailed information on employment experience, the analysis is restricted to 360 (58%: 184 males and 176 females) of the total sample for whom complete data were available. Although no IQ data are provided, a subgroup of 77 young people with 'mild/moderate learning difficulties' (M/MLD) is identified.

An employment rate of 13 per cent is reported for this group at school leaving, still extremely low compared with the immediate post-war period, but more than three times that reported by May and Hughes (1985) at the beginning of the decade. Employment levels tended to rise the further the cohort moved away from school, so that by age 22-plus, 34 per cent were in employment. This suggests that studies limited to the immediate post-school period may well present an overly pessimistic picture of long-term prospects. However, Thomson and Ward (1995) also note 'the low level, transient nature' of much of the work obtained and the ever-present threat of imminent unemployment. It should be noted that almost as many (32%) of the group were 'at home' as were in work, although how many of these were unemployed or were for various reasons (e.g. because they were married and/or were looking after children) not at that time seeking work, it is not possible to tell from the published data. A further 14 per cent had withdrawn from the labour market altogether and were receiving services for people with intellectual disabilities. As one might expect, there was a strong, positive correlation between employment and the demonstration of personal independence (including the ability to manage money, negotiate public transport, as well as carry out basic self-care tasks). Those who had high dependency needs were likely to end up in some form of sheltered placement.

The experience of open employment

In the three decades following World War II, as our review of the Scottish research reveals and the wider literature confirms, a generally buoyant labour market meant that a majority of young people with intellectual disabilities – somewhere between one-half and four-fifths – could expect to find work on leaving school. The young men were, by and large, more successful in this respect than the women (Ferguson and Kerr 1955, 1958; Jackson 1968; May and Hughes 1985; Richardson *et al.* 1988), a gender differential that widens as the latter move into their twenties and withdraw from the labour market – at least temporarily – to marry and raise families. But it is also the case that females are more likely to transfer to services for adults with intellectual disabilities on leaving school (May and Hughes 1985; Richardson *et al.* 1988).

By the late 1970s the prospects for intellectually disabled school leavers, along with those for all young people, had changed dramatically and, it would seem, notwithstanding some recent improvement in the employment figures, permanently. Now few if any young people (certainly not those with intellectual disabilities) find secure employment on leaving school. Even in good times young people with intellectual disabilities had consistently higher unemployment rates than their non-disabled peers (Richardson *et al.* 1988; Roberts 1975; Walker 1982). They took longer to find work in the first place (Roberts 1975) and were less likely to be recruited whenever labour was in surplus and employers could pick and choose, although this may have been less the result of direct discrimination than recruitment policies that emphasize appearance, general intelligence and mental alertness (Newton, Robinson and Pappenheim 1982; Walker 1982). Lack of interpersonal skills and basic literacy and numeracy confined them to unskilled and semi-skilled jobs with little prospect of advancement, and which are always the first to disappear in any recession or as the result of technological change (Ferguson and Kerr 1955, 1958; Jackson 1968; Richardson *et al.* 1988; Thomson and Ward 1995; Tuckey, Parfit and Tuckey 1973; Walker 1982). Thus the young women in the studies reviewed above worked in restaurants as cleaners and dish washers, but rarely waitresses, while the young men were delivery boys, but not van drivers.

The cross-sectional design of much of the research inevitably conceals the transitory nature of work for many, perhaps a majority, of unqualified young people. This is a point forcefully made by Kernan and Koegal (1984). In a study extending over 30 months of an admittedly unrepresentative sample of 48 'mildly retarded' people in Los Angeles, they found 21 who had spent some time in competitive employment, but only six who had held the same job for the whole of the period, and four of these were employed part time. Similar findings are reported by May and Hughes (1985). Of the nine young people in their sample of 63 'mildly mentally handicapped' school leavers, only one remained in the same job for the whole of the 18-month study period. The six who were no longer employed at the end of that period held on to their jobs for an average of 11 weeks, and in the case of one young woman for less than half a day. Rather better findings are presented in the national survey of employment commissioned by the Warnock committee in the late 1970s. Two-thirds of those ESN(M) youngsters who entered the labour market remained in continuous employment during the two years following school leaving, although as many as one-quarter had been out of work for at least half that time (Walker 1982). This is more in line with those studies which suggest that on job turnover the record of young people with intellectual disabilities is no worse than young unqualified people generally, and that in fact those who retain their jobs into their mid-twenties go on to develop employment records as stable, if not more so, than the non-disabled (Atkinson 1984; Clarke, Clarke and Adams 1960). The careful analysis of their data by Richardson *et al.* (1988) suggests that any problem is largely confined to a small subset of the population whose claim to employability in any event remains questionable. In the past employment rates seem to have been highest in the months immediately following school leaving, due largely no doubt to the activities of school and careers staff, but this may well be a trend that is reversing as post-school vocational training assumes increasing importance (Thomson and Ward 1995).

Employment rates *per se* tell us little about the conditions under which jobs are held. It is clear that in the past young people with intellectual disabilities who entered the labour market all too often found themselves abused and exploited, recruited in the first place for their docility and willingness to accept conditions at work which others would not put up with. Ferguson and Kerr (1958) report that the young men in their Glasgow cohort went into jobs that were 'dirty, unpleasant, or heavy, or which from their nature were not likely to be of universal appeal'. The girls likewise got work which was 'repetitive', 'unattractive', and 'often dirty' (Ferguson and Kerr 1955). A decade later special school leavers in Edinburgh were to be found in jobs characterized by 'impermanence of tenure, poor remuneration, and limited prospects' (Jackson 1968). Compared with other school leavers, Walker's (1982) 'handicapped' group worked longer hours, did heavier work, had fewer facilities at work, were more often isolated from their work mates and were more likely to feel insecure and unhappy. Richardson and Koller (1996) also found members of their cohort in jobs that 'were often repetitious and of little intrinsic interest, located in unpleasant physical environments, and offer[ing] little or no autonomy or responsibility in organizing the work' (p.267).

SEN school leavers are typically paid less for the same work than their non-disabled peers (Richardson and Koller 1996). Not infrequently they are (or were) expected to work for no wages at all or for little more than gratuities, their employment defined in therapeutic rather than economic terms (Baron, Riddell and Wilson 1999). One young man in Richardson and Koller's (1996) Aberdeen cohort worked for two years on first leaving school (in the late 1960s) at a stables cleaning out the byres and grooming the horses for 50p per week until he was summarily dismissed. Nor should we assume that a job necessarily implies a change of status. On the contrary, many of the jobs available to young people with disabilities are inherently stigmatizing, in part because of the nature of the work involved, but also because of their association with special schooling (Richardson and Koller 1996). To deny one's past or otherwise to challenge the implications of personal inadequacy that such employment announces is not only pointless, but risks dismissal (Clarke *et al.* 1960; May and Hughes 1985).

One final point needs to be made about the experience of young people with intellectual disabilities in the labour market. It is such a universal and consistent finding that it frequently goes unremarked upon by commentators and, especially in many of the earlier investigations, is simply incorporated into their research design. It is, however, a finding of great significance and like many taken for granted 'facts of life' tells us a great deal about the world in which we live, and in this particular case, the meaning of intellectual disabilities. I will return to this below, but for now it is sufficient to note that, even when demand is high, employment of young people with intellectual disabilities is by and large restricted to those with mild to moderate disabilities – generally those with IQs of less than 60 and almost invariably those with IQs of less than 50. Changes in educational practice and the organization of schooling, which might in the past have in part accounted for such exclusion, would seem to have made little difference. Although 'a small number' of Todd, Evans and Beyer's (1991) sample of people with 'severe learning disabilities' in South Wales took up 'transitional vocational activities' in the immediate post-school period, by their early twenties none was in open employment and the vast majority (88%) were attending day centres. Similarly 95 per cent of those with 'severe learning difficulties' in Thomson and Ward's (1995) Scottish sample were by the same age to be found in equally sheltered placements, while for all 35 of those with Down's syndrome 'the principal and consistent' placement was the supervised adult training centre (Thomson *et al.* 1995).

Youth training: the alternative to work

The severity of the early 1980s recession with its devastating effect on youth employment generally compelled government action. What resulted was a veritable alphabet soup of special programmes and training initiatives – TOPs, YOPs, YTS, YT, TVEI, WEEPs, WICs, TECs, LECs – all roundly dismissed by their less than enthusiastic participants as 'shit jobs' and 'govvie schemes'

(Coffield, Borrill and Marshall 1986; see also Roberts 1984; Wallace 1987). Nonetheless, by the mid-1980s upwards of two-thirds of all unqualified school leavers found their way onto such programmes (Brogan and Jennings 1993; Raffe 1990).

While much has been written about this initiative, it is mainly from the perspective of non-disabled young people. There are few critical evaluations of the experience of those with special needs. Two ethnographic studies – Shone and Atkinson (1980) in South Wales and May and Hughes (1986) in Tayside – in the early years of the programme emphasize its decidedly provisional and *ad hoc* status, with little central direction and particular schemes springing up in response to individual initiatives or the changing perception of need among local officials. Courses for SEN students tended to be marginalized, both physically and organizationally, and opportunities for integration were limited. Working practices and course content often bore only a tenuous relationship to formally stated goals, and curriculum development took on a highly improvised quality as staff struggled to reach students quite different, both intellectually and behaviourally, from those they were more used to dealing with. Young people with intellectual disabilities tended to be restricted to basic level courses, those emphasizing remedial and social education, rather than vocational training. More than half of all placements to YOPs in the Tayside study were to entry level courses (mainly Work Introduction Courses (WICs)) that offered no formal qualifications and very little prospect of work on completion. Those assigned to more advanced courses had a high failure rate – 53 per cent of such placements were prematurely terminated – and only two found work on completion, shortlived in both cases. Similar findings are reported from South Wales where 80 per cent of placements from the unit evaluated by Atkinson and his colleagues were to other government training schemes or to facilities reserved for people with disabilities (Doogan 1982).

It must be emphasized that both studies refer to the early years of youth training when careers officers, school authorities and training agencies, all overwhelmed by the magnitude of the crisis that confronted them, were very much driven to making policy 'on the hoof'. More recent descriptions (though, notably, not evaluations – see the collection in Closs 1993) suggest a much more established and articulated programme. Two related developments in particular are worth noting. The first is the extension of post–16 provision within the school system (Jones, Hemp and McIlhenny 1989; Wilson and Cherry 1993). Whereas continuation at school beyond minimum school-leaving age (MSLA) by those with special needs had in the past typically been a response to the lack of jobs and/or post-school provision generally (May and Hughes 1986), the development of a distinctive curriculum oriented to 'preparation for adult life through the development of social and intellectual competence' (Wilson and Cherry 1993) has made it a much more positive experience, encouraging many parents and young people to look on it as a valued 'bridge between school and post-school opportunities' (Ward *et al.* 1994). Almost half (47%) of Thomson and Ward's (1995) sample, for example, stayed on at school beyond MSLA and 6 per cent were still there at 19-plus.

The MSC (1977) and Warnock (1978) reports of the late 1970s were influential in opening up further education to school leavers of low attainment and limited social competence. By the early 1980s this was the first destination of about one in three SEN school leavers (Corrie and Zaklukiewicz 1983; Taylor 1986), while Thomson and Ward (1995) report as many as 71 per cent of their cohort with M/MLD leaving for 'post-school education and training' (a category that includes YT programmes). This compares with just 7 per cent of Walker's (1982) ESN(M) group who had received any further education in the two years since leaving school less than a decade earlier. 'Link' courses, which allow pupils with SEN to explore the possibilities of further education on a day release basis, have proved particularly effective in encouraging demand (McCallum 1993). An evaluation of FE provision for SEN students in inner London, for example, found that those who had completed a 'link' course were three times more likely to continue in FE on leaving school than those who had not. They were most helpful to those whose educational retardation was compounded by social disadvantage, especially when operated in conjunction with work experience schemes (Newton, Robinson and Pappenheim 1982).

Nevertheless, for all its more formalized and purposeful character, Riddell, Wilson and Baron (1999, p.451) found 'wide discrepancies [in practice] between different agencies, geographical areas and in relation to particular groups of people with learning difficulties'. Ward *et al.*'s (1994) survey of the views of users and providers suggests a system where practice still falls some way short of rhetoric. Among the problems they identified were: poor staffing levels, particularly in respect to specialist staff such as OTs and paramedics; inadequate support systems; a diffusion of responsibility that only encouraged 'buck-passing'; financial stringency and an overall lack of resources; and, perhaps most critical of all, a scarcity of appropriate work placements. In such circumstances it is all too easy for 'training' to degenerate into a succession of loosely related yet often repetitious courses, focused on 'life skills' rather than specific vocational skills in the vague belief that the one must precede the other, without in any way enhancing the realistic possibility of eventual employment. Particularly ill served are those young people who because of their disabilities – whether intellectual, physical or social – are unable to compete, or even to survive, in the open employment market without considerable support and encouragement, but yet are 'in some ways too able to fit easily within existing social work provision' (p.133).

The YT programme has had both positive and negative consequences for young people with intellectual disabilities. On the positive side, by substituting for the 'lottery of the labour market' (Newton *et al.* 1982), with its frankly exploitative tendencies, a formal programme of social and vocational education firmly focused on preparation for adult life, it promised a more orderly, and ultimately more successful transition. By including people with intellectual disabilities within a wider programme aimed at unqualified youth generally, it opened up opportunities for integration that had been largely absent from the school years. On the other hand, it could be said in practice merely to have pushed back the transition process while extending control and surveillance into the later teenage years without any compensating reduction of segregation or enhancement of long-term prospects.

So far as the great majority of young people with intellectual disabilities are concerned, YT, for all its rhetoric, operates in a highly selective and exclusionary fashion. In their Tayside study, May and Hughes (1986) report that all but two of twelve candidates put forward by the careers service for an entry-level WIC were rejected because they failed to meet required standards of literacy and numeracy, and in a further instance only one of nine young people from one special school was considered sufficiently competent even to be recommended for a WIC. More recent work suggests that little has changed meantime, and the situation may even be worsening as YT becomes increasingly employer led (Brogan and Jennings 1993). Riddell *et al.* (1999) note that those with 'more significant learning difficulties' were excluded from the programme altogether, while those who were accepted tended to be confined to college-based courses which offered few prospects of eventual employment:

> A common trajectory for people with learning difficulties is to move from a 2-year extension course at an FE college into a social work funded Adult Resource Centre (ARC). Although claiming that their activity is geared towards developing 'employment readiness' among disabled people, in reality people with learning difficulties tend to remain in ARCs for most of their adult lives. (Riddell *et al.* 1999, p.453)

The problem is not primarily one of individual deficiencies, but rather a system which is concerned with employability, if not necessarily actual employment, and which allocates resources accordingly. In a highly competitive job market people with intellectual disabilities will always be at a disadvantage, unattractive propositions for both employers and training agencies. As Baron (1998, p.102) notes: 'People with learning difficulties tend to learn slowly; slow learners are expensive. People with learning difficulties tend to produce slowly; slow producers are less profitable'. More disturbingly, Riddell *et al.* (1999) suggest that some groups and institutions, especially within social work, rather than seeking to move their clients on to open employment, have a vested interest in perpetuating dependency.

Intellectual disability and the meaning of work

Yet despite all this, the aspirations of the majority of young people and their parents remain fixed on work (Corrie and Zaklukiewicz 1983; Riddell *et al.* 1993; Todd *et al.* 1991). This is not simply the triumph of hope over experience, but rather speaks directly to the question of identity. On leaving school the real importance of work for young people with intellectual disabilities (and their families) lies not so much in the financial rewards it promises or the social contacts it facilitates, but rather that it is an indicator of social competence and thus provides a means of distinguishing those who are 'really' (intellectually) disabled from those who are not, being in this respect and at this time of greater significance than IQ (Wootton 1959, pp.254–267). Entry to the job market, however tentatively essayed, or placement on some vocational training programme, especially one in an actual or even simulated work environment, offering the possibility of working alongside non-disabled people, encourages the belief that one is after all more or less 'normal'. On the other hand, to be admitted to an ATC, or even to the more open and flexible ARC, is to be consigned to a status whose meaning remains wholly unambiguous. This is the significance of the unquestioned absence of the careers service from schools for those with severe intellectual disabilities in May and Hughes's (1986) Tayside study, or the exclusion of young people with severe and profound (learning) difficulties from the YT programme as reported by Riddell (1998).

To be excluded from the workforce is to risk being marginalized, civically and socially – a fate that intellectually disabled people share with children and the elderly (Hockey and James 1993) – but in the former case the more keenly felt because of their restricted access to those other markers of adulthood such as marriage, parenting and independent living (Jenkins 1990). It is ironic that just at the time when service providers and all those working with people with intellectual disabilities have accepted the legitimacy of their claims to be treated as adults (see Simpson, Chapter 6), structural changes to a labour market whose needs constructed the 'problem' of intellectual disabilities in the first place (Thomson 1998) should threaten to undermine those ambitions by rendering adulthood for young people generally 'less certain, more fluid' (Roberts 1984).

This has prompted two competing responses. The first would involve no retreat from the position that regards work as an essential component of adulthood:

> The idea that individuals can achieve reasonable status in society even if unemployed has yet to gain widespread acceptance. It requires great self-assurance for most young people to accept unemployment and considerable inventiveness to lead fulfilling lives without the disciplines and opportunities of work. Those with handicaps have difficulties enough in achieving an acceptable place in society ... To add the objective of significant living without work to the other burdens of disability is seen as wrong and manifestly unfair. (CERI 1983, p.17)

This has led some to call for more proactive policies including outlawing discriminatory practices, the enforcement of employment quotas, the promotion of supported employment and a generally more imaginative approach to the development of work opportunities, not excluding the provision of more sheltered placements (Baron *et al.* 1999; Riddell 1998; Riddell, Ward and Thomson 1993). The experience of youth training provides few grounds for optimism that such an approach would in practice result in any great improvement in participation rates: after all, to coin a phrase, 'you can't buck the markets'. Moreover, it is all too easy to romanticize work when it is scarce, but it is worth bearing in mind that for much of the time, as this review has shown, the majority of young people with intellectual disabilities have experienced it as exploitative, unpleasant and far from liberating.

An alternative approach recognizes the inherent limitations of the labour market, particularly insofar as people with intellectual disabilities are concerned, and would replace paid employment as a marker of adult status with more attainable, if also more nebulous, goals, such as 'productive daytime activity' or 'quality of life' (Thomson and Ward 1995). This builds on the Warnock (DES 1978) proposal of 'significant living without work' (see also Tizard and Anderson 1983), with the aim of maximizing purposeful and rewarding activities, enhancing social contact, reducing isolation and loneliness, providing opportunities for contributing to society and generally fostering a sense of belonging and self-esteem.

The transition from child to adult is a process universally experienced, but how it is defined and what are its essential features are historically and culturally specific (Mitterauer 1992). Certainly work continues to be an important component of adult identities, for working-class youths in particular, but there are others – marriage, parenting, independent living or, as one of Walmsley's (1991) informants put it, simply the right to 'say no to people' – which may assume greater salience for different groups at different times. Young women, for example, have traditionally attached more importance to marriage and motherhood (Leonard 1980; Wallace 1987). Work no longer separates the adult from the child – if it ever did (see the collection in Spencer (1990)). In a post-industrial age where paid employment occupies a shrinking proportion of our lives and the non-employed outnumber those with jobs, and where the nature and consequently meaning of work are radically changing, it no longer has the same significance it once did. Jenkins (1990) is surely correct to suggest that to confuse exclusion from the labour force with the denial of adulthood is to confuse rights with their actualization, means with ends. For much of the past century we assumed that intellectual disabilities necessarily implied incompetence, dependency and social exclusion, and were content to allow the more or less unfettered operation of the labour market to determine who should be assigned to that category. This is no longer a viable position, not simply because the economic conditions which made it possible no longer apply, but rather because the issue is less one of identifying who 'really' are the 'real intellectually disabled' (Gruenberg 1964) than of finding appropriate ways of meeting their legitimate demands, *as disabled people*, to be treated as fully participating adult members of society (Oliver 1990).

References

Aries, P. (1973) *Centuries of Childhood.* Harmondsworth: Penguin.

Atkinson, E. (1984) '30 years on: A study of former pupils of a special school.' *Journal of Special Education* (research supplement) *11*, 17–24.

Baron, S. (1998) 'The best burgers: The person with learning difficulties as worker.' In T. Shakespeare (ed) *The Disability Reader.* London: Cassell, pp.94–109.

Baron, S., Riddell, S. and Wilson, A. (1999) 'The secret of eternal youth: identity, risk, and learning difficulties.' *British Journal of Sociology of Education 20*, 4, 483–499.

Brogan, S. and Jennings, M. (1993) 'The specialist careers service: A pivotal role in post-school opportunities.' In A. Closs (ed) *Special Educational Needs Beyond 16...* Edinburgh: Moray House Publications, pp.68–82.

Centre for Educational Research and Innovation (CERI) (1983) *The Education of the Handicapped Adolescent: The Transition from School to Working Life.* Paris: OECD.

Cheston, R. (1994) 'The accounts of special educational leavers.' *Disability and Society 9*, 59–70.

Clarke, A.M., Clarke, A.D.B. and Adams, M. (1960) 'Problems of employment and occupation of the mentally subnormal.' In M. Adams (ed) *The Mentally Subnormal: The Social Casework Approach.* London: Heinemann Medical.

Closs, A. (ed) (1993) *Special Educational Needs Beyond 16... Meeting Special Education Needs: A Scottish Perspective.* Edinburgh: Moray House Publications.

Coffield, F., Borill, C. and Marshall, S. (1986) *Growing Up at the Margins.* Milton Keynes: Open University Press.

Corrie, M. and Zaklukiewicz, S. (1983) *Leaving Special School: Report on the First Phase of a Study of Leavers from Special Schools. Further Education for the Handicapped Project.* Edinburgh: Scottish Council for Research in Education.

Department of Education and Science (DES) (1978) *Special Educational Needs: Report of the Committee of Enquiry into the Education of Handicapped Children and Young People.* Cm 7212. London: HMSO.

Doogan, K. (1982) *The Careers of the Trainees of Two Industrial Training Units: A Follow-up Study of Disadvantaged Job-Seekers.* Cardiff: Sociological Research Unit, University College, Cardiff.

Ferguson, T. and Kerr, A.W. (1955) 'After histories of girls educated in special schools for mentally handicapped children.' *Glasgow Medical Journal 36,* 50–56.

Ferguson, T. and Kerr, J. (1958) 'After histories of boys educated in special schools for mentally handicapped children.' *Scottish Medical Journal 3,* 31–38.

Furlong, A. (1990) 'A decade of decline: Social class and post-school destination of minimum-age school-leavers in Scotland.' In C. Wallace and M. Cross (eds) *Youth in Transition: The Sociology of Youth and Youth Policy.* Lewes: Falmer Press, pp.113–128.

Goldstein, H. (1964) 'Social and occupational adjustment.' In H.A. Stevens and R. Heber (eds) *Mental Retardation: A Review of Research.* Chicago: University of Chicago Press, pp.214–258.

Gruenberg, E.M. (1964) 'Epidemiology.' In H.A. Stevens and R. Heber (eds) *Mental Retardation: A Review of Research.* Chicago: University of Chicago Press, pp.259–306.

Hockey, J. and James, A. (1993) *Growing Up and Growing Old: Ageing and Dependency in the Life Course.* London: Sage.

Jackson, R.N. (1968) 'Employment adjustment of educable mentally handicapped ex-pupils in Scotland.' *American Journal of Mental Deficiency 72,* 924–930.

Jenkins, R. (1990) 'Dimensions of adulthood in Britain: Long-term employment and mental handicap.' In P. Spencer *Anthropology and the Riddle of the Sphinx: Youth Maturation and Ageing.* London: Routledge, pp.131–146.

Jones, H., Kemp, C. and McIlhenny, F. (1989) *Still at School.* Jordanhill: Jordanhill College of Education.

Kernan, K.T. and Koegal, P. (1984) 'Employment experiences of community based mildly retarded adults.' In R.B. Edgerton (ed) *Lives in Process.* Washington DC: American Association of Mental Deficiency, pp.9–26.

Leonard, D. (1980) *Sex and Generation: A Study of Courtship and Weddings.* London: Tavistock.

McCallum, D. (1993) 'Developing a comprehensive further education service.' In A. Closs (ed) *Special Educational Needs Beyond 16…* Edinburgh: Moray House Publications, pp.93–107.

Manpower Services Commission (MSC) (1977) 'Young people and work: Report on the feasibility of a new programme of opportunities for unemployed young people.' (The Holland Report) London: Manpower Services Commission.

May, D. and Hughes, D. (1985) 'The prospects on leaving school for the mildly mentally handicapped.' *British Journal of Special Education* (Research Supplement) *12,* 151–158.

May, D. and Hughes, D. (1986) *An Uncertain Future: The Adolescent Mentally Handicapped and the Transition from School to Adulthood.* Dundee: Department of Psychiatry, University of Dundee.

May, D. and Hughes, D. (1988) 'From handicapped to normal: Problems and prospects in the transition from school to adult life.' In G. Horobin and D. May (eds) *Living with Mental Handicap: Transitions in the Lives of People with Mental Handicaps.* London: Jessica Kingsley Publishers, pp.62–80.

May, D. and Strong, P. (1980) 'Childhood as an estate.' In R.G. Mitchell (ed) *Child Health in the Community.* Edinburgh: Churchill Livingstone, pp.19–36.

Mitterauer, M. (1992) *A History of Youth.* Oxford: Blackwell.

Newton, J., Robinson, J. and Pappenheim, K. (1982) *Special School Leavers: The Value of Further Education in their Transition to the Adult World.* London: Greater London Association for the Disabled.

Oliver, M. (1990) *The Politics of Disablement.* Basingstoke: Macmillan.

Raffe, D. (1990) 'The transition from YTS to work: Content, context and the external labour market.' In C. Wallace and M. Cross (eds) *Youth in Transition: the Sociology of Youth and Youth Policy.* Lewes: Falmer Press, pp.52–72.

Richardson, S.A. and Koller, H. (1985) 'Epidemiology.' In A.M. Clarke, A.D.B. Clarke and J.M. Berg (eds) *Mental Deficiency: The Changing Outlook*, 4th edtn. London: Methuen.

Richardson, S.A. and Koller, H. (1996) *Twenty-Two Years: Causes and Consequences of Mental Retardation.* Cambridge MA: Harvard University Press.

Richardson, S.A., Koller, H. and Katz, M. (1988) 'Job histories in open employment of a population of young adults with mental retardation: 1.' *American Journal on Mental Retardation 92*, 6, 483–491.

Riddell, S. (1998) 'The dynamic of transition to adulthood.' In C. Robinson and K. Stalker (eds) *Growing Up with Disability.* London: Jessica Kingsley Publishers, pp.189–209.

Riddell, S., Ward, K. and Thomson, G.O.B. (1993) 'The significance of employment as a goal for young people with special educational needs.' *British Journal of Education and Work 6*, 2, 57–72.

Riddell, S., Wilson, A. and Baron, S. (1999) 'Captured customers: people with learning difficulties in the social market.' *British Educational Research Journal 25*, 4, 445–461.

Roberts, D.J. (1975) 'A survey of 235 Salford handicapped school leavers for 1970–72.' *Public Health 80*, 207–211.

Roberts, K. (1984) *School Leavers and their Prospects.* Milton Keynes: Open University Press.

Shone, D. and Atkinson, P. (1980) *Everyday Life in Two Industrial Units for Mentally Retarded Young People in Mid Glamorgan: Two Observational Studies.* Cardiff: Sociological Research Unit, University College, Cardiff.

Spencer, P. (ed) (1990) *Anthropology and the Riddle of the Sphinx: Youth Maturation and Ageing.* London: Routledge.

Taylor, J. (1986) *Mental Handicap: Partnership in the Community.* London: Office of Health Economics/Mencap.

Thomson, G.O.B. and Ward, K. (1995) 'Pathways to adulthood for children with special educational needs.' *British Journal of Education and Work 8*, 3, 75–87.

Thomson, G.O.B., Ward, K.M. and Wishart, J.G. (1995) 'The transition to adulthood for children with Down's Syndrome.' *Disability and Society 10*, 3, 325–340.

Thomson, M. (1998) *The Problem of Mental Deficiency: Eugenics, Democracy and Social Policy in Britain c 1870–1959.* Oxford: Clarendon Press.

Tizard, J. and Anderson, E. (1983) 'Alternatives to work for the handicapped. In Centre for Educational Research and Innovation *The Education of the Handicapped Adolescent: The Transition from School to Working Life.* Paris: OECD, pp.152–192.

Todd, S., Evans, G. and Beyer, S. (1991) 'Into adulthood: the vocational situations of young people with severe learning disabilities.' *British Journal of Mental Subnormality 36*, 5–16.

Tuckey, L., Parfit, J. and Tuckey, B. (1973) *Handicapped School-Leavers: Their Further Education, Training and Employment.* London: NFER.

Walker, A. (1982) *Unqualified and Underemployed: Handicapped Young People and the Labour Market.* London: MacMillan.

Wallace, C. (1987). *For Richer, For Poorer: Growing Up In and Out of Work.* London: Tavistock.

Walmsley, J. (1991) 'Adulthood and people with mental handicaps: Report of a research project.' *Mental Handicap Research 4*, 2, 141–154.

Ward, K., Thomson, G.O.B. and Riddell, S. (1994) 'Transition, adulthood, and special educational needs: an unresolved paradox.' *European Journal of Special Needs Education 9*, 2, 125–144.

Willis, P. (1984) 'Youth unemployment: Thinking the unthinkable.' *Youth and Policy 2*, 4, 17–24, 33–36.

Wilson, A. and Cherry, M. (1993) 'Young people staying on at special school.' In A. Closs (ed) *Special Educational Needs Beyond 16...* Edinburgh: Moray House Publications.

Wootton, B. (1959) *Social Science and Social Pathology.* London: George Allen & Unwin.

CHAPTER 6

Programming Adulthood

Intellectual Disability and Adult Services

Murray K. Simpson

With the implementation of care in the community policies and the run-down and closure of the mental handicap hospitals, the discussion of models and principles of service delivery has shifted somewhat. In particular, the pro- and anti-institutional focus which characterized the 1970s and much of the 1980s has given way to a more fragmented view of what adult services should actually look like. Normalization, which had seemed like a relatively straightforward idea when presented as a stark alternative to institutionalization, remained relatively unified as a model for a decade or so since its first appearance in an English language publication (Nirje 1969). With the increasing development of community-based services, marked differences of interpretation of normalization have emerged and some of its main tenets questioned by a number of individuals by no means hostile to the shift towards community services (see e.g. Brown and Smith 1989; Perrin and Nirje 1989; Simpson 1998; Szivos and Travers 1988). Lines of debate have opened up in relation to the principles and technicalities of the means, ends, planning and implementation of services.

One of the issues gaining prominence in some sections of the research literature is that of a perceived shift away from programmed environments, particularly in residential services. Improvements in social skills and adaptive behaviours were central to the development of the anti-institutional movement. Normalization gained much succour from the positive results obtained in behaviour modification and training and experiments in community living (see e.g.

O'Connor and Tizard 1956; Tizard 1964). The first wave of residential services in the 'care in the community' period of British social policy continued this ethos (Felce 1996a; Felce and Toogood 1988), having as central components the enhancement of community living skills and the reduction of 'maladaptive' behaviours. As Mansell put it in relation to one model of staffed housing studied:

> The aim is to help the people served take part in all the activities of daily living, instead of the typical arrangement where staff do all the housework and create large amounts of free time which they then find difficult to fill with constructive therapeutic activity. (Mansell 1996, p.50)

This chapter will explore some of the research literature from the past decade or so in order to unpack some of the issues and problems around the provision and researching of adult services. The question of programmed environments is particularly useful in this regard because it takes us to the heart of a number of debates, around the purpose of services, the nature of adulthood for people with intellectual disabilities and the setting of a research agenda. In addition, programming uncovers certain tensions and inconsistencies between a largely psychologically oriented research agenda and community care practices, particularly in relation to social work. Specifically, the apparent decline in the priority accorded to developmental objectives in residential care has coincided with the transfer of responsibility to social services and social work departments. This discrepancy in objectives points to the problematic nature of adulthood for people with intellectual disabilities.

In the first section, I shall explore the arguments put forward that such a shift in orientation has in fact happened. The nature of this 'debate' is that it is exclusively arguing against the desirability of such a change. There is little positive argument that services should not assign priority to developmental goals. Any change is, therefore, more likely to be the result of either drift or incremental divergence from such goals, rather than determined realignment. This interpretation is pursued in analysis of some of the factors suggested as lying behind the change in direction. The discussion leads on to the issue of how the objectives of services and research agendas are determined, specifically, in relation to the various perspectives of parents, researchers, service providers and people with intellectual disabilities themselves. The ambiguous and contestable nature of adulthood again surfaces in the context of research. As we shall see, this has tended to be an imposed concept, rather than one derived from people with intellectual disabilities.

In conclusion, I shall argue that, rather than carry on providing services and producing research in quite fundamental tension with each other as well as with the aspirations and perspectives of people with intellectual disabilities, a more constructive engagement is required. At present, there is little in the way of fruitful linkage between putative social work values – self-determination, respect for an individual's dignity, the promotion of choice, etc. – and the developmental aims of psychology. More seriously, there is very little attention being given to the views of adults with intellectual disabilities and the radically different views which they often hold of adulthood and intellectual disability to researchers and service providers.

The move away from the programmed environment

The initial results of creating intensively programmed environments seemed promising from the point of view of skills acquisition. Mansell (1996) reports that engagement in 'constructive' and 'meaningful' activities rose by between one-third and six times their pre-discharge level and that adaptive behaviour almost invariably improved by as much as one-quarter to double. Positive outcomes were also reported by Felce (1996a), with six main findings from studies comparing life in two innovative residential projects to that in hospitals. First, residents progressed better in skills acquisition than hospital patients or those living with parents at home. Second, residents enjoyed greater participation in domestic, leisure and social activities than hospital residents. Third, there was a higher level of staff–resident interaction. Fourth, their contact with family and friends was improved. Fifth, there was greater use of community services and facilities. Sixth, there was, however, no evidence of reduction in challenging behaviour.

For Mansell, and others, the development of competence and opportunities for meaningful activity are 'central measures of quality' (1996, p.55). Such a view is unsurprising, given that the emphasis on behavioural adaptation and competence has been crucial to the process of redefining intellectual disability itself, and not simply reorienting services (Race 1995; Simpson 1998; Stevens and Heber 1964; Wolfensberger 1975). At least one group of researchers even manage to invert the priority of the definitional elements of behaviour and intelligence:

> The definition of learning disabilities [used in Leicestershire] is based on adaptive behaviour problems (Heber 1955) associated with a moderate, severe or profound developmental intellectual impairment (WHO 1992). (McGrother *et al.* 1996, p.184)

Elsewhere, Felce and Toogood suggest that perhaps the reason why competence enhancement is so widely accepted is that it 'reverses the defining condition' (1988, p.14). The extent to which an individual has the opportunity to participate in activities up to the limit of their capabilities is, then, a measure of life quality, and the degree to which a service provides the necessary environment for skills to be realized in 'meaningful activity' is a measure of its appropriateness.

However, more recent evidence appears to suggest that such an orientation is declining. Research evidence points to a lack of clear linkage between staff: resident ratio and levels of staff: resident interaction. Neither is the inverse relationship between level of intellectual disability and level of staff engagement that one might expect necessarily present. Indeed, the more socially able the resident, the more staff time he or she got (Felce 1996b). Elsewhere, observers have pointed to the common failure of community living to produce increased social integration or participation in domestic living tasks (Rose 1993). Both Mansell (1996) and Felce (1996a, 1996b) point to a reduced training orientation of front-line staff. Of the three levels of service design which Felce (1996b) identifies – structure, orientation and procedures – attention has typically been paid to the former two at the expense of the latter. This is in spite of evidence, put forward by Felce and others, that the actual delivery of services at the individual level has a greater impact, that is, in terms of the criteria which they put forward as central to quality services, particularly improvements in adaptive behaviour.

Interestingly, Felce (1996a, 1996b) associates this trend as due, in part, to 'ideological' training replacing that of a more 'practical' nature. Normalization, or at least interpretations of it, are identified as producing a bias towards matters of structure and general orientation. The 'ordinary life' model is cited as producing such an emphasis on broad issues of service design and delivery, and for not being based around clear operational goals for client development. If true, this would mark a definite redefinition of normalization principles, given the dominance of the psychological-behavioural model of normalization during its early development, particularly in its classic formulation by Wolfensberger (1972). Both Felce (1996b) and Mansell (1996) posit another rather more banal explanation: the relative lack of any kind of training among front-line residential staff, ideological or otherwise. In addition, services are criticized for lacking clearly specified objectives for working with individuals: 'Thus, these community services are being set up without a cadre of well-trained staff at team leader level and with many striking gaps in the training offered to the unqualified staff in the team' (Mansell 1996, p.57).

The findings from one project reported on by Mansell (1996) indicate four key factors which produced significant improvements to such directionless services. First, the introduction of 'whole environment training' to improve the skills of staff in their interactions with residents. Second, changing the administrative structures and practices to improve the orientation and quality of management and, in particular, giving greater support to front-line staff. Third, improving systems for gathering information about the service's performance with clients, setting and monitoring objectives for programmed working. Fourth, procedures for reviewing such crises as do happen in order to prevent and/or better manage them in future so as to prevent complete placement breakdown. However, in spite of the implementation of such measures showing encouraging short-term results, follow-up research did not appear to show any lasting improvements in the service.

Pulling together?

The extent to which changes in adult services have been the result of deliberate theoretical reorientation rather than 'drift' produced by lack of training and leadership are difficult to ascertain. Rose (1993) suggests that what he calls 'secondary social policy', the unofficial influences on service design and implementation, such as normalization or advocacy, have been more influential than the official policies of successive governments in constructively shaping the lives of individuals with intellectual disabilities. The influence of Wolfensberger's model of normalization and John O'Brien's (1987) 'five accomplishments' are cited as having been particularly influential. Such a view seems to underestimate the importance of the macro-political level. Despite its near hegemony in progressive thinking about services for people with intellectual disabilities in the 1970s, comparatively few lives were transformed by the principle of normalization until official policies of community care developed in the 1980s. Even if these provided no more than the necessary conditions of opportunity for the creation of services by individuals and agencies operating with a different agenda, their significance should not be ignored. In addition, we also need to take into consideration the earlier point: that we are confronted with a number of different interpretations and mutations of normalization.

(1996a) makes the very interesting suggestion that the change from health to social services as the lead role in providing services (directly or otherwise) for people with intellectual disabilities may be partly responsible for a changing orientation. He argues that programmes of deinstitutionalization were too often based on naïve assumptions about the benefits which would accrue from the simple fact of living in the community. The belief that behaviour would markedly improve by simply removing people from the 'deviance-inducing' environment of the mental handicap hospital resulted in a diminution of attention to behavioural analysis and programming. If correct, this would be doubly ironic because psychology was pivotal in generating the anti-institutional critique in the 1960s and 1970s, and yet carried more professional weight in hospitals than in the social work dominated services that would come to replace them. Hitherto, the psychologist innovators were operating in the context of a medical regime hovering on the brink of moral, professional, political and organizational bankruptcy. The psychologists offered a way forward for health services which could scarcely be resisted. However, their organizational position in the context of local authority social services/work departments has been far less powerful than in health services, as has their conceptual leverage.

Social work did not have to fear the challenge of psychology. For better or worse, neither does it seem to have accepted its assistance, at least not whole-heartedly.

Social work approaches to services for adults with intellectual disabilities tend to be characterized by a stated orientation towards individual choice and independence. While neither of these is contradictory to the psychological approach, they do signify a subtle but important difference of emphasis, away from behavioural normality or adaptation. Felce opines:

> The status of developmental progress as a goal and allied processes such as assessment, goal-setting and skill-teaching were subordinated to the wider conceptualisation of the 'Five Accomplishments' (O'Brien 1987) – even though the achievement of competence was one of their number. Behavioural analysis and technology was consigned to the dustbin of the previous decade, only to be allowed out grudgingly in the extremis of severely challenging behaviour. (Felce 1996a, pp.138–139)

The important and unresolved question is whether the similarity of the approaches is indicative of a shared objective or because they are both attempting to find a way out of a similar problematic. The former interpretation suggests that common ground can be found; the latter that the different approaches are moving in opposing directions. While it seems improbable that Felce is exactly trying to suggest that objectives should not be informed by some value base, the suggestion that competence training should have overriding importance is at least contestable. Such a contest would then take us to another, more fundamental question, namely whose objectives are being considered in the first place? Nonetheless, Felce's contention that the relationship between the values and concepts employed by services and behavioural treatment is an unresolved and unsatisfactory one does not seem at all unwarranted.

This is all the more important in light of the perceived drift in orientation discussed above. We must take account of the fact that most of the homes in question are not directly run by social services/work departments, and that the majority of staff are not professionally trained. In addition, many housing and support agencies will not be large enough directly to employ a range of allied support professionals such as psychologists, and staff may lack both the know-how and opportunity to tap into such services.

Whose objectives: Parents, professionals and users

In this section, I pose the question of whose agenda is reflected in community care policy and practice. This is an important question, though not often explicitly addressed. Are 'adult services' services for *adults* or services for *adulthood?* Objectives and principles of service provision broadly expressed often present an air of apparently obvious meaning – 'ordinary living', 'independence', 'normality', 'inclusion', etc. In practice the ways in which these terms are mediated by the interpretation of various professions, parents and sections of society, and through the qualifications of risk management, informed choosing and 'best interests', result in a far more complex picture in which the voices of adults with intellectual disabilities are heavily muted. Indeed this is particularly noticeable when comparison is made with the wider field of disability and the relative balance of influence of disabled people, carers, service professionals and academics which exists there.

One of the most striking features of the literature on adult services – their proper function, effectiveness, form, methods, etc. – is the relative absence of the actual views of adults with intellectual disabilities (Atkinson, Chapter 9; Atkinson and Walmsley 1999). Walmsley (1991) comments on the general paucity of participatory research with this group. Whether from a strictly 're-search' perspective or from an ethically oriented one, this seems like a serious deficit. Why is it so? The answer relates to the question posed earlier, namely, how are the broad objectives of community care translated into services at the individual level? The extent to which services and models are genuinely empowering and focused on the needs of individuals, rather than aimed at social regulation and the reproduction of inequalities, is central to this debate. Apropos this critical discussion, Felce makes a revealing comment:

> Institutional reform is symbolic of the changing ideas in the post-war era about the place of people with disabilities in our society. The institutions had become purveyors of segregation as a deliberate act of social control. (Felce 1996a, p.127)

Such views encapsulate a not altogether unfamiliar, though hopelessly naïve, picture which separates approaches into some variation of a *care versus control* dichotomy. Consequently, certain programmes are characterized as being geared towards society's perceived interests (or perhaps those of dominant social groups) and, therefore, *controlling*, while others are based on individual needs and rights and are regarded as *caring* or *empowering*. The problem is that such views fail to grasp the complexity of social processes and that care and control are not mutual exclusives, just as any framework of services or theory involves complex exchanges between competing interests. If the key word in Felce's comment is 'deliberate', then the contrast is of minimal significance to the lives of people with intellectual disabilities, except that the counter-strategies are made that much more difficult when 'control' is not an intended outcome.

This is a central point, since it would be difficult to establish that normalization or community care were motivated by the intent to social control, at least at the operational level. Nonetheless, the majority of social regulation occurs by means which have little to do with conscious motivation. This is where the lack of sociological attention to the field becomes most keenly felt. There is a pervasive lack of awareness of some of the simplest tenets of social enquiry. It is essential that greater critical attention is brought to bear upon fundamental principles if the lack of influence on the research agenda or objectives of services by the people most directly affected is to be corrected.

'Choice' is a near ubiquitous concept and aim of services, one which few would reject. However, what it actually means in practice and the weight which it is accorded relative to other factors in the decision-making process are less straightforward. Felce and Toogood (1988) describe feeling obliged to consult a service user regarding a proposed move out of hospital on the grounds that the services are there, after all, for her and that it was important not to assume that even a profound level of intellectual impairment necessarily excluded all possibility of expressing a 'rational view'. Now, while the perceived absence of reason has for centuries been central to the deprivation of liberty and the social exclusion of people with intellectual disabilities, it is not clear that preference is always or ultimately a matter of reason. The desire to live in one kind of house as opposed to another, with this person as opposed to that, to prefer chocolate to strawberry milkshake, are not rational matters in any obvious sense. Why are such observations necessary? So long as professionals retain the right to overrule an 'uninformed' choice, they are absolutely crucial. We also need to ask why individual preference is not made more central than it is.

In fact, the objectives of services for individuals appear to most observers as more or less self-evident and determined largely by dominant social values. Brigden, for instance, suggests that the central aim should be to provide the necessary 'assistance [to adults with learning disabilities] to become more valued members of society' (1993, p.80). The underlying argument is that people with intellectual disabilities need social skills if they are to integrate and perform valued social roles. The objectives are essentialized inasmuch as they are rooted in an environment which is not in itself problematized; a reflection of the classic psychological conception of adaptation which underpins the field. 'Need' arises from the difference between what individuals are unable to do and what is deemed necessary for social survival, not between what they are able to do and what they want to do. Thus, the provision of services, and components thereof, such as choice, is only a means to ends which are already largely socially determined (albeit mediated and interpreted by professionals). 'Meaningful activity', for instance, is rarely, if ever, related back to the person to be engaged in it. Things such as 'leisure' and 'rest' have true 'meanings' which are only realized when the majority of one's time is taken up in other 'meaningful occupation' (Felce and Toogood 1988).

It should scarcely need to be stated that 'critical attention' does not mean rejection. However, there do seem to be grounds for rejecting the kind of self-evidential cultural uniformity behind most accounts. For instance, the widely held assumption that interaction between people with intellectual disabilities, as a devalued social group, and non-intellectually disabled others would not stand as a credible parallel for working with ethnic minorities. In addition, the whole concept, implicit or otherwise, of 'normality' has come in for intense criticism from the disability movement (Davis 1995; Oliver 1996). We also risk setting the standard of 'normality' for adults with intellectual disabilities much higher than for anyone else – the degree of understanding and responsibility which they must demonstrate before being allowed to enter into sexual relationships, for instance. Even more straightforward matters, such as friendship, assume far greater gravity. For instance, Brigden suggests:

> It is essential that adults with mild learning disabilities are fully conversant with the concept of friendship and what this means. They need to be able to demonstrate that they understand that friendship is a two-way process, involving give and take, and that certain types of behaviour are appropriate to certain levels of intimacy, such as kissing. (Brigden 1993, pp.81–82)

The consequences are not spelled out, but we should not forget that there are many other non-disabled people in society who do not understand or respect these concepts, but without this necessarily providing the grounds for intervention. If the justification is that they have an intellectual disability and the behaviour is pathologized, then we are clearly onto the terrain of social control. This example gives ample illustration of the danger of regarding social control and individual interests as mutual exclusives. When faced with the prospect of possible prosecution and incarceration for grossly inappropriate sexual behaviour, it will generally be possible to regard intervention as meeting everyone's view of desirable outcomes – 'it's better to be controlled in this way rather than that' – but we should be clear about one thing, the same argument could be made for people without intellectual disabilities. If we are treating them differently there remains a question of why. Intellectual disability will not provide a satisfactory basis for the answer, since we cannot regard social behaviours as unrelated to intellectual ability and antisocial as related. It remains to be established whether future competence enhancement forms part of the life goals of the majority of people, or if they even conceive of their future in terms of life goals at all.

However, it is not only among service users, professionals and researchers that discrepancies between agendas may arise. As has been noted, many parents of adults with intellectual disabilities entertain real doubts about the extent to which normalization gives sufficient recognition to the 'differentness' of their sons and daughters, particularly in relation to 'high risk' issues such as sexuality and independent living (Brown, Orlowska and Mansell 1996; Rose and Jones 1994). There is also the ambiguous status of services as meeting parents' needs and those of the rest of the family as well as the family member actually using them. What is clear is that there is a pronounced tendency of many parents and most professionals and researchers to emphasize or construct the 'otherness' of intellectual disability and those who have it. However, in the context of larger populations – in research, or service planning and delivery – sharp divisions give way to continua. In spite of this quantitative variation, the language of research, policy and practice produce and sustain binary division – a process which Derrida refers to as *différance*(Corker 1998). Thus, in spite of the fact that no such clear division exists in the properties of the population, a body of professional and lay knowledge exists which implies that such a division does in fact exist. Of course, put another way, the division does indeed exist it is accomplished in the act of knowing itself. So even given the arbitrary nature of the statistically based division of intellectual disability, there may be a group of people, in a broad or narrow band of functioning range, around the threshold of intellectual disability, whose status is subject to the contingencies of testers' orientation and mood, the error margin of the tests, the view of parents and professionals and other variables. In spite of this, the division, once accomplished, is still largely binary.

If the aim of community care services is to provide opportunities and support for 'adulthood', then there may be a problem squaring this with the perspective of service users. This is even more true when we consider those who do not take up adult services on school leaving. The significance of adulthood itself has been the occasional subject of research. Walmsley (1991) reported that interviewees found it difficult to engage with the concept of adulthood *per se*. The nearest point at which the researcher's focus and the research participants' concerns coincided was 'independence'. Walmsley found that living more independently was a primary issue for most of the participants (all attendees at an adult training centre). The definition of 'independence' employed by the participants and researcher is a typical one, meaning doing things for one's self. As one participant related:

> She [Mum]'s been training me all these years to be independent. I've learnt cooking, do me own breakfast every morning, washin', ironin', shoppin', cleaning, looking after me own animals. I go shopping with my mum, but I'm soon going to do it on me own. (Walmsley 1991, p.147)

What is interesting here is that alternative views of independence and independent living from the wider disability movement are nowhere in evidence. As Brisenden (1986) comments, the alternative view of independence is about being in control of one's life; about how, when and by whom assistance is provided, rather than necessarily 'doing things for one's-self' (see also Morris 1993). In one sense this is unsurprising, since this view of independence requires the individual to accept that they are disabled, albeit by social barriers. What comes through very clearly in other research is that for most people with intellectual disabilities entering adult life, the key issue is to detach themselves altogether from an intellectually disabled status (Bogdan and Taylor 1982; Edgerton 1967; Richardson and Koller 1996). Survival with as little support as possible assumes a much greater significance in this regard.

Adulthood as a research problem

It may be that the relationship between researchers and the views and aspirations of adults with intellectual disabilities are themselves at odds. Walmsley (1991) attempts to adopt a 'participatory' research methodology based on feminist principles, most notably in trying to avoid imposing the researcher's agenda and assumptions on the interviews. However, despite establishing early on that 'adulthood' did not figure as a key concept for the participants, the findings end up being fitted into this conceptual framework. Thus the comments of interviewees are fed back to them in terms of how they equate to adulthood: 'Being an adult means: independent living; managing your own money; getting married; having a home of your own; being treated right; not being told what to do' (Walmsley 1991, p.151). This seems especially interesting in view of the established finding, noted above, that it is escape from the status of intellectual disability which preoccupies most adults so designated or at risk of being so, rather than 'adulthood'.

However, it is not only in relation to adulthood as a research question itself that research problems arise. There is a general inattention to the views of adults with intellectual disabilities about their lives, experiences and use of services. This, and the general bias towards issues relating more or less directly to adaptive behaviour, is reflected in the findings of Emerson and Hatton's (1996) review of research into the impact of deinstitutionalization programmes on individuals. (Table 6.1 summarizes these findings.) The four top measures – engagement, competence, use of community facilities and staff contact – form a clear group in terms of their frequency in measuring service outcomes, appearing in roughly two-fifths of all studies. The rest form a tail dwindling down to 'satisfaction with services' and 'life satisfaction' at the lower end of the scale. It is also noteworthy that disposable income seldom figures as an issue for researchers. McGrother *et al.* (1996) found that financial assistance was by far the most significant area of unmet need as expressed by adults with intellectual disabilities and carers in their study in Leicestershire (37 per cent). In spite of this, the authors give the issue little discussion.

Table 6.1 Summary of research into the effects of deinstitutionalization	
Measure	Percentage of studies[1]
Engagement	40
Competence	37
Use of community facilities	37
Staff contact	37
Service organisation	17
Opportunities	16
Social relationships	12
Costs	11
Physical environment	10
Carer outcomes	8
Satisfaction with services	7
Social status/community acceptance	6
Disposable income	3
Possessions	3
Life satisfaction	3

1 Figures are estimates read from a bar chart

As much as this might reflect what researchers think is important for adults with intellectual disabilities, it also highlights what they think counts as knowledge, i.e. empirical, objective, scientific and quantifiable data. Elsewhere, Brown *et al.*

(1996) construct a continuum of activities among parents' groups – 'preventing, improving, maintaining, extending, augmenting or replacing current service provision' (p.235). The authors attempt to create an apolitical and semi-quantifiable scheme of classification. This again reflects the tendency of researchers to stick to a predetermined research framework which sets the issues, determines the methodology and directs the findings. What it does not do is give a clear picture of what being an adult with an intellectual disability actually means.

Conclusion

The thrust of this chapter may seem to imply that the orientation of most current research is fatally flawed and that we should back off from such 'scientifically' and psychologically oriented studies. This would be a mistaken interpretation; the research in question has been too important and invaluable to too many people to be so summarily dismissed. The research literature is replete with examples of well-programmed interventions bringing about radical improvements to the lives of individuals as well as of non-programmed, superficially 'progressive' services making little impact. Felce makes this point very succinctly:

> I believe that the results of our research on the Andover houses did not show that they were better than the other services we compared them against because they were small, ordinary houses, or even small, ordinary, well-staffed houses in the community, but because these attributes were coupled with a well-operationalised orientation and a set of working procedures and staff training methods to match. (Felce 1996b, pp.127–129)

Instead, this chapter points to two broad areas in which improvement could be made: first, in relation to specific points of reorientation; second, in terms of making up for considerable gaps in the present shape of research.

To take the gaps first, the review of Emerson and Hatton (1996) gives a clear picture of where the areas of underactivity lie, and it does seem important to put it in these terms, rather than of overactivity in other areas. There is a serious lack of studies attempting to elucidate or analyse the views of adults with intellectual disabilities (see Atkinson, Chapter 9). This seems to be true in all areas: personal accounts of intellectual disability, experiences of receiving services, involvement in research planning, and so on. The difficulty in solving this particular problem is that no one has any clear strategic responsibility for ensuring that such a balance is achieved – an issue which the reserch funding bodies might address more seriously than they have hitherto. That said, this does not overcome the problem of how to stimulate greater interest among researchers in areas such as sociology, social policy and a wider range of psychology. In this respect this problem is easier to identify than to solve.

The second area in which progress might be more easily made is in relation to points of reorientation. First of all, this chapter echoes the view expressed by Felce that the current relationship, in both theory and practice, between values and technology is unsatisfactory. However, Felce does not offer any convincing explanation for his own conclusion that developmental objectives should be given automatic priority, and nor has any been forthcoming from other quarters. This remains, therefore, an unresolved issue, and one that can only be satisfactorily dealt with in conjunction with people with intellectual disabilities themselves.

Second, people with intellectual disabilities are an oppressed social group (Williams 1989). Points of difference with other marginalized social groups should certainly not be ignored, but points of similarity almost entirely are in large sections of the research literature. Attempts to make links to gender issues (Brown and Smith 1992; Szivos and Travers 1988), ethnicity (Baxter 1989; Ferns 1992) and disability more generally (Walmsley 1994) highlight some possible directions here.

Third, and leading on from these points, there needs to be a greater attention to the question of what it is that services are and ought to be trying to achieve for users and carers. The tendency to root itself in the apparently self-evidential model of adaptation, borrowed from evolutionary thought, is typical of the dominant forms of psychological thinking. While useful and important in some respects, this tends to downplay the relative importance of self-determination, political consciousness, collective identity and the need for societal changes.

Fourth, research into the nature and meaning of 'adulthood' for people with intellectual disabilities has to come to terms with the fact that it may not form part of the outlook of the people being studied. It is important to be clear about when, how and why the analytical concepts and categories of the researcher are being used, and to recognize also that these are not intrinsically illegitimate.

Equally, this chapter has implications for the direction of social work services. The dogmatic commitment to social work values can become more of an impediment than a help if they are allowed to become excuses for non-engagement with other professional perspectives and contributions. A number of conclusions may be drawn. First, 'self-determination' fits uneasily with the reality of empty lives with little meaningful activity; though, neither does it go away. It is important to find more constructive means of identifying life choices and facilitating their realization. Second, social work services need to regain a much clearer sense of purpose. What specifically are they trying to achieve for service users? More to the point, what do service users want professionals to achieve for them? It is an inescapable fact that small does not in itself necessarily mean better, whatever 'better' might mean. Third, most users and potential users of adult services do not wish to have the status of 'intellectually disabled' by any name (Baron, Riddell and Wilson 1999). Indeed, most of those able to survive without them prefer not to access services at all, rather than accept such a status.

What does this mean for service providers? There are a number of issues that need to be addressed. Are people really better off in services than out of them, particularly for those who are also out of employment and otherwise socially excluded? If there are benefits, what are they? Insofar as service provision is a central part of the constitution of the intellectually disabled identity (i.e. not self-identity, but the socially imposed or expected one), to what extent can this be made less stigmatizing and promote a positive collective and personal self-image? At the very least, this discrepancy between what most individuals want and what service providers are typically prepared to acknowledge must be tackled.

As Baron *et al.* (1999), Jenkins (1989) and others have noted, the 'adulthood' of people with intellectual disabilities is highly problematic. Their access to the social roles, opportunities and status which provide the cultural markers of being an adult are generally more restricted for people with intellectual disabilities coming of age (see May, Chapter 5). This has left a number of critical ambiguities and conflicts in the design and provision of services. For example, one of the things that comes across very clearly in most direct observational and experiential studies of life as an adult with intellectual disability is that even 'progressive' services are geared towards creating adults with intellectual disabilities (e.g. Angrosino 1998; Devlieger 1998; van Maastricht 1998). In other words, the thrust of community care policies (used in the widest possible sense) is to challenge the assumption that being intellectually disabled is an intrinsic barrier to achieving adulthood. With such a strategy, the concept of intellectual disability mutates to accommodate a change in values and perspective. But in no sense does this mark a challenge to the intellectually disabled status *per se*. It is about the integration of people with intellectual disabilities rather than disintegration of intellectual disability. This may be a defensible position, but it is at odds with the aspirations of many of the people it is designed to serve. At the very least, service providers and researchers do need to become more sensitive as to whether it is adulthood or intellectual disability which is the overarching cultural category since this fundamentally affects the extent to which those subject to their attentions have control over their lives.

References

Angrosino, M.V. (1998) 'Culture, classification and (in)competence.' In R. Jenkins (ed) *Mental Disability in the United States: An Interactionist Perspective.* Cambridge: Cambridge University Press.

Atkinson, D. and Walmsley, J. (1999) 'Using autobiographical approaches with people with learning difficulties.' *Disability and Society 14*, 2, 203–216.

Baron, S., Riddell, S. and Wilson, A. (1999) 'The secret of eternal youth: Identity, risk and learning difficulties.' *British Journal of Sociology of Education 29*, 4, 483–499.

Baxter, C. (1989) 'Parallels between the social role perception of people with learning difficulties and black and ethnic minority people.' In A. Brechin and J. Walmsley (eds) *Making Connections: Reflecting on the Lives and Experiences of People with Learning Difficulties.* London: Hodder and Stoughton.

Bogdan, R. and Taylor, S.J. (1982) *Inside Out: The Social Meaning of Mental Retardation.* Toronto: University of Toronto Press.

Brigden, P. (1993) 'Personal relationships.' In P. Brigden and M. Todd (eds) *Concepts in Community Care for People with a Learning Difficulty.* Basingstoke: Macmillan.

Brisenden, S. (1986) 'Independent living and the medical model of disability.' *Disability, Handicap and Society 1*, 2, 173–178.

Brown, H., Orlowska, D. and Mansell, J. (1996) 'From complaining to campaigning.' In J. Mansell and K. Ericksson (eds) *Deinstitutionalisation and Community Living: Intellectual Disability Services in Britain, Scandinavia and the USA.* London: Chapman and Hall.

Brown, H. and Smith, H. (1989) 'Whose "ordinary life" is it anyway? A feminist critique of the normalisation principle.' *Disability, Handicap and Society 4*, 2, 105–119.

Brown, H. and Smith, H. (1992) 'Assertion, not assimilation: A feminist perspective on the normalisation principle.' In H. Brown and H. Smith (eds) *Normalisation: A Reader for the Nineties.* London: Routledge.

Corker, M. (1998) *Deaf and Disabled, or Deafness Disabled? Towards a Human rights Perspective.* Buckingham: Open University Press.

Davis, L.J. (1995) *Enforcing Normalcy: Disability, Deafness and the Body.* London: Verso.

Devlieger, P.J. (1998) '(In)competence in America in comparative perspective.' In R. Jenkins (ed) *Questions of Competence: Culture, Classification and Intellectual Disability.* Cambridge: Cambridge University Press.

Edgerton, R. (1967) *The Cloak of Competence: Stigma in the Lives of the Mentally Retarded.* Cambridge: Cambridge University Press.

Emerson, E. and Hatton, C. (1996) 'Impact of deinstitutionalisation on service users in Britain.' In J. Mansell and K. Ericsson (eds) *Deinstitutionalisation and Community Living: Intellectual Disability Services in Britain, Scandinavia and the USA.* London: Chapman and Hall.

Felce, D. (1996a) 'Changing residential services: From institutions to ordinary living.' In P. Mittler and V. Sinason (eds) *Changing Policy and Practice for People with Learning Disabilities.* London: Cassell.

Felce, D. (1996b) 'Quality of support for ordinary living.' In J. Mansell and K. Ericsson (eds) *Deinstitutionalisation and Community Living: Intellectual Disability Services in Britain, Scandinavia and the USA.* London: Chapman and Hall.

Felce, D. and Toogood, S. (1988) *Close to Home: A Local Housing Service and its Impact on the Lives of Nine Adults with Severe and Profound Mental Handicaps.* Kidderminster: BIMH Publications.

Ferns, P. (1992) 'Promoting race equality through normalisation.' In H. Brown and H. Smith (eds) *Normalisation: A Reader for the Nineties.* London: Routledge.

Heber, R. (1955) 'A manual on terminology and classification in mental retardation.' *American Journal of Mental Deficiency, 64*, 1–11.

Jenkins, R. (1989) 'Barriers to adulthood: long-term unemployment and mental handicap compared.' In A. Brechin and J. Walmsley (eds) *Making Connections: Reflecting on the Lives and Experiences of People with Learning Difficulties.* London: Hodder and Stoughton.

McGrother, C.W., Hauk, A., Bhaumik, S., Thorp, C. and Taub, N. (1996) 'Community care needs for adults with learning disability and their carers: Needs and outcomes from the Leicestershire register.' *Journal of Intellectual Disability Research 40*, 2, 183–190.

Mansell, J. (1996) 'Issues in community services in Britain.' In J. Mansell and K. Ericsson (eds) *Deinstitutionalisation and Community Living: Intellectual Disability Services in Britain, Scandinavia and the USA.* London: Chapman and Hall.

Morris, J. (1993) *Independent Lives? Community Care and Disabled People.* Basingstoke: Macmillan.

Nirje, B. (1969) 'The normalisation principle and its human management implications.' In R.B.Kugel and W. Wolfensberger (eds) *Changing Patterns of Residential Care for the Mentally Retarded.* Washington DC: Presidential Committee on Mental Retardation.

O'Brien, J. (1987) 'A guide to life style planning: using The Activities Catalogue to integrate services and natural support systems.' In B.W. Cox and G.T. Bellamy (eds) *The Activities Catalogue: An Alternative Curriculum for Youth and Adults with Severe Disabilities.* Baltimore MD: Paul H. Brookes, pp.175–189.

O'Connor, N. and Tizard, J. (1956) *The Social Problem of Mental Deficiency.* London: Pergamon.

Oliver, M. (1996) *Understanding Disability: From Theory to Practice.* Basingstoke: Macmillan.

Perrin, B. and Nirje, B. (1989) 'Setting the record straight: A critique of some frequent misconceptions of the normalisation principle.' In A. Brechin and J. Walmsley (eds) *Making Connections: Reflecting on the Lives and Experiences of People with Learning Difficulties.* London: Hodder and Stoughton.

Race, D. (1995) 'Historical development of service provision.' In N. Malin (ed) *Services for People with Learning Disabilities.* London: Routledge.

Richardson, S.A. and Koller, H. (1996) *Twenty-two Years: Causes and Consequences of Mental Retardation.* Cambridge MA: Harvard University Press.

Rose, J. and Jones, C. (1994) 'Working with parents.' In A. Craft (ed) *Practice Issues in Sexuality and Learning Disabilities.* London: Routledge.

Rose, S. (1993) 'Social policy: a perspective on service developments and inter-agency working.' In P. Brigden and M. Todd (eds) *Concepts in Community Care for People with a Learning Difficulty.* Basingstoke: Macmillan.

Simpson, M.K. (1998) 'The roots of normalisation: a reappraisal: guest editorial.' *Journal of Intellectual Disability Research 42*, 7, 1–7.

Stevens, H.A. and Heber, R. (eds) (1964) *Mental Retardation: A Review of Research.* Chicago: University of Chicago Press.

Szivos, S. and Travers, E. (1988) 'Consciousness raising among mentally handicapped people: A critique of the implications of normalisation.' *Human Relations 41*, 9, 641–653.

Tizard, J. (1964) *Community Services for the Mentally Handicapped.* Oxford: Oxford University Press.

van Maastricht, S. (1998) 'Work, opportunity and culture: (In)competence in Greece and Wales.' In R. Jenkins (ed) *Questions of Competence: Culture, Classification and Intellectual Disability.* Cambridge: Cambridge University Press.

Walmsley, J. (1991) 'Adulthood and people with mental handicaps: Report of a research project.' *Mental Handicap Research 4*, 2, 141–154.

Walmsley, J. (1994) 'Learning disability: Overcoming the barriers.' In S. French (ed) *On Equal Terms: Working with Disabled People.* London: Butterworth-Heinemann.

Williams, F. (1989) 'Mental handicap and oppression.' In A. Brechin and J. Walmsley (eds) *Making Connections: Reflecting on the Lives and Experiences of People with Learning Difficulties.* London: Hodder and Stoughton.

Wolfensberger, W. (1972) *The Principle of Normalisation in Human Services.* Toronto: National Institute of Mental Retardation.

Wolfensberger, W. (1975) *The Origin and Nature of our Institutional Models.* Syracuse: Human Policy Press.

World Health Organization (WHO) (1992) 'The ICD-10 classification of mental and behavioural disorders.' Geneva: World Health Organization.

CHAPTER 7

Marriage and Parenting

David May and Murray K. Simpson

If school leaving can be said to mark the end of childhood and the formal beginning of that journey to full adult status, then marriage, and even more so,
parenthood, publicly announces its completion: indeed in some European societies still a successful transition cannot otherwise be achieved (Mitterauer
1992). The significance of both is not lost on the majority of people with intellectual disabilities, especially those who might aspire to social acceptance and
anything like an 'ordinary' life. Edgerton (1967), for example, notes that for his
sample of ex-hospital residents marriage and parenthood remained 'cherished
goals', essential components of self-esteem, despite the fact that for many it was
their sexuality – their proclivity, 'real or fancied', for sexual misconduct – that
had prompted their removal from the community in the first place; a confinement from which they were only released by their agreement to sterilization.

It is perhaps difficult today to appreciate just how entrenched and unquestioned was the opposition to the idea of people with intellectual disabilities
forming relationships with the opposite sex, let alone having children. 'It is
agreed,' asserted the Board of Control in 1949, with a spurious authority that in
fact rested on little more than prejudice and anecdote, 'that mentally defective
persons are generally unfit for the responsibility of marriage and parenthood'
(quoted in Mattinson 1970, p.47). Mabel Cooper describes some of the extraor-
dinary strategies adopted by the authorities at St Lawrence's in the early 1950s
to control social intercourse between the sexes and ensure that undesirable attachments did not form:

> You couldn't mix with the men. You could go to a dance but you'd have men one side, women the other. You could dance with them, but they had to go back men one side, women the other side. Even in the dance hall there was two loads of staff in the middle, one full of women and one full of men, and you just danced around the staff in the middle. (Atkinson, Jackson and Walmsley 1997, p.25)

Even with the adoption of community care and 'normalization' and the formal abandonment of the institution as the cornerstone of government policy, opposition to (perhaps one should more accurately say, incredulity with) the idea of people with intellectual disabilities marrying persisted, if perhaps in a less overt fashion. *Like Normal People* (Myers 1978) celebrates the marriage of two 're-tarded' people in the USA in the late 1970s as a major breakthrough (as it then surely was), achieved despite the reservations of support workers and family. The couple involved describe the obstacles they encountered to their burgeoning relationship from the staff in the residential home where they were both living before their marriage: 'They wouldn't let us be alone together, and if we were in the same room, we had to leave the door open. It was as if they didn't trust us ... Houseparents would criticize us if we held hands or if I put my arm around her' (p.148). At much the same time, Craft and Craft (1979), pioneers in the field, were reporting on their failure, 'despite three years of staff counselling', to open up one UK institution to married residents. In this way, denied the opportunity to engage in meaningful adult relationships, the public image of people with intellectual disabilities as 'eternal children' was reinforced.

We note such attitudes in part to remind ourselves of the distance we have travelled over the past two to three decades. It is a journey that is clearly reflected in the research literature. In her groundbreaking study of marriage and intellectual disability first published in 1970, Mattison states that she was unable to find any published work which 'dealt in detail with the relationships in a marriage made by two individuals, once weak in social functioning, handicapped by low intelligence and having experienced care and training in a hospital' (pp.18–19). This is perhaps to overstate the lack of interest in marriage and parenting among the research community even at that time and certainly ignores Edgerton's (1967) important and enormously influential study which appeared only three years earlier and presents a picture of marriage in a formerly institutionalized population not too dissimilar from her own. But her general point is well taken. Of nearly 150 references identified by the present authors, less than 13 per cent were published prior to 1970, while almost two-fifths have appeared in the last decade.

Not only does this illustrate the recent, remarkable growth of interest in the area, but closer inspection of the work reveals an equally significant shift in the research focus, since all but two of the more than fifty papers appearing since 1990 are concerned specifically with parenting rather than marriage *per se.* The question posed at the very outset of Mattison's book – 'Is marriage a viable proposition for the subnormal and their children?' – is not only no longer thought appropriate, it is simply irrelevant. The task for researchers is now not so much to establish the fitness (or otherwise) of people with intellectual disabilities for marriage and parenthood, but to assist them more effectively to discharge those roles (see, for example, the papers in the special issue of the *Journal of Intellectual and Developmental Disabilities 24*, 1, 1999).

In this chapter we consider this shift of emphasis and present a selective review of the findings on marriage and parenting before offering some data of our own as a contribution to the debate. We do not, however, presume to add to the many existing comprehensive reviews of the literature. For this the reader is referred especially to Dowdney and Skuse (1993); Llewellyn (1990); Sheerin (1998); Tymchuk and Andron (1994). For earlier work focusing particularly on marriage see Craft and Craft (1979). The most important, and certainly most interesting work of recent years is that by the Booths, an ethnographic study very much in the Edgerton tradition. This has produced two books (Booth and Booth 1994, 1998) and a number of papers, of which see especially Booth and Booth (1993).

From marriage to parenthood

In many ways the shift of emphasis we have referred to merely acknowledges the changing reality consequent upon the policy developments of the past 30 years. As Booth and Booth (1993) note: 'Parenthood is a choice and consequence of ordinary living.' The numbers of people with intellectual disabilities who are becoming parents are (or so it is assumed) inevitably increasing, and are likely to continue to do so – whether we wish it or not – and the research agenda must needs change in response to this new reality. But at the same time research does not simply reflect the world, it helps shape it. Changing attitudes to marriage and parenting are in large measure the result of the quite different way we have come to view people with intellectual disabilities and their relationship to the wider society, and much of the responsibility for that, both in the general and the particular, must rest with the research community.

One of the earliest, and certainly most influential, studies of marriage is Mattinson's (1970) study of 36 couples discharged on licence from one large hospital in the south-west of England in the 1950s and 1960s. They had spent up to 42 years in institutions, although the mean length of time was 14 years. The mean IQ of the group was 61, but Craft and Craft (1979) note that 'nearly a quarter had a tested IQ of over 70 on admission' and others who had originally been admitted for work training or whose IQ was depressed as a result of 'grossly deprivative upbringings'. In short, the status of 'a high proportion' of the sample was at least contestable. Most had known one another while in the institution and some had discreetly embarked on their courtship there, but others had not met until after their discharge. Only 4 of the 36 couples were at the time of the study divorced or separated. A further three were rated as 'unsatisfactory', characterized by 'a negative, stormy relationship'. On the other hand, 19 of the 32 had a relationship that Mattinson described as 'supportive and affectionate', 'able to give to each other both practically and emotionally and safe enough to afford considerable flexibility and freedom within the relationship and with the organisation of their marital affairs. Their togetherness was the most real, as it allowed them still to be separate individuals and at times within the togetherness to be "alone"' (pp.133–134).

Craft and Craft's (1979) study of 45 Welsh couples, in which at least one of the partners was 'mentally handicapped', i.e. with an IQ of less than 70, adopted a similar methodology (although with a significant action component) and produced very similar results. At the time of the study 41 of the 45 marriages were still intact. The average length of marriage was 7.5 years, with one having lasted for 27 years. The mean age at marriage was early thirties, somewhat older than in the general population, although whether this resulted from their incarceration or reflects the social isolation of people with intellectual disabilities more generally is hard to say.

Craft and Craft (1979), like Mattison (1970) and Edgerton (1967) before them, drew a generally positive picture of the ability of people with intellectual disabilities to forge and sustain productive and meaningful relationships: 'with adequate education, a counselling programme, current government allowances, social work support and standard council houses or flats, far more handicapped married couples can make a success of marriage, and achieve happiness in life, than previous studies have suggested' (p.125). Yet, as with Mattison's study, the precise status of their sample is ambiguous and it is far from clear just how generalizable are their results. More than one in four had IQs in excess of 70, and while some of these had other mental and physical problems, others were described as 'normal or dull normal [with] no overt disability'.

Perhaps surprisingly, neither Mattison (1970) nor Craft and Craft (1979) have a great deal to say about children or their samples' parenting abilities. This is no doubt in part because for many of their couples children were simply not a major consideration. Between one-half and two-thirds of the couples were childless, and the average family size, of 1.5 and 2.1 respectively, was lower than for women of comparable age in the general population. However, it was also clear that for those families with children child care was an issue: almost all were receiving regular support from health visitors or social workers, in many cases of a quite intensive nature, and the children themselves were performing less well than children from other families.

Parenthood was marginal to the concerns of Mattison and Craft and Craft because what they were offering was a form of companionate marriage largely unburdened by the demands and risks of children. It is no coincidence that such ideas commanded the attention of researchers and campaigners alike in the late 1960s and early 1970s when widespread use of 'the pill' and the emergence of a much more liberal social climate were generally effectively decoupling sex from procreation and elevating the former to the status of a universal human right. But these same social trends also led to a decoupling of sex from marriage and a rise in cohabitation and single parenthood among the general population, inevitably detracting from the significance of marriage as the decisive threshold to adult status.

Parenting

For all these reasons, by the early 1980s marriage was no longer the issue on which the battle for the rights of intellectually disabled people was to be fought; it was instead, parenthood, transformed from a practical into a moral issue. As Greenspan and Budd (1986) declare: 'allowing individuals labelled as mentally retarded to exercise their desire to participate in the life-giving process is the ultimate test of living in a free and humane society'. But this is to introduce other equally vulnerable parties to the equation with 'rights' that are increasingly being recognized and, indeed, accorded primacy (Brodeur 1990; Hayes 1993), which may well help explain the continuing controversy surrounding this issue. However, as Sheerin (1998) has pointed out, even here there has been a significant shift in emphasis in the research agenda over the past two decades, from an initial concern with parental inadequacies to a much more positive approach which seeks to emphasize the abilities of intellectually disabled parents, and identify means by which those abilities may be further strengthened.

Three assumptions dominate much of the early research on parenting by people with intellectual disabilities: that such people lack the intellectual and social competencies for adequate parenting; that they are incapable of acquiring the necessary skills; and that as a result their children are at risk of serious developmental delays, or worse. At first sight the evidence would seem to support the first and last of these assumptions, while opinion on the second is somewhat divided. Closer inspection, however, reveals a much more confused and inconclusive picture (Dowdney and Skuse 1993). Certainly, there is a good deal of evidence to suggest that women with intellectual disabilities (there has been little work carried out on fathers) make for poor housekeepers and are frequently overwhelmed by their parenting responsibilities, their difficulties not surprisingly increasing with the size of their families (Accardo and Whitman 1990; Mickleson 1947; Shaw and Wright 1962; Sheridan 1956; Zetlin, Weisner and Gallimore 1985). Although Borgman (1969), it must be added, found no such relationship. At the same time, it would appear that above a minimum level of intellectual competence – the consensus seems to suggest somewhere in the region of an IQ of 50 (Borgman 1969; Mickelson 1947) –

there is no clear relationship between parental competence and intelligence (Brandon 1957; Galliher 1973; Schilling *et al.* 1982; Shaw and Wright 1960).

There is a common belief – Espe-Sherwindt and Crable (1990) prefer to call it a 'myth', but it is buttressed by considerable research evidence – that the children of parents with intellectual disabilities will themselves be intellectually disabled, or at the least are more likely to experience significant developmental delays, to suffer from health problems, exhibit behavioural problems and generally invite the concern of health visitors, social workers and teachers, and as a consequence are more likely to be taken into care (Brandon 1957; Craft and Craft 1979; Gillberg and Giejer-Karlsson 1983; Kaminer, Jedrysek and Soles 1981; Mattison 1970; Reed and Reed 1965). At the same time, it is clear that this is by no means an inevitable progression. In their ethnographic study of the long-term effects of parenting by people with intellectual disabilities, Booth and Booth (1998) conducted in-depth interviews with 30 now adult children of parents, at least one of whom had intellectual disabilities. Half of their sample were themselves identified as intellectually disabled. They found that the relationship between parental competence and child outcomes is far from straightforward or deterministic, but is rather shaped by such contingencies as 'the birth of another child, the death of a grandparent, a change of school, the separation of parents, the onset of unemployment, a move to a new house'. Many of the children showed 'considerable resilience' in the face of life's vicissitudes and overall they seemed to fare no better or worse than other children from the same social background. Far from their surviving (and in some cases, prospering) in spite of the handicaps imposed by their upbringing, the idea of family exerted an important and positive influence on their behaviour and on the parent–child relationship that extended well into adulthood. Booth and Booth concluded that 'children's destinies are not fixed by having a mother or father with learning difficulties'.

While the specific factors that account for success or failure remain elusive, Booth and Booth identified three broad sets of variables that enhance the prospects for a positive outcome. The first of these centre on the personality of the individual child: 'sociability, responsiveness to others, and an outgoing nature as shown by a readiness to join in activities and take on responsibility' enable the child to cope with the negative effects of the environment. Second, is a secure and stable family environment characterized by warmth and mutuality. Finally the existence of supportive relationships outside the home encourages participation and involvement by child and family in the wider society. These factors operate, not in some mechanistic way, but rather in a highly contingent fashion:

> [They] may be missing for some people, or they may change over time, or they may be insufficient to buttress the individual against the pressures bearing on them. The balance between the stresses that heighten vulnerability and the protective factors that enhance resilience varies for different individuals and at different points in people's lives. (Booth and Booth 1998, p.84)

In this and their earlier study of parents with intellectual disabilities (Booth and Booth 1994), Booth and Booth are at pains to counter 'the presumption of incompetence' that characterizes so much social services, involvement with such families and which encourages premature removal of children from the home, not because of inadequate care, but simply because their parents have intellectual disabilities. They criticize the agencies working with these families for: using inappropriate standards of care when assessing parental competence; focusing on parenting deficits or failure and ignoring achievement and success; attributing inadequate child care or unsatisfactory outcomes to those parenting deficits, while failing to take into account wider environmental influences – the poverty and social deprivation that mark their lives; and generally for adopting a one-dimensional approach to what is the much more complex reality of people's lives and relationships. They do not, however, deny that there is a problem, and research has shown that many such parents lack the skills necessary for effective child rearing. They note specifically:

> the failure to adjust parenting styles to changes in their child's development, a lack of verbal interaction with the child, insufficient cognitive stimulation especially in the area of play, a tendency to overgeneralize instructions, inconsistent use of discipline (and, in particular, a reliance on punishment at the expense of praise), and a lack of expressed warmth, love and affection in relationships. (Booth and Booth 1993, pp.463–464; see also McGaw 1993)

The issue, however, is not so much whether some parents with intellectual disabilities are deficient in these respects, but rather how extensive is the problem?

Is it peculiar to parents with intellectual disabilities and can it be remedied, or at least countered, by education or other special measures?

To take this last point first, Feldman (1994) reviewed 20 studies published since 1983 that reported on educational interventions for parents (almost exclusively mothers) with low (less than 80) IQ. The parenting skills examined included: basic child care, safety, nutrition, problem solving, positive parent–child interactions and child behaviour management. The most common instructional approach used was behavioural (e.g. task analysis, modelling, feedback, reinforcement). While the results overall were encouraging, the numbers involved were small; the median sample size was four, and only three of the studies examined had more than ten participants. Moreover, more than half included persons with IQs less than 70, generally considered outside the range of intellectual disability. The relevance, therefore, of much of this work to persons with lower IQ, and especially to persons who may be considered to have severe intellectual disabilities, remains questionable. It is also unclear whether the skills learnt largely in the clinic or psychology lab can be generalized to real life situations in the home or are sustainable over time (Feldman 1994; Whitman and Accardo 1990). Finally, we should note that much of this work is restricted to North America, which may limit its applicability. In the UK parent education programmes have been described, often as an adjunct to more extensive support services, but with insufficient detail provided to permit an evaluation of their effectiveness (McGaw 1993; Young, Young and Ford 1997).

Problems with the research

There are two principal reasons why the results of research into parenting by people with intellectual disabilities appear at first sight so confused, and even contradictory. The first may be termed ideological; that is, it relates to the underlying aims and purpose of the researchers. As we noted above, the emphasis of research into the parenting abilities of people with intellectual disabilities has changed quite significantly over the past two decades. The implicit middle-class standards by which they were judged, and for which earlier research has been rightly criticized, have now given way to the idea of 'good enough' parenting, where aspirations and endeavour seem to count for more than performance. The presumption of incompetence that previously dominated the work of researchers (and practitioners) and which focused attention on parental shortcomings has largely given way to a more positive approach which seeks to identify and develop what is seen as an existing (even natural) capacity for parenting (see, for example, the papers in Craft 1993). It is in many respects a question of perspective, of whether we wish to see the glass as half empty or half full. Certainly, while there was a tendency in the past to overlook findings which suggested that a good many people with intellectual disability provide adequate parenting, equally, it seems to us, the data offered by more recent researchers who wish to assert the rights of people with intellectual disabilities to parenthood are capable of supporting more than one conclusion. We are in no way suggesting that the interpretation placed on the evidence is wrong, or that the refocusing of activity more generally is misplaced – indeed, the position adopted is one with which we have a great deal of sympathy; only that it is a value position to which the findings of research are ultimately subordinate, even irrelevant.

The second reason for treating the findings of research in this area with some caution is that so much of the work is methodologically and conceptually flawed:

> The perspectives presented in the professional literature on parents with intellectual disability are contradictory and equivocal. Sound empirical research is lacking. Judgements based on adequacy of child care are frequently subjective or from third party sources. Much of the data has been gathered indirectly or is presented as clinical observations of 'extreme cases'. Comparison groups when used have been inadequately formed, generally relying on only one variable, tested intelligence. (Llewellyn 1990, p.377; see also Booth and Booth 1994; Dowdney and Skuse 1993; Sheerin 1998 for other detailed critiques).

At its most basic level we are confronted with the all-too typical problem in taking an overview of research on intellectual disability that the studies in question are not necessarily talking about the same thing. Terms such as 'learning/intellectual disabilities', 'low intelligence', 'feeble-minded' are used interchangeably, often without any attempt to define them more precisely or to provide details of just how particular samples are constituted. Yet what is meant by intellectual disability, and specifically how it is to be operationalized for research purposes, are crucial issues here. Given the heterogeneous nature of the intellectually disabled population and the vagaries of definition, assessment and identification, there is the very real possibility that many of the studies include a significant proportion who are not really intellectually disabled at all, or whose status is at least contestable (Whitman and Accardo 1990). Although, since few studies provide detailed descriptions of the samples employed, this is not always easy to establish with any confidence.

Much of the early work, for example, relied heavily on previously institutionalized samples. Not only do these include many with IQs temporarily depressed by grossly deprived upbringings and others who were admitted for reasons that often had little to do with intellectual disability, but their long years of confinement deprived them of a family life that might have informed their own subsequent efforts, and on discharge frequently found themselves socially isolated. Other studies rely on samples drawn from those known to social services, often because of problems with child care. These are important sources of bias. Dowdney and Skuse (1993) note that studies which include people with IQs in the normal range tend to draw optimistic conclusions, while those whose samples contained families already known to welfare agencies were generally pessimistic. Finally, the heterogeneous nature of many of the samples used is rarely explicitly acknowledged. Subjects are typically drawn from across the adult range, bringing together parents at very different stages of the child-rearing process and thus with very different perspectives on that experience, but also from sampling frames that are rarely described in any detail. Therefore, not only are they unrepresentative, often in unknown ways, limiting the kind of conclusions that may safely be drawn, but their very unrepresentativeness and heterogeneity conceal both the nature and extent of any problem.

Marriage and parenting in a Scottish cohort

One study that avoids many of these problems, in that it examines marriage in a complete, epidemiologically defined population of people with intellectual disabilities, is that by Richardson and Koller (1996), also reported in Koller, Richardson and Katz (1988). As part of a wider study of intellectual disability they followed into early adulthood a cohort of young people (N = 191), all those identified as having intellectual disabilities from a total population born between 1951 and 1955 and resident in one UK city. At age 22, 43 (19 males and 24 females) were (or had been) married. A further 3 (2 males and 1 female) were cohabiting. Although no precise figures are given, Koller *et al.* (1988) report that 'most' of those married (by which, it appears, they mean around two-thirds) had one or two children.

Two features of this group stand out. The first is that those who were married were among the most able of the cohort, even when comparisons exclude those with IQs of less than 50, none of whom were married: mean IQ 68 compared with 64 for those not married. Exactly half (13 males and 8 females) of those with IQs of 70 or more were married by age 22, while only one married male and four females had IQs under 60. The young men had significantly higher IQs than the women: mean IQ 71 compared with 67. Second, and related to the previous point, none of those who were (or had been) married at age 22 were at that time receiving services for people with intellectual disabilities. Five had briefly entered services in the immediate post-school period, but by age 22 all 43 had dropped out: they had ceased for all practical purposes to be regarded as intellectually disabled. Whether they were receiving other forms of social work support is not clear, but the fact that Koller *et al.* (1988) make no explicit reference to this suggests that they were not.

'Significantly fewer' (about half as many, with the women more likely to marry than the men) of the intellectually disabled group were married compared with a non-disabled comparison group matched by age, gender, residence and social class. The great majority (38 of the 43) had married people who did not themselves have intellectual disabilities. It seems clear that many had not told their spouse of their status and some were concerned lest they find out, while others reported feelings of anguish or shame at the way their partners had reacted on learning of their past. All when asked rated their marriage as 'well' or 'very well'. This is either a methodological artefact or a sad reflection of the generally low expectations held by people with intellectual disabilities (see Mattinson 1970). Koller *et al.* concluded that while around half of these marriages did indeed appear to be going well, nevertheless the group experienced 'significantly more problems, discord, separation, and divorce than their matched comparisions'. This was particularly true of the young women, whose marriages were twice as likely as their non-disabled counterparts to be rated as having problems. Financial difficulties, unemployment and sex-related problems seem to have predominated, but the women in the intellectually disabled group were also seven times more likely to report being physically abused by their husbands than those in the comparison group.

For all its general methodological soundness, the value of the Aberdeen study is limited for the obvious reason that the data extend only to age 22 and therefore present a partial and incomplete picture of marriage and parenting in this group. Twenty years later a further follow-up was carried out, although restricted on this occasion to those in the sample (N = 73) who at age 22 were receiving services for people with intellectual disabilities (May and Hogg 1999). Of the 54 people recontacted (83% of survivors) 7 (3 males and 4 females) were or had been married (although this underestimates the rate of marriage in this population since of the 11 survivors not contacted, two women were definitely known to be married with children, and three others possibly so, while one of the five 'not contacted' males was cohabiting). Of the three ever-married males contacted, one was divorced. None had children. All four women, on the other hand, had children, a total of ten between them. One of the women was a single mother, her marital history somewhat unclear. It is possible that she had been twice married, but this is not certain. What is clear is that as a young woman she had had a number of liaisons. She was presently living with her 9-year-old daughter, but had had another child in her teens who had been adopted. Now in his twenties he was living in Aberdeen but had no contact with his mother.

With the exception of the single mother just referred to, all these marriages had taken place relatively late in life – late twenties/early thirties. One of the men had waited until he was 39 before marrying 'for company' a woman with physical disabilities 12 years his senior. In at least three cases (although again this is likely to be an underestimate) the spouse also had intellectual disabilities. One woman had met and married her husband in the long-term hospital in which they were then resident. One of the men had met his wife at the occupational centre they were both then attending, while another met his wife at a social club for people with intellectual disabilities.

As a group these seven were perhaps somewhat less able than those who had married by age 22 (mean IQ 63) and appeared to have a greater range of other disabilities. They were, however, far more able than those from the 'adult services' group who had not married (mean IQ 45) and their status as 'intellectually disabled' in mid-life ambiguous. The three men (mean IQ 65) all had quite serious physical limitations, which had been the principal reason for their being diverted into special education in the first place and had certainly prevented them from obtaining employment on school leaving. They had drifted into occupational centres, but it was always likely that they would find these both restrictive and further stigmatizing. All three left in their late twenties, two to find work, but with mixed results. At the time of the follow-up all three were living independently, two in fact unknown to services for people with intellectual disabilities, while the third received only minimal support from the social work department, centred round budgeting and general household finance.

The four women were quite different, although intellectually hardly less able (mean IQ 61). All four had presented with behavioural problems in their late teens and as a consequence had been institutionalized. They remained in hospital for between 7 and 14-plus years. One met and married her husband in hospital and had her first child there. This child was initially fostered before being returned to the couple, against social work advice, shortly after they were discharged. Two others were married not long after coming out of hospital, to men they appear to have met on the outside. The most successful of the four, somewhat surprisingly, was the single mother. With considerable help from an older married sister who lived nearby and with more limited support from the social work department, she was holding down a part-time job and had achieved a measure of domestic independence.

The other three women were being supported by the child and family unit of the social work department, although the intensity of the support varied considerably. All the children involved gave cause for concern: in two families all four school-age children were in special education, and the two infants were developmentally delayed, while in the third there was a child with cerebral palsy who was thought not to be receiving adequate care largely because of her mother's continuing mental health problems. In one further family all three children were at one stage subject to a temporary Place of Safety order prompted by suspicions of sexual abuse in which the father was in some way implicated. There were in addition other problems of varying complexity and seriousness – with money, with the police and with neighbours.

Although numbers are small and the data incomplete, nevertheless it is possible to draw some general conclusions from this study concerning marriage and parenthood by people with intellectual disabilities. First, marriage rates are low, especially when compared with the general population (Coleman 1988). Second, those people with intellectual disabilities who do marry are among the most able of that population, and are likely to be drawn disproportionately from those whose status as intellectually disabled is, at the very least, contestable. Whereas 36 per cent of those who dropped out of services at school leaving were married by their early twenties (the figure for women is 53%), less than 20 per cent of those who continued in adult services had married by the time they reached middle age, compared with more than 80 per cent of the general population. Even among this group it was the most able and those who now stood in an ambiguous relationship to services who were most likely to marry. No one currently attending a day centre or residing in a facility reserved for people with intellectual disabilities was married.

The Aberdeen data tell us little about the quality of marriages or the nature of the parenting experience. Those who did not continue in services were more likely to marry early (although generally later than their non-disabled counterparts) to people who were not themselves formally intellectually disabled, and to have children. Their marriages were far from problem free, yet for the most part they seemed to hold together, although they still had a long way to go. Koller *et al.* (1988) have nothing to say on the quality of their parenting. Those whose status as intellectually disabled was reaffirmed at school leaving were not only less likely to marry, but more likely to marry late and to marry other intellectually disabled people. No doubt this is in part explained by the more closely supervised and restricted world of adult services.

Conclusions

It may indeed be the case that 'as a result of changing attitudes towards sexuality, deinstitutionalization, decreased segregation and wider opportunities for independent living and participation in the community' the numbers of people with intellectual disabilities who are marrying and having children are 'steadily increasing and will probably continue to do so' (Booth and Booth 1993). Nevertheless, as the Aberdeen data suggest, the majority (a great majority, depending on how one defines intellectual disability) do not marry, have children, or for that matter, sexual relations, and those who do are far from representative of this sector of the population. While it may be that developments in the organization of services, and even more in the rhetoric of policy makers and service providers, offer proof of a kind for the 'discovery of adulthood', it remains the case that the kinds of adult roles to which people with intellectual disabilities have access are restricted: the acknowledgement of a right does not necessarily result in its realization.

The point is underlined by two further statistics from the Aberdeen data. More than half of those who were living in the family home at age 22 were still there 20 years later, the majority still attending the same day centre they had entered on school leaving. For this group leaving home was typically delayed until their late thirties or early forties, and then only prompted by the death or failing health of parents. Sheerin (1998) insists with reference to the situation in Ireland that 'current social attitudes do not promote an equal and inclusive approach towards learning disabled people', but rather continues to support 'a custodial view-point, albeit within the context of community-based units' (p.131). Equally we would argue that accompanying the well-motivated push to facilitate and support marriage and even more, parenting, there is an unacknowledged extension of surveillance and intervention into the lives of adults with intellectual disabilities. The right to parenthood has not brought any substantive retrenchment of control over their lives; rather there has been an extension and reconfiguration of the field in new areas. For this reason, we wonder whether it is actually more accurate to suggest that, rather than being granted a right to become parents, they are instead being accorded the right to become *intellectually disabled* parents, there being fundamental differences in the assumptions which are made about when and how it is legitimate for statutory agencies to take an active interest in their lives. Surveillance and intervention by social work agencies are not routine aspects of parenting, but are predicated on at least prima facie evidence of a problem. In the case of adults with intellectual disabilities the opposite seems to apply, intellectual disability itself providing the grounds for attention. The issue, therefore, is what the role of statutory agencies might be, not whether or not they have one.

References

Accardo, P.J. and Whitman, B.Y. (1990) 'Children of mentally retarded parents.' *American Journal of Disease of Children 144*, 69–70.

Atkinson, D., Jackson, M. and Walmsley, J. (1997) *Forgotten Lives: Exploring the History of Learning Disability.* Kidderminster: BILD Publications.

Booth, T. and Booth, W. (1993) 'Parenting with learning difficulties: Lessons for practitioners.' *British Journal of Social Work 23*, 459–480.

Booth, T. and Booth, W. (1994) *Parenting Under Pressure: Mothers and Fathers with Learning Difficulties.* Buckingham: Open University Press.

Booth, T. and Booth, W. (1998) *Growing up with Parents who have Learning Disabilities.* London: Routledge.

Borgman, R.D. (1969) 'Intelligence and maternal inadequacy.' *Child Welfare 48*, 301–304.

Brandon, M. (1957) 'The intellectual and social status of children of mental defectives.' *Journal of Mental Sciences 103*, 710–738.

Brodeur, D.A. (1990) 'Parents with mental retardation and developmental disabilities: Ethical issues in parenting.' In B.Y. Whitman and P.J. Accardo (eds) *When a Parent is Mentally Retarded.* Baltimore: Paul H. Brookes.

Coleman, D.A. (1988) 'Population.' In A.H. Halsey (ed) *British Social Trends Since 1900.* Basingstoke: Macmillan, pp.36–134.

Craft, A. (ed) (1993) *Parents with Learning Disabilities.* Kidderminster: BILD Publications.

Craft, A. and Craft, M. (1979) *Handicapped Married Couples: A Welsh Study of Couples Handicapped from Birth by Mental, Physical or Personality Disorder.* London: Routledge & Kegan Paul.

Dowdney, L. and Skuse, D. (1993) 'Parenting provided by adults with mental retardation.' *Journal of Child Psychology and Psychiatry 34*, 1, 25–47.

Edgerton, R. (1967) *The Cloak of Competence: Stigma in the Lives of the Mentally Retarded.* Berkeley: University of California Press.

Espe-Scherwindt, M. and Crable, S. (1990) 'Parents with mental retardation: moving beyond the myths.' *Topics in Early Childhood Special Education 13*, 2, 154–174.

Feldman, M.A. (1994) 'Parenting education for parents with intellectual disabilities: A review of outcome studies.' *Research in Developmental Disabilities 15*, 4, 299–332.

Galliher, K. (1973) 'Termination of the parent/child relationship: Should parental IQ be an important factor?' *Law and the Social Order 4*, 855–879.

Gillberg, C. and Geijer-Karlsson, M. (1983) 'Children born to mentally retarded women: A 21 year follow-up study of 41 cases.' *Psychological Medicine 13*, 891–894.

Greenspan, S. and Budd, K. (1986) 'Research on mentally retarded parents.' In J. Gallagher and P. Vietze (eds) *Families of Handicapped Persons: Research Programmes and Policy Issues.* Baltimore MD: Paul H. Brookes.

Hayes, M. (1993) 'Child care law: An overview.' In A. Craft (ed) *Parents with Learning Disabilities.* Kidderminster: BILD Publications.

Kaminer, R., Jedrysek, E. and Soles, B. (1981) 'Intellectually limited parents.' *Journal of Developmental and Behavioral Pediatrics 2,* 39–43.

Koller, H., Richardson, S.A. and Katz, M. (1988) 'Marriage in a young adult mentally retarded population.' *Journal of Mental Deficiency Research 32,* 93–102.

Llewellyn, G. (1990) 'People with intellectual disability as parents: Perspectives from the professional literature.' *Australia and New Zealand Journal of Developmental Disabilities 16,* 4, 369–380.

McGaw, S. (1993) 'Working with parents on parenting skills.' In A. Craft (ed) *Parents with Learning Disabilities.* Kidderminster: BILD Publications.

Mattinson, J. (1970) *Marriage and Mental Handicap.* London: Duckworth.

May, D. and Hogg, J. (1999) 'Is there a "hidden" population of adults with intellectual disabilities? Evidence from a follow-up study.' *Journal of Applied Research in Intellectual Disabilities 12,* 3, 177–189.

Meyers, R. (1978) *Like Normal People.* London: Souvenir Press.

Mickelson, P. (1947) 'The feebleminded parent: A study of 90 family cases.' *American Journal of Mental Deficiency 51,* 644–645.

Mitterauer, M. (1992) *A History of Youth.* Oxford: Blackwell.

Reed, E. and Reed, S. (1965) *Mental Retardation: A Family Study.* Philadelphia: Saunders.

Richardson, S.A. and Koller, H. (1996) *Twenty-Two Years: Causes and Consequences of Mental Retardation.* Cambridge MA: Harvard University Press.

Schilling, R., Schinke, S., Blythe, B. and Barth, R. (1982) 'Child maltreatment and mentally retarded parents: Is there a relationship?' *Mental Retardation 20,* 5, 201–209.

Shaw, C. and Wright, C. (1960) 'The married mental defective: A follow-up study.' *The Lancet,* 30 January, 273–274.

Sheerin, F. (1998) 'Parents with learning disabilities: A review of the literature.' *Journal of Advanced Nursing 28,* 1, 126–133.

Sheridan, M. (1956) 'The intelligence of 100 neglectful mothers.' *British Medical Journal 1,* 91–93.

Tymchuk, A. and Andron, L. (1994) 'Rationale, approaches, results and resource implications of programmes to enhance parenting skills of people with learning disabilities.' In A. Craft (ed) *Practice Issues in Sexuality and Learning Disabilities.* London: Routledge, pp.202–216.

Whitman, B.Y. and Accardo, P.J. (1990) 'Mentally retarded parents in the community.' In B.Y. Whitman and P.J. Accardo (eds) *When a Parent is Mentally Retarded.* Baltimore: Paul H. Brookes, pp.3–10.

Young, S., Young, B. and Ford, D. (1997) 'Parents with learning disability: Research issues and informed practice.' *Disability and Society 12,* 1, 57–68.

Zetlin, A.G., Weisner, T.S. and Gallimore, R. (1985) 'Diversity, shared functioning and the role of benefactors: A study of parenting by retarded parents.' In S.K. Thurman (ed) *Children of Handicapped Parents: Research and Clinical Perspectives.* Florida: Academic Press.

CHAPTER 8

Rights of Passage

Life Course Transitions for Women with Intellectual Disabilities

Patricia Noonan Walsh

Introduction

For many years people with intellectual disabilities lived separate and unequal lives. At best, they were buffered by their special status in society. In the worst of times, thousands lingered in hospitals and other institutions. Sporadic family contact, removal from the regular workforce, indifferent health and nutrition, dearth of civic responsibility and lifelong segregation of the sexes in residences were but a few of the hallmarks of daily life prescribed by this bleak form of care. Whether bounded socially or built in stone, generations of men and women lived and died in a place apart. They paid a high price for safekeeping, denied access to the life experiences and also to the social roles typical for their own people bred in the same place and time. The impact of this closed world was not uniform. Women with intellectual disabilities living in cultures where gender inequality prevailed were especially at risk of being excluded from a full part in everyday life. In addition, they missed the defining moments typically available in their cultures to young, middle-aged and older women.

Institutional care may have had its day, supplanted by policies in favour of supporting individuals with intellectual disabilities to achieve a satisfying quality of life in their own communities. But remnants of the old regimes linger in pockets of every country, woven into modern fabric or unreconstructed in countries of central and eastern Europe with economies now in transition

(Walsh 1997). In developing countries – the majority world where most people with disabilities live – traditional attitudes and poverty often impede the inclusion of people with disabilities in their own culture (Epstein 1997; O'Toole and McConkey 1995).

Although prevailing winds freshen towards social inclusion for all citizens, equality remains an elusive landfall for the 60,000,000 men and women estimated to have some level of intellectual disability (WHO 1997). New rights-based criteria for supporting people with intellectual disabilities throughout their lives – Quality of Life indicators, for example – have yet to be attained in service systems of many countries (Rapley and Beyer 1998). Around the globe, the levels at which women have achieved gender equality and visible participation in political and economic life vary widely from region to region (UNDP 1997). How do these contextual factors influence the lives of women with intellectual disabilities? How do personal characteristics interact with their social, economic and political environments as these women grow and, increasingly, mature into middle and old age? In countries with formal support systems, does status as a service user blur the distinctive experiences at rites of passage across lifespan developmental stages typically experienced by other women?

This chapter addresses some of the issues arising from the longer, more visible lives of women with intellectual disabilities. They are important for women taking charge of themselves, as well as for their family members, advocates and those providing supports for them at different stages of their lives. First, it is suggested that gender interacts with other social roles assumed by women with intellectual disabilities within their culture to enrich or perhaps compromise their health and other aspects of quality of life. Second, the opportunities presented at stages of transition and the potential problems in adjustment for young, middle-aged and older women with intellectual disabilities are explored. Guidelines for practice and policy emerging from a recent WHO-IASSID initiative on health and ageing among women with intellectual disabilities are drawn. Finally, research strategies are proposed to deepen an understanding of the specific environmental, social and personal characteristics associated with a satisfying quality of life for women throughout their lives.

Gender, rights and quality of life

As women live longer than men, the quality of their longer life becomes of central importance (WHO 1998, p.105). At the start of the twenty-first century, social inclusion is the leading policy target for all citizens, whether or not they have disabilities or are otherwise at risk of living marginal lives. How aptly does this single target fit all aspirations – feminine well-being among them?

Global perspectives

To think globally about women with intellectual disabilities is to evoke their human rights for social inclusion and self-determination. The United Nations Standard Rules for Equalization of Opportunities apply universally (UN 1994). Although without status in international law, these 22 Rules exert a compelling moral force. The European Union of 15 member states endorses a rights-based rather than a welfare-based model of disability as the engine of its social policy for this population of citizens (CEC 1996). Yesterday's hard and fast human services aimed at accommodation and rehabilitation for people with intellectual disabilities have been recast in the light of the new focus on their rights. Societies must offer personalized, more flexible supports to individuals, helping them to determine how they will achieve inclusion in their own homes, workplaces and communities throughout their lives.

Quality of life

New forms of services and supports demand new forms of appraisal. Quality of life has emerged as a 'potentially unifying construct in setting the goals for services and measuring their impact on the character of people's day-to-day lives' (Felce 1997, p.126). It measures the effectiveness of supports by how well they achieve desired personal outcomes for people with intellectual disabilities. A lifespan developmental approach to quality of life does not mete out prescribed patterns of social behaviour on a fixed schedule. Rather, it takes into account the age, gender and other distinctive attributes of the individual whose life is central to the process of determining whether valued outcomes have been attained (Stark and Faulkner 1996).

Quality of life appeals as a commonsense answer to the question, what do all men and women prize? In the field of intellectual disabilities, it fuels continuing debate about philosophical underpinnings as well as methodological problems arising from attempts to measure and apply this guiding principle. Questions about the reliability of measures of subjective well-being – for example, among people with severe intellectual disabilities or with no communication skills – militate against its uncritical embrace (Hatton 1998). Nonetheless, consensus emerges. Quality of life is a multidimensional construct, both subjective and objective components must be assessed, and it is a suitable yardstick to appraise outcomes of services for individuals with developmental disabilities.

Working within this model, service providers are obliged to consult about, strive for and measure valued outcomes for individuals. Good practice may then be appraised by how effectively supports for service users achieve such outcomes (Conliffe and Walsh 1999). A core element in measures of quality of life is the degree to which the individual exercises autonomy about everyday decisions (Schalock 1996). However, as Stalker and Harris concluded in their literature review, overwhelming evidence suggests that 'people with intellectual disabilities often lack the opportunity to make choices for themselves' (1998, p.70). Recent attempts to conceptualize and measure self-determination have helped to illuminate how individuals may be encouraged to make choices. This dispositional characteristic is expressed in self-regulation, psychological empowerment, self-realization and autonomy, emerging as individuals become competent at directing their own lives (Wehmeyer 1996). How do women make choices at different stages of their lives and what outcomes do they achieve for themselves? These are worthy questions for further research.

Gender and health

While health and well-being are positive indicators of quality of life, they are not prizes in a free-for-all game which all can play. Good health depends in part on the individual's access to medical and health care generally, nowadays named as prerequisites in order for people with disabilities to secure equal opportunities in society (UN 1994). Political and economic constraints set obvious limits to key health indicators such as life expectancy: a Norwegian woman may expect to outlive her counterpart in India (UNDP 1997). As life expectancy increases, the quality of life among older people expressed as disability-free life expectancy looms large as a health target. Gender plays a part in reaching these targets. Robine, Romieu and Cambois (1999) examined health expectancy calculations across 49 countries, mostly developed market economies. They observed that the proportion of morbidity-free years to life expectancy is slightly lower for females, possibly because of their longer survival after the development of disability or handicap.

In some countries, women do not live as long as they might relative to men. Social circumstances and cultural practices compromise the greater longevity they might otherwise expect. The link between gender and health reflects the complex influences of their social, economic and cultural environments on women's lives at each stage of the lifespan.

Gender and health policies

Globally, the World Health Organization (WHO) is increasing efforts toward gender-sensitive approaches to health care delivery: promotion of women's health – ensuring that they take part in planning and monitoring interventions; making health systems more responsive to women's needs; and enacting policies to improve gender equality. National health policies address these targets by devising strategies to achieve local outcomes. These may also apply to the distinctive health needs of particular groups, such as people with intellectual disabilities (Turner and Moss 1996). In the Republic of Ireland, health gain and social gain are targets for all citizens: a complementary strategy focuses on the good health of women, including women with disabilities (Government of Ireland 1994, 1997).

Women have different health concerns and circumstances as they age. Arguably these are not yet fully understood for the general population of women, and certainly the factors associated with health among women with intellectual disabilities have only recently been explored. While people with intellectual disabilities share the same health needs as the general population – including surveillance measures relevant to women's health – they have additional, special health needs. Yet adequate primary health services for this population remain an unmet target (Kerr 1998).

In summary, health is a positive indicator of each person's quality of life, arguably the gold standard for measuring the outcomes of services and supports for people with intellectual disabilities. Personal characteristics and gender as well as the social, economic and political environment help to determine health status. Access to health and medical care is necessary, if not sufficient, for women and all people with intellectual disabilities to enjoy equal opportunities for social inclusion. Strategic actions are required to target specific outcomes throughout the lifespan as women experience developmental transitions. In the next section, the experiences of women at key stages of their lives are explored.

Lifespan transitions

Enchanting photographs of three or more generations of handsome, multicultural families of girls and women abound in general textbooks on human lifespan development (Santrock 1995). Readers search behind the soft focus in vain for any sign of diversity apart from chronological age. Girls or women with any visible disabilities are rarely pictured. Offstage, they are daughters, sisters-in-law, cousins, friends, bridesmaids, sisters, aunts, although few are mothers and even fewer grandmothers. Their understudy role is apparent from the start, at adolescence, a stage signalled by the young person's endeavours to create a sense of identity, manage startling physical growth, adjust family ties and attune to the tug of peers. The families of girls with intellectual disabilities must temper their offsprings' surge towards independence with a heightened awareness of special vulnerabilities for their daughters (Redmond 1996).

Physical change is the outward sign of adolescence, with menarche an outstanding rite of passage for adolescent girls. Recent research suggests that, although it may be experienced a little earlier, both the age of onset and the ensuing pattern of menstruation are much closer to those of women in the general population than had been thought, even for women with Down's syndrome (Schupf *et al.* 1997). Coverage of educational programmes, levels of information available to girls and attitudes of teachers and other caregivers vary considerably. Social markers typical for the culture, such as school-leaving ex-

aminations, graduation from secondary education, deepening of intimate relationships, university matriculation or vocational apprenticeship may be absent
for the young woman with intellectual disabilities.

Early adulthood

Moving into young adulthood, a stage at which women in the general population reach for independence, deepen intimate attachments and find productive
work, women with intellectual disabilities may carry the developmental
baggage of exaggerated dependency. Their gender identity may be ignored
(Brown 1996), even if the particular risks related to their sexuality are apparent
(McCarthy and Thompson 1998). These authors point out that the average age
of a group of women in the USA with intellectual disabilities who had been
victims of sexual abuse – 72 per cent of the sample surveyed – was 30 years.

Many women live with their families well into adulthood, years or decades
past the time when their peers launch themselves into independent living. Is
co-residence the first refuge for very dependent adult children with intellectual
disabilities? Is it, rather, an agreeable living arrangement providing companion-
ship to ageing parents who share an increased household income from disability
entitlements? Or is prolonged family caring a desperate remedy for years of
waiting for residential supports from formal service systems? Doubtless, homes
with an adult family member with intellectual disabilities share some of these
elements and more. Equally, it is likely that women try to redress the caregiving
imbalance and to achieve more reciprocal relationships in their families as they
age (Walmsley 1996).

General attitudes in society and the fears of older parents may be expressed
as denial or trivializing of the sexual development and health needs of women
with intellectual disabilities (Walsh *et al.* 1999). While families may diminish
steps to affirm women's sexual maturity, they continue to bolster the social
support available to adults with intellectual disabilities. Young adults typically
strengthen friendships and form a few intimate attachments. For young women
with intellectual disabilities, the texture of their friendships may reflect sporadic
contact with peers, or perhaps none at all with other young women without disabilities. Young women with intellectual disabilities may be out of step as their

peers – in the developed countries, for example – find a spouse or partner, or become parents. Krauss, Seltzer and Goodman (1992) studied the social support networks available to men and women aged 15–66 years with intellectual disabilities living with their parents. While both men and women had large, active and diverse networks with family members predominant, women were less at risk of social isolation.

Young women with intellectual disabilities may expect mixed fortunes as productive citizens, even though regional policies encourage women in the general population to enter the workforce. In the European Union (EU), women accounted for almost 90 per cent of the overall increase in the labour force between 1994 and 1996, although they still constituted only 42.5 per cent of the total (CEC 1997, p.39). Evidence as to whether women with intellectual disabilities have gained a comparable share of employment is incomplete, even though 'employment issues should therefore be considered as a central part of the overall European Community Disability Strategy' (DG-V 1998, p.5).

Traditionally women were pressed into unpaid domestic service if resident in old-style institutional settings (Walsh 1988). Still underrepresented in the ordinary labour force, they may also be more likely to find lower paid jobs there (Levy *et al.* 1994). When women with intellectual disabilities reach the workplace, will feminine stereotypes await them? A social structural model of sex differences in behaviour assumes that gender roles co-exist with other social roles within the family and workplace. Gender roles emerge from the productive work of the sexes. The characteristics that are required to perform sex-typical tasks become stereotypic of women or men – communal (feminine) versus agentic (masculine) behaviours (Eagly and Wood 1999). Thus, men and women should converge in their psychological attributes when, in the future, the traditional sexual division between wage labour and domestic labour disappears.

Women with intellectual disabilities have often been barred from assuming typical female roles, whether or not these may be perceived nowadays as desirable or correct. They have to date entered supported employment less often than men (Walsh 1999). Is this disparity widespread? It remains to be seen whether their heightened presence in ordinary workplaces will signal compliance with tradition or break new ground.

Although work settings are second only to the family in their importance as a social context, little is known about the impact of employment on the health of women with intellectual disabilities. Supported employment has flourished for more than two decades in North America, more recently throughout Europe (Walsh and Beyer 1999). Yet we do not know enough about the texture and extent of friendships which women with intellectual disability may build with co-workers, the presence of self-disclosure in their interactions and the social benefits that may accrue. For example, friendships at work may lead to an enhanced probability of psychological well-being (Ohtake and Chadsey 1999). Some evidence from studies within the general population of working women strengthens the link between positive social interactions and well-being. Walters *et al.* (1998) studied the occupational and domestic roles of women nurses in Canada, finding that overall life stress was related to an increase in health problems. By contrast, a confiding relationship with a friend was associated with better health. These authors concluded that it is important to examine the effects of both paid and unpaid work on women's health, and particularly to develop meaningful indices of women's work experiences.

In developing countries, ordinary employment may be elusive, notwithstanding the pressures on women and men with intellectual disabilities to help to earn their, and their family's, livelihood. Those who find work are likely to do so in traditional agriculture, production or forms of self-employment. In many developing countries thousands of people with disabilities and their families 'are waiting for an opportunity to make ends meet' (Sutton and Walsh 1999, p.197).

Middle adulthood

Today's older women with intellectual disabilities form a unique cohort. They are twice blessed: they are living longer and, thanks to inclusive social policies, have a greater presence in the community. Yet they have few role models to emulate for their experiences of middle and elder years. In Ireland, a relatively youthful member of the EU, more people with intellectual disabilities now reach middle and older adulthood. The percentage of persons aged 35–54 years has risen markedly since 1981, with nearly one-third of all Irish people with intellectual disabilities in this age group (HRB 1997). Adults with intellectual disabilities in the prime of life – in prosperous countries with long life expectancy, the fifth and sixth decades – have had lopsided personal and social histories. Only a few were formally educated. Few have voted in elections. In some countries, they were as likely as their peers to have married or had children of their own, particularly those with lesser levels of disability. Elsewhere only a handful of women did so (HRB 1997; Mulcahy and Reynolds 1984). With fewer social roles to play, do women with intellectual disabilities in middle adulthood find fewer resources to buffer stress? No model of healthy ageing for this group has been developed. In its absence, there are few guidelines on how best to prepare for a healthy older adulthood. Life course changes which women themselves experience, or which they witness, such as changing relationships, brothers and sisters growing up and moving to their own homes, older relatives becoming frail or dying, are perplexing. Older women with intellectual disabilities may find it difficult to grasp the meaning of life course changes without validation from others, or even to understand their own age and what this may mean (Walsh *et al.* 1999).

Women with intellectual disabilities may need particular support in understanding the impact of the menopause, commonly experienced earlier compared with women in the general population. Appropriate advice on problems related to changed hormonal levels is often inaccessible, or delivered by insensitive or ill informed health care professionals. How can the health of this group of women be enhanced? Common problems for them include high blood pressure, osteoarthritis and heart disease, conditions exacerbated by very sedentary lifestyles, poor nutrition and limited access to preventive health care.

Increased life expectancy also brings greater exposure to age-related risks for breast cancer and other illnesses typical for women in this age group, although it is possible that sexual inactivity may diminish their risks for cervical cancer. Rigorous screening for problems related to reproductive health often eludes women with intellectual disabilities. Communication difficulties, insensitive attitudes, untrained health professionals and inaccessible medical procedures disadvantage their health (Walsh *et al.* 1999). Other conditions which arise more frequently at this age mirror those in the general population of middle-aged women: heart disease, thyroid problems, sensory impairments and musculoskeletal disorders (van Schrojenstein Lantman de Valk 1998).

Women in mid-life are also vulnerable to depression, anxiety and adjustment disorders, conditions more prevalent among people with developmental disabilities than within the general population (Stavrakaki 1999). A woman in her forties or fifties may suffer the loss of a very elderly parent, but manifest signs of depression belatedly. Those with more severe levels of intellectual disability or communication difficulties may do so in behaviours such as aggression, sleep disturbance or lethargy. Adults who have lived in deprived settings may have poorer health and fewer coping resources to deal with abrupt life changes or other stresses (Davidson and Thorp 1999).

Relationships with kin continue to develop throughout the lifespan. Adults with intellectual disabilities may hold unique ties with sisters and brothers as they age, especially those who assume caregiving responsibilities after parents have relinquished their role (Seltzer *et al.* 1991). Caregiving is an exchange, and thus an adult sibling and a family member with intellectual disability influence each other's lives. Consider three women in their fifties and sixties who make up a quiet and comfortable suburban household in Ireland. As in many other countries with developed economies, these women are approaching retirement age, although only two of the three worked in paid employment while the third sister devoted herself to home duties. For decades, they have shared the care of the fourth, youngest sister with intellectual disability who has known no other home and who has for her entire adult life dressed and spent her time just as her sisters do. Did each remain single because she had charted her own life course as a carer? Was each influenced by her sisters' choices, by covert pressure from their parents, by diffidence among suitors who, one by one, fought shy of marrying into a tightly knit quartet? Were their chances of marriage further constrained by economic hardships and the waves of emigration of eligible men during the 1940s and 1950s? The lives of the woman with intellectual disabilities and those of her sisters are interwoven to shape the roles they adopt in middle and older adulthood, not merely in their family, but in society.

Middle-aged adults aged 50 years or more are greying. They are more likely to have suffered the loss of a parent and to have left the family home. They begin to look towards a fulfilling life beyond the world of work as they grow into the seventh or eighth decade of life. Yet only a handful of middle-aged women with intellectual disabilities will experience retirement from years of paid, productive employment as this life stage is defined in countries with developed market economies.

Late adulthood

Old age is more visible in better-off countries of the developed world, where 12.6 per cent of the population are elderly, than in developing countries where only 4.6 per cent are elderly (WHO 1995, p.3). In common with their peers, more people with intellectual disabilities enjoy greater life expectancy – those with an aetiology other than Down's syndrome will reach their sixties and beyond (Janicki 1994). As they grow older, they require supports for living and working matched to their changing needs and vulnerabilities to age-related diseases such as dementia. When they reach old age, they are at greater risk for developing the diseases of age – cardiovascular disease, for example. Older women who have lost oestrogens after the menopause are at greater risk of developing weaker, more porous bones, which in turn increases the risk of fracture. Some groups have particular vulnerabilities. For example, people with Down's syndrome age earlier than other adults with or without intellectual disabilities, and have lesser life expectancy. They are more at risk of developing Alzheimer's disease. Paradoxically, the very oldest people with intellectual disabilities may prove to be the healthiest as they are the 'healthy survivors' of their birth cohort (Moss and Patel 1997; Zigman *et al.* 1994). Evidence as to whether the prevalence of Alzheimer's disease may be greater among women with Down's syndrome is incomplete.

Patterns of living for older people vary, even within regions such as Europe. In the Netherlands a majority of older people with intellectual disabilities lives in group homes, special residences often placed near villages and towns (van Schrojenstein Lantman-de Valk 1998). By contrast, just one-quarter of Irish adults aged over 54 years has moved outside the family home and now lives in a group home or other residence.

Supports for older adults

As more adults with intellectual disabilities grow to maturity and become old, family members and service providers regard their longevity with some surprise. It was not expected that those born in the 1920s and 1930s would grow old alongside other citizens. Service organizations throughout Europe, for example, bear names more suited to the children for whom they were established. But yesterday's *bambini* or *angeli* are today's men and women, just as charming, if just as awkward as any cohort of middle-aged Europeans. In better-off countries, special workshops built to occupy young adults for a brief period in the 1950s have long abandoned their initial purpose. At the start of the new century, they offer shelter to groups of older people who lived decades of their productive lives in 'pre-vocational' programmes. Many have now been reassigned by service providers to 'pre-retirement' programmes – without ever working in regular paid employment for even a single day. Should they be encouraged to retire – even if they have never worked? Should they spend productive leisure time with older people who do not have disabilities? Or should they enter separate, convenient residences designed only for older adults with intellectual disabilities? Countries already seek their own solutions to fit local circumstances. In France, older people, with and without disabilities, have embarked on shared living schemes in special residences, growing old together (Fondation de France 1995). But choosing between special and generic supports is spurious if integration is a recipe for blending older adults with intellectual disabilities into groups already impoverished. Services for the elderly in Europe, as elsewhere, are by no means exemplary (Blaney 1992). Thus, older women with intellectual disabilities entering services for their peers in the third age may find their own second-class status exacerbated.

For women with intellectual disabilities who attain old age, developmental themes such as life satisfaction and successful ageing are best served by policies to achieve a society where older people may live healthy, productive and economically secure lives. Programmes of support and education targeting the needs of older people with intellectual disabilities are in their infancy. Friendships, family ties, continuing personal development and an active role in the local community are typical mainstays for older people with more time following retirement from paid employment. How can these pursuits be extended to women and men with intellectual disabilities as they age (Harris, Bennet and Hogg 1997)?

In summary, women with intellectual disabilities – as all other women – grow and develop in a particular social and economic context, living lives in times (Elder 1994). Their experiences of friendship, intimacy, family life, employment, leisure and personal satisfaction both reflect these times and are tempered by cultural expectations. Gender and other social roles are linked to distinctive behaviours that may become stereotyped in cultures where gender inequality holds sway and traditional male and female occupations diverge. It is evident that social, economic and political disadvantages have a detrimental effect on women's health. Teasing out the influence of their gender or their disability on women's development and well-being at transitional stages will prove a complex task. In the next section, a fresh international initiative to identify factors related to health and well-being of women with intellectual disabilities is presented.

Policy and practice

Mindful of the increased life expectancy of people with intellectual disabilities in the context of global trends towards ageing, the World Health Organization (WHO) initiated a collaborative work programme with the International Association for the Scientific Study of Intellectual Disability (IASSID). The aim was to produce a summative report to inform policy, practice and future research strategies on health and ageing within this population. Four reports were presented to the Tenth International Roundtable on Aging and Intellectual Disabilities held at WHO headquarters in Geneva in April 1999 (Bigsby *et al.* 1999; Davidson and Thorp 1999; Evenhuis *et al.* 1999; Walsh *et al.* 1999). In pursuit of the WHO's gender approach to health, a working paper on 'Women's health and related issues' (Walsh *et al.* 1999) was prepared in collaboration with professionals, women with intellectual disabilities, their advocates and family members in many countries. Summaries of recent research literature in three areas were compiled: sexual and reproductive health; health promotion; and the social and economic contexts of health for this population.

Health, ageing and gender: core themes

An overarching theme of the Geneva meetings was the shift in focus towards the majority world, the developing and least developed countries, where most people on the globe live, as well as the countries of central and eastern Europe whose economies are in transition. Policies typically underrepresent the distinctive needs and aspirations of people with intellectual disabilities, particularly of women, in these countries. Core themes emerged:

1.   The need for greater sensitivity in areas related to family life, sexuality and relationships in planning health promotion and interventions across *diverse cultures.*

2.   It was recognized that women have distinctive needs by virtue of their *gender and the social roles* adopted in their communities. These characteristics and experiences help to determine their health status and should be taken into account in planning health strategies on behalf of women with intellectual disabilities.

3.   *Ethical issues,* for example, securing informed consent, raised perplexing but important questions. How can women with intellectual disabilities give their consent to health procedures, to guardianship, to life roles valued in their communities – marriage, having children – to education, to risk? How can their rights be safeguarded?

4.   Finally, notwithstanding cultural sensitivities, how can women's educational needs be identified? What methods of *health education* are most effective for them and their families? How might interdisciplinary, continuing education for professional workers be organized?

Policy guidelines

Roundtable participants drew up a set of guidelines to form policies related to health for women with intellectual disabilities. Access to health care and thus to an enhanced quality of life should be available to women with intellectual disabilities in their communities. A lifespan approach is recommended, so that the changing health needs of women at different stages and transitions in their lives are met. Suitable supports should be provided so that women may be consulted about their needs and helped to plan their own health care.

Minimum standards of long-term care consistent with the WHO guidelines on healthy ageing should be developed. These standards should encompass older women with intellectual disabilities and their families with particular supports for their mothers and sisters, typically the family carers who directly support women with intellectual disabilities in their homes and communities.

Throughout the world, the role of women in families should be recognized. Strategies to raise awareness of the potential long-term stresses on caregiving families, and to promote the well-being of carers, are priorities. Especially as they age, caregivers' own health needs become interwoven with those of the women for whom they care.

Good practice

While the diversity of cultures was recognized, participants concluded that in each country the same standards of health care, adherence to ethical guidelines and respect for informed consent should apply equally to women with intellectual disabilities as to any other citizens.

Echoing the WHO principle of ensuring that women themselves help to design and monitor health interventions (WHO 1997, p.83), the Geneva meeting recommended that women with intellectual disabilities should be informed about and involved in education about health matters. The voice of the person should be heard. Two actions were specifically endorsed:

- Education, including sex education, for women with intellectual disabilities in ways they can understand and which respect cultural sensitivities is a priority. For example, popular health guides for women could include a chapter on ageing and developmental disabilities.

- Research and practice should be integrated. Dissemination of research findings should target women with intellectual disabilities, their family members, advocates and professional helpers.

More trained women health professionals should be encouraged to take part in health promotion and health care on behalf of women with intellectual disabilities. Health care practices should be accessible in both physical and cognitive domains. For example, gynaecological and other medical equipment should be adapted to meet the needs of women, using assistive technology as appropriate.

In summary, health policies for women with intellectual disabilities should promote their health and well-being by adopting a lifespan approach, meeting distinctive needs for access to health care at different stages of their lives. Women's health should be approached in the context of their lives with their families, typically the first source of caregiving and livelihood. Practice guidelines should build on respect, consultation, cultural sensitivity, improved professional training and accessibility for all.

Participants at the Geneva Roundtable based these recommendations on evidence from the scientific literature as well as qualitative experiences of women with intellectual disabilities, their advocates and family members. In the next section, strategies for further research aimed at informing both policy and practice in promoting health with this population are proposed.

Research strategies

First principles

Little enough is known about how young, middle-aged and older adults with intellectual disabilities will weather life transitions and indeed prevail. Gender differences have yet to be fully documented, let alone explained. What are the environmental, social, occupational and physical factors associated with life expectancy among women with intellectual disabilities when compared with men? Why do women with intellectual disabilities not live longer than they do? While their numbers are steadily increasing, there remains a dearth of gender-specific evidence. The ageing women of the mid-twenty-first century have already been born. Descriptive data are necessary, if not sufficient, to identify the personal and environmental factors related to women's well-being at different life stages. Cohort studies, in particular, adopting a longitudinal perspective would advance our understanding of their personal growth and development over the life course.

Gender and health

More specific research questions need to address the policy issues. Will age-related changes in health impact on the lives of women with intellectual disabilities as they age? What do we know about their reproductive health and attendant risks – and what do we need to know? Will greater participation in the social and economic life of the community – higher rates of paid employment, for example – influence their health and well-being?

Supports for living

Second generation research is founded on what has been learned already, following the time when landfall has taken place on new territory. Once gained, the domain must now be explored so that useful maps may be drawn. This strategy has been proposed to test the effectiveness of various elements of early intervention programmes (Guralnick 1998), and also to refine the supports provided for satisfying employment in ordinary settings on behalf of people with intellectual disabilities (Chadsey 1998). This research strategy may be applied fruitfully to a broader agenda to determine the effectiveness of interventions focused on specific personal and environmental characteristics – gender, age and the social and economic context of the daily lives of women with intellectual disabilities (Walsh 1999). If useful interventions depend on the direct involvement of women themselves, what supports might they require to write the script for their own health education and intervention programmes? Can self-determination in this complex area be accomplished while respecting ethnic and cultural sensitivities, especially given the wide diversity of experience between rich and poor countries?

Epilogue

Longer, richer and more visible lives carry risks as well as marvellous possibilities for women with intellectual disabilities. They will gain little of lasting value by adopting stereotyped social roles currently available for women in the general population. The contextual features and depth of their life experiences at stages of transition are as yet imperfectly understood. It is not so much that they have a good deal to learn. Rather, women and men living in the same place and time have some way to go in understanding the nature of these newly discovered risks and opportunities, whether they are worth taking and how we might make them so. A woman from Amherst, Massachusetts, left such questions unanswered:

> Bred as we, among the mountains,
> Can the sailor understand
> The divine intoxication
> Of the first league out from land?

Emily Dickinson

References

Bigsby, C., Bjorkman, M., Botsford, A., Haveman, M.J., Hogg, J., Lucchino, R., Janicki, M.P., Robertson, B., San Nicholas, H., Smit, L., Takashashi, R., Walker, A. and Wang, K. (1999) 'Healthy aging – adults with intellectual disabilities: Ageing and social policy.' Background Paper prepared for 10th International Roundtable on Aging and Intellectual Disabilities, WHO, Geneva, Switzerland, 20–23 April.

Blaney, B. (1992) 'The search for a conceptual framework.' In S. Moss (ed) *Aging and Developmental Disabilities: Perspectives from Nine Countries.* New Hampshire: IIEIR, Institute on Disability, University of New Hampshire, pp.93–96.

Brown, H. (1996) 'Ordinary women: Issues for women with learning disabilities. A keynote review.' *British Journal of Learning Disabilities 24*, 2, 47–51.

Chadsey, J. (1998) 'Examining personal and environmental variables for social integration success in employment settings.' In J.G. Chadsey and D.L. Shelden (eds) *Promoting Social Relationships and Integration for Supported Employees in Work Settings.* Urbana-Champaign IL: Transition Research Centre, University of Illinois at Urbana Champaign, pp.126–145.

Commission of the European Communities (CEC) (1996) *A New European Community Disability Strategy.* Brussels: CEC. Document no. 96/0216, pp.23–24.

Commission of the European Communities, DG-V (1997) *Employment in Europe 1997.* Brussels: CEC. Catalogue no. CE–05–97–729-EN-C.

Commission of the European Communities, DG-V (1998) Brussels: CEC.

Conliffe, C. and Walsh, P.N. (1999) 'An international perspective on quality.' In S. Herr and G. Weber (eds) *Aging, Rights and Quality of Life.* Baltimore MD: Paul H. Brookes, pp.237–252.

Davidson, P. and Thorp, L. (1999) 'Healthy aging – adults with intellectual disabilities: Biobehavioral issues.' Background paper prepared for 10th International Roundtable on Aging and Intellectual Disabilities, WHO, Geneva, Switzerland, 20–23 April.

Eagly, A.H. and Wood, W. (1999) 'The origins of sex differences in human behavior: Evolved dispositions versus social roles.' *American Psychologist 54*, 6, 408–423.

Elder, G.H. (1994) 'Time, human agency and social change: Perspectives on the life course.' *Social Psychology Quarterly 57*, 1, 4–15.

Epstein, S. (1997) *We Can Make It – Stories of Disabled Women in Developing Countries.* Geneva: ILO.

Evenhuis, H., Beange, H., Chicoine and Henderson, M. (1999) 'Healthy aging – adults with intellectual disabilities: Physical health issues.' Background paper prepared for 10th International Roundtable on Aging and Intellectual Disabilities, WHO, Geneva, Switzerland, 20–23 April.

Felce, D. (1997) 'Defining and applying the concept of quality of life.' *Journal of Intellectual Disability Research 41*, 2, 126–135.

Fondation de France (1995) *Pouvons-nous Vieillir Ensemble?* Paris: Fondation de France.

Government of Ireland, Department of Health (1994) *Shaping a Healthier Future.* Dublin: Stationery Office.

Government of Ireland, Department of Health (1997) *A Plan for Women's Health.* Dublin: Stationery Office.

Guralnick, M. (1998) 'Second-generation research in the field of early intervention.' In M. Guralnick (ed) *The Effectiveness of Early Intervention.* Baltimore MD: Paul H. Brookes, pp.3–20.

Harris, J., Bennett, L. and Hogg, J. (1997) *Ageing Matters: Pathways for Older People with a Learning Disability.* Kidderminster: BILD Publications.

Hatton, C. (1998) 'Whose quality of life is it anyway? Some problems with the emerging quality of life consensus.' *Mental Retardation 36*, 2, 104–111.

Health Research Board (HRB) (1997) *National Intellectual Disability Database Annual Report.* Dublin: Health Research Board.

Janicki, M.P. (1994) 'Policies and supports for older persons with mental retardation.' In M.M. Seltzer, M.W. Krauss and M. Janicki (eds) *Life Course Perspectives on Adulthood and Old Age.* Washington DC: AAMR, pp.143–166.

Kerr, M. (1998) 'Primary health care and health gain for people with a learning disability.' *Tizard Learning Disability Review 3*, 4, 6–14.

Krauss, M.W., Seltzer, M.M. and Goodman, S.J. (1992) 'Social support networks of adults with mental retardation who live at home.' *American Journal on Mental Retardation 96*, 4, 432–441.

Levy, P., Botuck, S., Levy, P.H. and Kramer, M.E. (1994) 'Differences in job placements between men and women with mental retardation.' *Disability and Rehabilitation 16*, 2, 53–57.

McCarthy, M. and Thompson, D. (1998) *Sex and the 3Rs: Rights, Responsibilities and Risks.* 2nd edn. Brighton: Pavilion.

Moss, S. and Patel, S. (1997) 'Dementia in older people with intellectual disability: Symptoms of physical and mental illness, and levels of adaptive behaviour.' *Journal of Intellectual Disability Research 41*, 1, 60–69.

Mulcahy, M. and Reynolds, A. (1984) *Census of Mental Handicap in the Republic of Ireland.* Dublin: Medico-Social Research Board.

Ohtake, Y. and Chadsey, J.G. (1999) 'Social disclosure among co-workers without disabilities in supported employment settings.' *Mental Retardation 37*, 1, 25–35.

O'Toole, B. and McConkey, R. (eds) (1995) *Innovations in Developing Countries for People with Disabilities.* Chorley: Lisieux Hall Publications.

Rapley, M. and Beyer, S. (1998) 'Daily activity, community participation and quality of life in an ordinary housing network: A two-year follow up.' *Journal of Applied Research in Intellectual Disabilities 11*, 1, 34–43.

Redmond, Bairbre (1996) *Listening to Parents.* Dublin: UCD Family Studies Centre.

Robine, J-M., Romieu, I. and Cambois, E. (1999) 'Health expectancy indicators.' *Bulletin of the World Health Organization 77*, 2, 181–185.

Santrock, J.W. (1995) *Life-span Development.* Madison WI: Brown and Benchmark.

Schalock, R. (1996) *Quality of Life. Vol.1: Conceptualization and Measurement.* Washington DC: American Association on Mental Retardation.

Schupf, N., Zigman, W., Kapell, D., Lee, J. and Levin, B. (1997) 'Early menopause in women with Down syndrome.' *Journal of Intellectual Disability Research 41*, 264–267.

Seltzer, G., Begun, A., Seltzer, M.M. and Krauss, M.W. (1991) 'Adults with mental retardation and their aging mothers: Impacts of siblings.' *Family Relations 40*, 310–317.

Stalker, K. and Harris, P. (1998) 'The exercise of choice by adults with intellectual disabilities: A selected literature review.' *Journal of Applied Research in Intellectual Disabilities 11*, 1, 60–76.

Stark, J. and Faulkner, E. (1996) 'Quality of life across the life span.' In R. Schalock (ed) *Quality of Life. Vol.1: Conceptualization and Measurement.* Washington DC: American Association of Mental Retardation, pp.23–32.

Stavrakaki, C. (1999) 'Depression, anxiety and adjustment disorders in people with developmental disabilities.' In N. Bouras (ed) *Psychiatric and Behavioural Disorders in Developmental Disabilities and Mental Retardation.* Cambridge: Cambridge University Press.

Sutton, B. and Walsh, P.N. (1999) 'Inclusion International's open project on inclusive employment.' *Journal of Vocational Rehabilitation 12*, 3, 195–198.

Turner, S. and Moss, S. (1996) 'The health needs of adults with learning disabilities and the Health of the Nation strategy.' *Journal of Intellectual Disability Research 40*, 5, 438–450.

United Nations (UN) (1994) *The Standard Rules on the Equalization of Opportunities for Persons with Disabilities.* New York: United Nations.

United Nations Development Programme (UNDP) (1997) *Human Development Report 1997.* New York: Oxford University Press.

van Schrojenstein Lantman-de Valk, H. (1998) *Health Problems in People with Intellectual Disabilities.* Maastricht: Unigraphic.

Walmsley, J. (1996) 'Doing what Mum wants me to do: Looking at family relationships from the point of view of adults with intellectual disabilities.' *Journal of Applied Research in Intellectual Disability 9*, 4, 324–341.

Walsh, P.N. (1988) 'Handicapped and female: Two disabilities?' In R. McConkey and P. McGinley (eds) *Concepts and Controversies.* Galway: Woodlands Centre, pp.65–82.

Walsh, P.N. (1997) 'Old world – new territory: European perspectives on intellectual disability.' *Journal of Intellectual Disability Research 41*, 2, 112–119.

Walsh, P.N. (1999) 'Jobs for the girls.' *Clinical Psychology Forum, 137*, 31–35.

Walsh, P.N. and Beyer, S. (1999) 'Guest editor's introduction.' Special issue on European perspective on employment and disability. *Journal of Vocational Rehabilitation 12*, 3, 127–129.

Walsh, P.N., Heller, T., Schupf, N. and van Schrojenstein Lantman-de Valk (1999) 'Women's health and related issues.' Report prepared for 10th International Roundtable on Aging and Intellectual Disabilities. Geneva: WHO and IASSID.

Walters, V., Eyles, J., Lenton, R., French, S. and Beardwood, B. (1998) 'Work and health: A study of the occupational and domestic roles of women registered nurses and registered practical nurses in Ontario, Canada.' *Gender, Work and Organization 5*, 4, 230–244.

Wehmeyer, M. (1996) 'Essential characteristics of self-determined behavior of individuals with mental retardation.' *American Journal on Mental Retardation 100*, 6, 632–642.

World Health Organization (WHO) (1995) *Aging and Health: A Programme Perspective.* Geneva: WHO.

World Health Organisation (WHO) (1997) *The World Health Report 1997.* Geneva: WHO.

World Health Organisation (WHO) (1998) *The World Health Report 1998. 'Life in the 21st century: A vision for all.'* Geneva: WHO.

Zigman, W., Seltzer, G.B. and Silverman, Wayne P. (1994) 'Behavioral and mental health changes associated with aging in adults with mental retardation.' In M.M. Seltzer, M.W. Krauss and M. Janicki (eds) *Life Course Perspectives on Adulthood and Old Age.* Washington DC: American Association of Mental Retardation, pp.67–91.

CHAPTER 9

Bringing Lives into Focus

The Disabled Person's Perspective

Dorothy Atkinson

Introduction

The voices of people with intellectual disabilities have, by and large, gone unheard. Theirs are the 'ultimate lost voices' of the twentieth century (Atkinson and Walmsley 1999). Often separated from their families and local networks, people with intellectual disabilities became 'invisible' in their own communities (Bornat 1992). Unseen and unheard, they were the last people to be consulted in any research into learning disability – until now, that is. In recent years people with intellectual disabilities have become increasingly involved in research in ways hitherto unthinkable.

In the past, including the recent past, people with intellectual disabilities were invisible because they were excluded from everyday life. For much of the twentieth century they were regarded as a threat to society, responsible for many of the social problems of the day; at other times they have been seen as vulnerable people, potential and actual victims of an uncaring society. Either way, many people with intellectual disabilities led separate and segregated lives in special schools, day centres and in institutional or residential care. This made them invisible.

They were silent, or silenced, because as Bogdan and Taylor (1982) pointed out, the rest of us chose not to listen to them. We thought they had nothing to say: they had no awareness of their situation, no capacity for understanding it, nor the means to speak about it. As a result, many people with intellectual disabilities gave up the struggle to speak out and instead remained silent (Sinason 1995). Now people with intellectual disabilities are 'speaking up' and the rest of us, including researchers and practitioners, are beginning to listen. The 'lost voices' of the twentieth century are at last being recovered.

This chapter looks at the developments in research and practice in the last 20 years or so which have set that recovery in motion. In particular, the focus here is on life story research (and practice) because that is where people become most visible and have most to say. The life story is the ultimate means of self-representation. It allows otherwise oppressed and powerless people to speak for themselves, to reclaim their past and, in so doing, to rediscover their identity.

Why life story research?

Only in recent years have researchers sought the views of people with intellectual disabilities. Surveying the twenty or so years up to 1984, Richards (1984) could identify only five British studies in which people with intellectual disabilities were informants. During the 1980s a steady stream of studies appeared in which they were accorded the status of interviewees in their own right (see, for example, Atkinson 1988; Flynn 1986; Sigelman *et al.* 1981; Wyngaarden 1981). In the 1990s a further shift towards greater involvement of people with intellectual disabilities in research occurred: not only were they now treated as potential informants, they also came to be seen as full participants, even as co-researchers, with the potential for involvement in all stages of the research process. Life story research is part of the dramatic move towards a more participative and inclusive research approach. Indeed it could be said to be the ultimate expression of such an approach.

Life story research has come a long way from those first tentative interviews with people with intellectual disabilities reported in the literature only ten to twenty years ago. What has made such a swift turn around possible? There are five possible explanations. First, the run-down and closure of many of the long-stay institutions and the movement of people with intellectual disabilities into the community has helped change the research agenda. One way of finding out about life in the community is through the lived experiences of those people out there. Researchers needed to access those experiences. Thus, the accounts by people with intellectual disabilities of their lives on the outside, as well as on the inside, have provided evidence of their everyday experiences in the community and how they compare with institutional life.

The process of deinstitutionalization itself has played its part in the development of life story research. It has resulted in the return to the community of a good number of relatively able and articulate people who had been incarcerated, often for many years, but who as a result had important and fascinating stories to tell. Their stories are of significance too because of what they can tell us about their former lives in a closed and alien world. Their stories are from the inside of institutions managed in our name, but which have remained largely hidden from us.

Second, there has been a growing recognition that people with intellectual disabilities are an oppressed group, sharing the same predicament as all other oppressed groups (including for example, women, black people, homosexuals and mental health survivors) and subject to much the same public prejudices and stereotypes (Williams 1992). One way to counter this is to work with people with intellectual disabilities in order to help them more accurately to represent themselves and their lives. The development of people's own life stories can prove an effective countervailing force to the misconceptions that otherwise may arise.

Third, the increase in life expectancy, in the context of intellectual disabilities, has brought about the 'discovery of adulthood'. With adulthood comes biography and the need to make sense of one's life, past and present. This has manifested itself in two ways. On the one hand, the capacity of people to 'speak up' about themselves and their lives has become apparent through the self-advocacy movement of the 1980s and 1990s. Alongside this has been the steady flow of published and unpublished autobiographies of people with intellectual disabilities (see, for example, Barron 1996; Burnside 1991; Cooper 1997; Deacon 1974; Hunt 1967). These two developments have demonstrated that people with intellectual disabilities have the capacity to express themselves and to make sense of their lives; to tell their own stories. Inevitably the stories are different, and more complex, than the stories told by others on their behalf. They cast themselves not as the perpetrators of social ills, as the eugenicists would have them, nor simply the victims of an oppressive system, as they are seen by the proponents of normalization, but as individuals with 'a personal history, a culture, a class, a gender, as well as an impairment' (Atkinson and Williams 1990, p.8).

Fourth, the life story provides a unique window on an otherwise hidden world – and researchers have begun to see the potential of this vantage point. The use of life stories makes it possible for researchers to look at life through the eyes of people who have been labelled and to see their world as they see and experience it. A life story approach allows for 'insider perspectives', where people with intellectual disabilities have a central place in the telling of history – and are no longer silent (Goodley 1996). Personal accounts can also act as an antidote to the professional 'case history' which is put together for different reasons (to identify, to categorize, to diagnose and to treat people). Case records, by their nature, do not draw on the voices of the people themselves, nor do they represent their lived experiences, or capture their uniqueness – only the life story can do that (Gillman, Swain and Heyman 1997).

Fifth, there is a wider and more general move towards what Booth and Booth (1996) have called the 'age of biography'; including storytelling and narrative methods of research. The methods used in sociological and oral history research to recover other 'excluded voices', such as the voices of black people, of women and of mental health survivors, for example, are transferable to people with intellectual disabilities. Such methods make it possible for people with intellectual disabilities to speak and to be heard. Although the importance of listening to people with intellectual disabilities was recognized quite late (Williams and Shoultz 1982), there is now an increasing readiness to listen to their own accounts of their lives and experiences.

What is life story research?

Life story research, as it is used here, is an inclusive term. It covers both *biographical* (or narrative) research, which seeks to draw out and compile individual auto/biographies or life stories, and *oral history* which involves individuals and groups in recording their lives within an historical context.

Life story research is powerful. It has the capacity to change people's lives – through the telling and the understanding of those lives. It has an impact on two levels: the personal and the social. At a personal level, life story research gives people with intellectual disabilities the opportunity to look at and make sense of their lives; in effect, to do a life review. At a social level, the bringing together of life stories can highlight the commonalities as well as the differences in people's experiences, commonalities with other people with intellectual disabilities as well as with the rest of society. This has the potential to become a collective account, to encourage a group identity as well as a personal identity, and to bring about social and historical awareness in people with intellectual disabilities (Atkinson 1997).

Three recent developments, in particular, have been influential in boosting life story research: refinements in qualitative research, especially in the use of interviews; the growth of self-advocacy; and an increasing interest in autobiography. I will look briefly at each of these developments in turn.

In qualitative research, the process is often as important as the outcomes. The process in intellectual disability research is a complicated one because it involves people with little or no recourse to the written word and, for some, few spoken words. Until the last few years, as noted above, it was widely assumed that people with intellectual disabilities had little or nothing of interest to say about themselves and their lives – and so were rarely asked. There were exceptions to this rule. Pioneering work by Edgerton (1967), Edgerton and Bercovici (1976) and Bogdan and Taylor (1976, 1982) showed how people with intellectual disabilities could be interviewed about their lives.

At first only a handful of research projects in the 1980s involved people with intellectual disabilities as respondents (Atkinson 1988; Flynn 1986; Sigelman *et al.* 1981, 1982). However, refinements in interviewing techniques meant that researchers began to spend time getting to know people, helping them relax, creating an informal atmosphere and enabling them to talk – sometimes in depth – about their lives. Some researchers spent time simply 'being there' with people when formal interviewing proved difficult; others spent time relaxing with interviewees before interviews or outside the research (see, for example, Atkinson 1988; Booth, Simons and Booth 1990; Cattermole, Jahoda and Markova 1987; Flynn 1989; Lowe, de Pavia and Humphreys 1986; Wilkinson

1989). Now research awareness (Goodley 1996) and a reflective approach (Atkinson 1997) are considered important assets in working with people with intellectual disabilities.

Further refinements are still being sought, as researchers seek to overcome the barriers of 'inarticulateness, unresponsiveness, a concrete frame of reference and problems with time' (Booth and Booth 1996). What is emerging is the need sometimes to build life stories in situations where the words are hard to find, and where researchers have to listen to the silences and proceed using 'creative guesswork' (Booth and Booth 1996). The fact that someone is inarticulate is no reason to exclude them from life story research – the challenge is to overcome the barriers through sensitivity and innovation on the part of the researcher (Ward 1997). 'Guided tours' of familiar places, and 'guided conversations' with props such as photographs and drawings may be needed to help dismantle the barriers (Stalker 1998).

Alongside the developments in qualitative research, where more and more attempts have been made to give people with intellectual disabilities a voice, has been the growth of the self-advocacy movement in which people have been finding and using their own voices, separately and together. The growth of self-advocacy has paralleled the development of research studies which have aimed to include people with intellectual disabilities. This was no coincidence. The phenomenon of people 'speaking up' helped convince both researchers and people with intellectual disabilities that the involvement of the latter in research was feasible and desirable.

This led to people with intellectual disabilities becoming the subjects in research – and, for example, being interviewed about their lives and experiences. Subsequently their role in research has become more central, as researchers and self-advocates have challenged the status of 'subjects'. The participatory paradigm has begun to hold sway in some parts of intellectual disability research, with the result that some people with intellectual disabilities are contributing to the design and execution of research projects; even in some instances working as co-researchers (see, for example, Minkes, Townsley and Weston 1995; Mitchell 1998; Rolph 1998; Townsley 1995; Whittaker, Gardner and Kershaw 1991; Williams 1999). The aim of participatory research is to make research relationships more equitable. It is based on the belief that not only do people have a right to be involved in research which affects their lives, but the research is also the richer for their involvement (Stalker 1998). The closeness of contact between researcher and participants, or between co-researchers, can result in 'reverse commodification', where the researcher becomes involved in the lives of people with intellectual disabilities – acting as advocate, scribe or supporter as well as researcher (Ramcharan and Grant 1994). Such involvement can continue long after the research has ended (Booth 1998). This closeness of contact is particularly the case in life story research, a point I return to later.

Pre-dating self-advocacy, but growing in importance alongside the movement, has been the steady stream of autobiographies produced by people with intellectual disabilities. They represent the clearest and most direct means by which people with intellectual disabilities can account for their own lives. The autobiography is the ultimate life story; and the best possible means of self-representation. In a sense, the autobiographical voice is the voice of the self-advocacy movement. The person who 'speaks up' may yet be the person who 'writes up' their life. As noted earlier, there is now a modest list of published and unpublished autobiographies by people with intellectual disabilities.

Oral history has its place in this context. The techniques and approaches of oral history have enabled people with intellectual disabilities, singly or in groups, to talk about their lives in a wider social and historical context (Atkinson 1997: Potts and Fido 1991). The telling of the life story against the backcloth of the policies and practices of the time has meant that people with intellectual disabilities have had the role of historical witness and informed insider of past regimes and practices (Atkinson 1998a). This is a means to reclaiming not only a personal past, but a collective past or a shared history of intellectual disability.

How are life stories told?

My current research falls into the participatory paradigm. It may also fit the emancipatory paradigm now advocated in disability research (French 1992; Morris 1992; Oliver 1992; Zarb 1992) where disabled people control the research process and outcome. My work fits this context – and can therefore serve as a case study – because it is life story research, but set up at the request of the people concerned. The impetus for the research came from the would-be storytellers. Our paths crossed initially by chance when I was looking for stories for a forthcoming Open University course (Open University 1996) and Mabel Cooper, then Chair of People First, London, was acting as facilitator for a new and inexperienced self-advocacy group. I visited the group with a view to involving some of the members in an oral history project. This project never took off, but something much more important did. On the train home Mabel confided that she had long wanted to tell her life story, but had no means of doing so. We arranged to meet and in an informal and relaxed atmosphere (as outlined in the literature) we tape-recorded our conversations about Mabel's life. The transcriptions of these and subsequent conversations have led to an evolving life story, as more and more is remembered or revealed (Cooper 1997; Cooper 2000).

The first version of Mabel's life story was told entirely from memory; later versions have been supplemented by access to photographs, records and case notes. The following transcript is an extract from one of those subsequent conversations, where we looked at photographs of St Lawrence's Hospital in Caterham where Mabel was a resident for over 20 years. The photographs triggered many memories:

Dorothy: This is an external shot of St Lawrence's taken from the air. It looks huge.

Mabel: Yes, it was. On the female side it was A to H; on the male side it was A to D. There was more females than men. I think it was because the women were sent from the courts, some of them, and in the old days if you had a child and you wasn't married, it was a disgrace so they used to take the child away, put it in a home, and then the mother went into a workhouse. And St Lawrence's was something like that, and that's why it was called the loony bin in them days because it was a workhouse as well. Even when I went there, even for me, you could hear the racket of it going in. It's something you get used to, even being in one of them places. Unless you know what it's like it's hard to imagine.

Dorothy: This one is taken on the inside, it looks like some sort of workshop.

Mabel: That is a workshop, it looks like the needlework room. Or is it the laundry room? They both had long benches like that, so it's either the laundry or the needlework room, because they were both together you know.

Dorothy: There are people there, on the picture, but you can't see anybody's face. Why is that, do you think?

Mabel: In the olden days, even when you went to church and they used to take photographs, they always took them from the back. So you didn't actually see our faces, you just saw the back of us.

Dorothy: Why? Did they want to hide you?

Mabel: Yes, in them days they used to hide us because the people were frightened, they didn't understand [...]

The use of photographs took our exchanges into new realms of insider knowledge. They revealed aspects of the institutional regime, and Mabel's place in it, which I would not otherwise have known nor thought to ask. Compiling the life story has also involved consulting records. This is not a straightforward process. Records tell a different story. They may reveal new and sometimes painful insights into past personal and family events, and they may use the language of 'mental deficiency'. This is Mabel Cooper's account of what her personal records revealed:

There is so much that I didn't know that I'm finding out now. I went to St Lawrence's and I went to the archives. Some of it, like the names they called you in them days, hurt a bit but otherwise I think it was great. It was something I needed to find out. And going to the archives, that was great again, that was somewhere I've never been, and I enjoyed it. It would be smashing if half of this could be put in another book so it would say this is what Mabel said about this.

> I went with Dorothy to St Lawrence's, and Gloria came, and we went up, and we had a look. They said we could look through their records, my records, and they were very nice to us. We sat in a little room for ages, it was 12 o'clock when we stopped, and then we asked could I take some of them away, that I would like some of them. They said to me 'The ones you want you put on one side, and the ones you don't want put on the other side.' The ones I didn't want were not about the family, and they're not about anything that would interest people outside. I put to one side everything about me and my family. (Cooper, 2000)

The need to find out, to know rather than not know about the past, proved compelling for Mabel, in spite of the language in which it was cast. Finding her records, seeing them and owning at least some photocopied extracts from them, has proved to be a major step forward in understanding the past. Mabel could remember much, though by no means all, of what had happened to her but she had never known why. The records began to uncover some of the reasons. The telling of the life story, and its clearly beneficial effects, has led to three of Mabel's friends deciding to tell theirs. This includes Gloria Ferris, referred to in Mabel's extract above, who was also an ex-resident of St Lawrence's Hospital.

Gloria started her life story in the same way – from memory. We set up a similar series of informal conversations, which I tape-recorded, based on Gloria's memories of the past. The tapes were transcribed and the written words were reordered into a chronological and flowing account – checked, amended and approved by Gloria. This was not enough. Memory can only account for so much of the past, so we looked for documentary evidence. Again the process was both enlightening and hurtful as light was shed on long-forgotten, or never known, past events and people, but it was written in the language of 'mental deficiency' still prevalent in the 1950s. In the final version of her life story, Gloria incorporates what she found from records with what she can remember:

> I didn't know it at the time but I found out from records that I was born before the midwife could get to the house, and I fell on the floor. Then I had pneumonia when I was six months old, so I didn't get a very good start in life. I also know from records that I was put into residential nurseries when my mother was having more children. Then the Women's Voluntary Services for Civil

Defence came round to see about evacuation for me because of the war and the bombs falling on London. They thought I was very small and because I wasn't talking they thought I was, in their words, a 'mental defective'.

I've been away all my life from home, since I was three years old. I went to the Fountain Hospital which was for people with learning difficulties, which is what they thought I was. My parents said I couldn't walk, or whatever. They said they wouldn't come and get me there, I wouldn't be able to come home, or they wouldn't come and see me any more. That was depressing. I used to cry when I had to go away from home at weekends. I've got used to it. I've grown out of that now. (Ferris, 2000)

Since Gloria took up the challenge two more of their friends decided to follow suit. Mary Coventry told her own story of life in the community with her parents, and subsequently in a group home, first by writing out what she could remember and then supplementing this through taped and transcribed conversations. Mary's story was not hidden in records. It was known to her. She had a family, a family home, letters, photographs and other memorabilia to draw on. Subsequently, Doris Thorne, another friend and ex-resident of St Lawrence's, decided to tell her story. This time we are using individual and shared memories, songs and hospital case notes to reconstruct the past. Memories are increasingly shared as the storytellers have formed a naturally occurring group. This adds a new dimension as ideas are sparked off between them and we enter new realms of insider experience. It is to this insider research that we turn next in looking at what life stories tell us.

What do life stories tell us?

Life stories recount the lives and experiences of individuals. In so doing, they capture the period details of the past and give substance to the social world in which people lived. They are historical documents and, taken together, the life stories of people with learning difficulties begin to tell a shared history of intellectual disability. The life stories of the people who are co-researching with me are thus important social and historical documents. As such they tell us a great deal – about the people themselves and their personal experiences, but they go beyond that. Life stories give an *insider perspective*, they offer a *corrective account*, they demonstrate people's *resilience*; and they invite a *reflective view*. I will take each of these points in turn.

Life stories provide glimpses into otherwise hidden worlds. They give us the insider's perspective into the past, allowing us to look at the everyday routines and rhythms of long-stay hospitals as people experienced them. They allow us to see into the day-to-day life and workings of past systems. The following extract is from Mabel Cooper's life story, where she describes her first impressions of St Lawrence's Hospital and what it was like to be a child there in the 1950s:

> When I first went in there, even just getting out of the car you could hear the racket. You think you're going to a madhouse. When you first went there you could hear people screaming and shouting outside. It was very noisy but I do think you get used to them after a little while because it's like everywhere that's big. If there's a lot of people you get a lot of noise, and they had like big dormitories, didn't they? And the children were just as noisy, in the children's home, and they were all the same sort of people.
>
> I went to St Lawrence's in 1952. I went to A2, that was the admissions ward. They didn't used to have many in there, they used to just take the new ones what came in. You were only there for a week or two weeks. And they moved you on to another ward where there was all children. I stayed there till I was 15 and then I went to another ward where I was with adults.
>
> There was bars on the windows when I first went to St Lawrence's, it was just like a prison. Of course it was called a nuthouse in them days, so it used to have bars on it. You couldn't open the windows. Well, you could, but not far enough to get out of them. You didn't have toys, no toys whatsoever. You couldn't have toys because they would just get broken and thrown through the bars in the window, and get caught in them. (Cooper 1997, pp.22–23)

In the public world, people with intellectual disabilities are seen as people who have to be cared for – they are 'the other, the disregarded and excluded' (Walmsley, 2000). However, in their own accounts people with intellectual disabilities are able to offer a corrective view in which they emerge as rounded and complex human beings, with the capacity to care about, to care for and to reciprocate 'caring' in relation to other people. A main strand in Gloria's life story, for example, is her 40-year caring relationship with Muriel, another former resident of St Lawrence's:

> I met Muriel in St Lawrence's when she was very young. She was on C1 and I met her there when I took over and helped the staff out. Muriel's family came from Shepherd's Bush. I think her father owned a café or shop there. They were good parents, they never missed a week without going to see her. Twice a week they'd come, even when they retired to Brighton. They never missed. They were good people, they never complained. Her parents were very good to me. We used to go out together because they couldn't lift Muriel, they couldn't manage her. We used to have tea in the pavilion in the hospital grounds.
>
> I helped the staff out on C1. They quite enjoyed it because it helped them out. I dressed them, put them in nightdresses, I was a good help to them. I quite enjoyed being with them, especially Muriel. She is a happy sort of person. She's got a lovely smile. When you take pictures, sometimes she's not in the mood for people taking pictures of her – and she won't smile, won't even look at you. She'll look the other way. I'd never forget her. I told her parents that if anything happened to them I would never forget her. And now I'm registered as an advocate to her, so I'm near enough the next of kin. (Ferris, 2000)

In the telling of her own life story, Gloria portrays herself as a family friend and supporter, and as a nurse working (unpaid) alongside the staff of St Lawrence's Hospital. Years later, in the community, she is now Muriel's informal carer and advocate. This story confronts and contradicts many of the stereotypes of people with intellectual disabilities which cast them solely as dependants.

Many accounts by people with intellectual disabilities attest to their experiences of prejudice, stigma and segregation. Yet they are more than victims of an oppressive system, they are the survivors of it – and their accounts echo the 'human resilience' noted by Goodley (1996). Gloria's resilience was expressed through the caring roles she adopted throughout her institutional and post-institutional life. Mabel, on the other hand, expressed her resilience through a deliberate policy of staying silent. Although the case notes described her as timid and shy, her own account made clear that her silence was a form of protest:

> I never said anything in the hospital because there was no point. Nobody listened, so why speak? If you spoke they told you to shut up, so I stopped saying anything. I didn't talk, it was a protest really rather than anything else. I only said two words, 'yes' and 'no', and mostly I only said 'no'! (Atkinson and Cooper, 2000)

Since leaving hospital, Mabel has become involved in the self-advocacy movement and has begun to speak for herself and others. Just as she used silence to express her resilience in the hospital, now she uses the spoken and written word as a means of speaking out against injustice, prejudice and discrimination.

The telling of the life story is not just a recounting of events – it is a way of making sense of those events and, indeed, of life itself (Gillman *et al.* 1997). But it can go even beyond that, to make sense of the lived experiences against the backcloth of social and historical events and alongside the experiences of others. Mabel spent over 20 years of her life in a long-stay institution; her life story describes those years but it goes beyond the descriptive to the *reflective*. In making sense of her life, Mabel reflects on the role of institutions in society and, in so doing, shows an historical awareness of the context of her own story (Atkinson and Walmsley 1999):

> In them days, if you had learning difficulties or anything, that's where they used to put you. They didn't say 'Oh, you could go into a house and somebody would look after you'. They would just say 'You, you've gotta go in a big hospital' and that's it. Years ago, if you wasn't married and you had a baby, that was a disgrace and they would say 'Oh the mother goes in a workhouse or a loony bin' as they had in them days, or the mother went into a workhouse or a loony bin and the child was put into care. I think that's why there was more women. (Cooper 1997, p.29)

Why do life stories matter?

Life stories do matter. They matter to the people who tell them and they matter – or should do – to those who hear them. Mabel Cooper is quite clear about why her life story matters to her:

> I think it was nice for me to be able to do something, so that I could say 'I've done it'. It made me feel that it was something I had done. You've got some-

thing so that you can say, 'This is what happened to me'. Some of it hurts, some it's sad, some of it I'd like to remember. My story means a lot to me because I can say, 'This is what happened to me', if anyone asks. So it's great, and I will keep it for the rest of my life. I will keep the book. (Atkinson, Jackson and Walmsley 1997, p.11)

Mabel's life story matters because it is an expression of her *identity*, a statement about who she is; it is a means of *reclaiming her past*, it is 'my story'; it has the *enduring quality* of the written word; and it represents a major and much longed for *achievement* on her part. What Mabel does not say here, but which comes through in her various accounts of her life, is that telling her story has been an *empowering process*. She is strong and confident – well able to speak up and be heard – but also more knowledgeable. She knows and understands her own life within a wider social and historical context. This is empowerment through knowledge – perhaps the most enduring kind of empowerment (Atkinson 1998b).

Mabel Cooper came to understand what happened to herself and to other people; so too, in our life story research, did Gloria, Mary and Doris. The process of reclaiming a personal past, and understanding it in context, proved enlightening and empowering. Life story research has worked for them. Presumably it can also work for others.

Conclusion: What are the implications for social work?

Life story research is about the *process* of finding out about the past: through individual and shared reminiscence; guided conversations; planned visits to archives and record offices; and supported access to contemporary written accounts, photographs and family/community informants. The process of self-discovery and indeed social discovery (the growing awareness of a wider historical context) are both enlightening and empowering. But there is also a *product* at the end of it – the written life story. This is a particularly valued outcome, as Mabel Cooper pointed out:

You've got something to show for your life. You've got something so that you can say, 'That's what happened to me'. It will keep history in my mind for years

> to come, what's happened to me and a lot of others like me. (Atkinson 1998b,
> p.115)

Life story books have, of course, been used in social work practice, particularly in relation to children (Usher 1993), but also with older people involved in reminiscence and life review and those with intellectual disabilities in transition from hospital to the community. They have the potential to transform lives – as well as maintain them – if they are given due time and space. The life story, or biography, is a way of understanding the actual lived experience of a person who has suffered because they are poor, or old, or black, or disabled (or because they are poor *and* disabled or any other combination). Life stories are both unique accounts of individual lives and part of a shared experience of a particular time and place in history. A life story reveals the person and that person's history, identity and social networks, but also locates the individual in a social and historical context. Life stories have the capacity to reveal the *resilience* of individual people with learning difficulties but, as more and more stories are told, collectively they may yet come to form – with the help of social workers and other allies – a 'resistance movement' (Gillman *et al.* 1997).

Life story work has practical benefits for social workers. It provides a mechanism for establishing a relationship between the social worker and the person with intellectual disabilities. This is important in itself. However, the telling of the story can lead to a greater understanding, not only on the social worker's part in seeing their intellectually disabled client as a unique person with a distinctive biography, but also on the part of the person with intellectual disabilities who comes to understand him or herself better.

Life story research contributes to social work practice, but also draws on it. The reflective social worker becomes the reflective researcher. Good research practice means working within individual and group relationships; being supportive, diplomatic and even-handed. It involves tracking down people, case records, archives, documents and photographs. It means facing the raw truth about the past with the person who wants to find out; softening the blow, while reading aloud the pejorative comments from a bygone era.

But life story research goes beyond social work practice, because it goes beyond the telling and into the *recording* of lives – into written testimonies which will last. And not only that. The written life story is the person's *own account*, not a case history compiled *about* them. It is the 're-authoring' of events (Gillman *et al.* 1997) and thus the ultimate reclaiming of a life.

References

Atkinson, D. (1988) 'Research interviews with people with mental handicaps.' *Mental Handicap Research 1*, 1, 75–90.

Atkinson, D. (1997) *An Auto/Biographical Approach to Learning Disability Research*. Aldershot: Ashgate.

Atkinson, D. (1998a) 'Autobiography and learning disabilities.' *Oral History 26*, 1, 73–80.

Atkinson, D. (1998b) 'Reclaiming our past: Empowerment in oral history and personal stories.' In L. Ward (ed) *Innovations in Advocacy and Empowerment for People with Intellectual Disabilities*. Chorley: Lisieux Hall Publications.

Atkinson, D. and Cooper, M. (2000) 'Parallel stories.' In L. Brigham, D. Atkinson, M. Jackson, S. Rolph and J. Walmsley (eds) *Crossing Boundaries*. Kidderminster: BILD Publications.

Atkinson, D., Jackson, M. and Walmsley, J. (1997) *Forgotten Lives. Exploring the History of Learning Disability*. Kidderminster: BILD Publications.

Atkinson, D. and Walmsley, J. (1999) 'Using autobiographical approaches with people with learning difficulties.' *Disability and Society 14*, 2, 203–216.

Atkinson, D. and Williams, F. (eds) (1990) *'Know Me As I Am'. An Anthology of Prose, Poetry and Act by People with Learning Difficulties*. London: Hodder and Stoughton.

Barron, D. (1996) *A Price to be Born*. Harrogate: Mencap Northern Division.

Bogdan, R. and Taylor, S. (1976) 'The judged, not the judges: An insider's view of mental retardation.' *American Psychologist 31*, 47–52.

Bogdan, R. and Taylor, S.R. (1982) *Inside Out: The Social Meaning of Retardation*. Toronto: University of Toronto Press.

Booth, T. and Booth, W. (1996) 'Sounds of silence: Narrative research with inarticulate subjects.' *Disability and Society 11*, 1, 55–69.

Booth, T., Simons, K. and Booth, W. (1990) *Outward Bound: Relocation and Community Care for People with Learning Difficulties*. Buckingham: Open University Press.

Booth, W. (1998) 'Doing research with lonely people.' *British Journal of Learning Disabilities 26*, 4, 132–134.

Bornat, J. (1992) 'The communities of community publishing.' *Oral History 20*, 2, 23–31.

Burnside, M. (1991) *My Life Story*. Halifax: Pocket Well College.

Cattermole, M., Jahoda, A. and Markova, J. (1987) *Leaving Home: The Experience of People with a Mental Handicap*. Stirling: Department of Psychology, University of Stirling.

Cooper, M. (1997) 'Mabel Cooper's life story.' In D. Atkinson, M. Jackson and J. Walmsley (eds) *Forgotten Lives. Exploring the History of Learning Disability*. Kidderminster: BILD Publications.

Cooper, M. (2000) 'My quest to find out.' In D. Atkinson, M. McCarthy, J. Walmsley *et al.* *Good Times, Bad Times: Women with Learning Difficulties Telling Their Stories.* Kidderminster: BILD Publications.

Deacon, J. (1974) *Tongue Tied.* London: NSMHC.

Edgerton, R.B. (1967) *The Cloak of Competence.* Berkeley: University of California Press.

Edgerton, R.B. and Bercovici, S.M. (1976) 'The cloak of competence: Years later.' *American Journal of Mental Deficiency 80*, 485–497.

Ferris, G. (2000) 'Muriel and me.' In D. Atkinson, M. McCarthy, J. Walmsley *et al.* *Good Times, Bad Times: Women with Learning Difficulties Telling Their Stories.* Kidderminster: BILD Publications.

Flynn, M. (1986) 'Adults who are mentally handicapped as consumers: Issues and guidelines for interviewing.' *Journal of Mental Deficiency Research 30*, 369–377.

Flynn, M.C. (1989) *Independent Living for Adults with Mental Handicap: A Place of My Own.* London: Cassell.

French, S. (1992) 'Researching disability: The way forward.' *Disability and Rehabilitation 14*, 183–186.

Gillman, M., Swain, J. and Heyman, B. (1997) 'Life history or "case" history: The objectification of people with learning difficulties through the tyranny of professional discourse.' *Disability and Society 12*, 5, 675–693.

Goodley, D. (1996) 'Tales of hidden lives: A critical examination of life history research with people who have learning difficulties.' *Disability and Society 11*, 3, 333–348.

Hunt, N. (1967) *The World of Nigel Hunt.* Beaconsfield: Finlayson.

Lowe, K., De Paiva, S. and Humphreys, S. (1986) *Long Term Evaluations of Services for People with a Mental Handicap in Cardiff: Clients' Views.* Cardiff: Mental Handicap Wales, Applied Research Unit.

Minkes, J., Townsley, R. and Weston, C. (1995) 'Having a voice: Involving people with learning difficulties in research.' *British Journal of Learning Disabilities 23*, 94–97.

Mitchell, P. (1998) 'Self advocacy and families.' Unpublished PhD thesis, Open University.

Morris, J. (1992) 'Personal and political: A feminist perspective on researching physical disability.' *Disability, Handicap and Society, 7*, 2, 157–166.

Oliver, M. (1992) 'Changing the social relations of research production.' *Disability, Handicap and Society 7*, 2, 101–114.

Open University (1996) *K503 Learning Disability: Working As Equal People.* Milton Keynes: Open University.

Potts, M. and Fido, R. (1991) *A Fit Person to be Removed.* Plymouth: Northcote House.

Ramcharan, P. and Grant, G. (1994) 'Setting one agenda for empowering persons with a disadvantage in the research process.' In M. Rioux and M. Bach (eds) *Disability is Not Measles: New Research Paradigms in Disability.* Ontario: Roeher Institute.

Richards, S. (1984) 'Community care of the mentally handicapped: Consumer perspectives.' University of Birmingham, unpublished manuscript.

Rolph, S. (1998) 'Ethical dilemmas: Oral history work with people with learning difficulties.' *Oral History 26*, 2, 65–72.

Sigelman, C.K., Budd, E.C., Spanhel, C.L. and Schoenrock. C.J. (1981) 'When in doubt say yes: Acquiescence in interviews with mentally retarded persons.' *Mental Retardation 19*, 53–58.

Sigelman, C., Budd, E., Winer, J., Schoenrock, C. and Martin, P. (1982) 'Evaluating alternative techniques of questioning mentally retarded persons.' *American Journal of Mental Deficiency 86*, 511–518.

Sinason, V. (1995) *Mental Handicap and the Human Condition.* London: Free Association Books.

Stalker, K. (1998) 'Some ethical and methodological issues in research with people with learning difficulties.' *Disability and Society 13*, 1, 5–19.

Townsley, R. (1995) 'Avon calling.' *Community Care*, 12–18 January, 26–27.

Usher, J. (1993) *Life Story Work: A Therapeutic Tool for Social Work.* Social Work Monographs. Norwich: University of East Anglia.

Walmsley, J. (2000) 'Caring: A place in the world?' In K. Johnson and R. Traustadottir (eds) *Women with Intellectual Disabilities: Finding a Place in the World.* London: Jessica Kingsley Publishers.

Ward, L. (1997) *Seen and Heard. Involving Disabled Children and Young People in Research and Development Projects.* York: Joseph Rowntree Foundation.

Whittaker, A., Gardner, S. and Kershaw, J. (1991) *Service Evaluation by People with Learning Difficulties.* London: King's Fund.

Wilkinson, J. (1989) '"Being there": Evaluating life quality from feelings and daily experience.' In A. Brechin and J. Walmsley (eds) *Making Connections: Reflecting on the Lives and Experiences of People with Learning Difficulties.* London: Hodder and Stoughton.

Williams, F. (1992) 'Women with learning difficulties are women too.' In M. Langan (ed) *Women, Oppression and Social Work.* London: Routledge.

Williams, P. and Shoultz, B. (1982) *We Can Speak for Ourselves: Self-advocacy by Mentally Handicapped People.* London: Souvenir Press.

Williams, V. (1999) 'Researching together.' *British Journal of Learning Disabilities 27*, 2, 48–51.

Wyngaarden, M. (1981) 'Interviewing mentally retarded persons: Issues and strategies.' In R. Bruininks, C. Meyers, B. Sigford and K.C. Lakin (eds) *Deinstitutionalisation and Community Adjustment of Mentally Retarded People.* New York: American Association on Mental Deficiency.

Zarb, G. (1992) 'On the road to Damascus: First steps in changing the relations of disability research production.' *Disability, Handicap and Society 7*, 2, 125–138.

CHAPTER 10

Older Family Carers

Challenges, Coping Strategies and Support

Gordon Grant

Introduction

As the life chances of people with intellectual disabilities improve, many more will continue to experience a life at home and in the community as older citizens. Survival to old age is also an achievement, due largely to improvements in pharmacology, standards of health care and levels of living. What matters now is that adding 'life to years' for people with intellectual disabilities becomes just as important as 'years to life'. This applies equally well to older family carers.

For families who continue to support older people with intellectual disabilities there are some good demographic reasons for being concerned about expectations for continued support from this source (Seltzer, Krauss and Heller 1991). Increasing life expectancy will prolong caregiving among older family carers. As a consequence this may implicate more siblings in middle age than at present. At the same time shifts in fertility ratios towards smaller family size may in future years reduce the supply of sibling carers and hence the dependency ratio (proportion of caregivers to recipients) is likely to become less favourable, while the ratio of older to younger families of people with intellectual disabilities will increase, creating a different balance in service demands. Changes in the structure of families, the emergence of black and ethnic minority elders and the impact of divorce may have significant consequences for patterns of family caregiving which are as yet uncharted.

More difficult to anticipate are the effects of societal values which often follow political directions and economic fortunes, these being most likely to influence the way in which disability, and responses to it, are socially constructed. The emergence, for example, of the social model of disability (Oliver 1996) may signal a very important shift in enabling families to recognize that responsibility both for creating and dealing with disabling barriers in people's lives is everyone's, not just that of disabled people themselves, their families or services. The National Strategy for Carers (DoH 1999), while not exactly endorsing the social model, at least recognizes how structural factors like labour market conditions, educational opportunities, service designs, information systems and a lack of official 'joined-up' policy thinking can serve to keep family carers trapped within the private world of caring. Time will tell whether or not the strategy creates new opportunities for carers to realize their aspirations.

The first part of this chapter therefore addresses challenges that older family caregivers face. It is argued that if these challenges are to be understood they also need to be contextualized, theoretically and empirically. An attempt is therefore made to locate demands and associated stresses that families may face within models of caregiving that avoid an undue emphasis on pathology. The second part of the chapter will then consider the kinds of coping strategies that older carers use in their everyday lives to manage demands and circumstances. Finally, practice implications will be considered in the light of what we are learning about the support needs of older family caregivers and their experiences of support from front-line practitioners in health and social care services.

With growing interest in the issue around the world, the last few years have witnessed an explosion of literature in this connection. It cannot be comprehensively summarized in a short chapter like this so what follows is more of a personal interpretation of the main themes and issues.

Challenges
Demography

The scale of the potential challenge is indicated by the results of some recent surveys. Following a population survey in Leicestershire, McGrother *et al.* (1996) found that family caregivers aged 60 and over were responsible for looking after 44 per cent of all adults with intellectual disabilities who were living in a family home. Similar results (40%) were found in Watson and Harker's (1993) report. The vast majority of these carers, 89 per cent in the McGrother *et al.* study, were women. In their recent literature review Hogg and Lambe (1998) estimated that there are 30,000–35,000 caregivers in the UK of 60 years of age or older supporting relatives with intellectual disabilities at home.

Such bald figures tell us little of the challenges faced by older carers of people with intellectual disabilities or of the factors that mediate these challenges in some way. Much of the early literature conceptualizes challenges in relation to stress or else in terms of what some writers refer to as non-normative caregiving. Theoretical perspectives linked to these interests need to be considered separately.

Stress among older family carers

In regard to stress experienced by carers, the transactional stress coping model credited to Lazarus and Folkman (1984) has been particularly influential. Basically it lays an emphasis on the cognitive appraisals people bring to situations and to the secondary and consequent appraisals made of the coping resources they can draw upon to deal with these. Hence, stress is not the direct by-product of a set of problematic or challenging circumstances – rather it is the outcome of how those circumstances are first appraised and then evaluated against personal resources for coping.

This model has been exhaustively tested among samples of younger and older parents of people with learning disabilities (Quine and Pahl 1991; Orr, Cameron and Day 1991; Smith, Tobin and Fullmer 1995) and seems to have extremely good explanatory power. A key point to take away from these studies is that a linear link does not exist between the personal characteristics, physical or behavioural dependencies of the person with intellectual disabilities and the experience of stress among family caregivers.

Studies by Seltzer and Krauss (1989) and Hayden and Heller (1997) suggest that risk factors in maternal burden and parenting stress are tied to the physical health of their offspring, with poorer health leading in turn to poorer health in the parent. However, demographic factors also seem to be implicated with fewer years in education, lower income and not being married influencing maternal physical health and life satisfaction. These findings alert us to a difficulty with stress studies. Unless stress concepts are operationally tied into how family carers manage their affairs, there is a danger that many factors external to caregiving but important to an understanding of stress in general (the well-known connection between social disadvantage, ill health and stress being one) will not only confuse the outcomes but obscure practical applications of the findings.

None of the foregoing should be used to obscure the fact that many older carers suffer ill health and disablement, that they may already have experienced bereavement through the loss of a partner, that their support networks may be shrinking, that they may be dependent more than others on forms of income support from the state or that a significant onus of responsibility falls on the shoulders of lone elderly family carers (Grant 1993; Prosser and Moss 1996; Walker and Walker 1998). However, studies suggest that caregiver age on its own is not a good predictor of caregiver stress and that common assumptions about surviving parental carers being lonely do not hold (McDermott *et al.* 1996; McGrath and Grant 1993). There is evidently a complex of compensatory mechanisms which needs to be understood, the first of which are the 'non-normative' circumstances in which many older carers find themselves.

Non-normative caregiving

Tobin (1996) describes older parents of people with intellectual disabilities as 'perpetual parents' as they have not finished and may never complete launching their offspring towards a more independent life. In comparison to the vast majority of parents they find their adult child still living at home and making demands on their parenting and caregiving resources. They may seek to conceal their continued parenting from peers and neighbours in order to create the appearance of a 'normal' lifestyle, something they often accomplish by severing social relationships and accomplishing their caregiving within a very privatized world. Concerned about the future of their offspring, perpetual parents are threatened by unfinished business as the life cycle nears its end.

They harbour anxieties about the future, their own capacity to continue caring, and what will happen to their offspring when they themselves die (Grant 1990; Prosser 1997). Time, in short, has entrapped them in what might be regarded as 'non-normative' circumstances.

However, Tobin's (1996) work shows that through caregiving these older parents maintain intimacy, assertiveness and a sense of control which can be missing from the lives of their age-related peers. Consequently, they experience many gratifications in caregiving and derive a sense of meaningfulness from their caregiving efforts. Suspended in social time, perpetual parents evidently encounter rewards in spite of their fears for the future. This may explain why some older parents have been found to be healthier, have better morale and report no more burden or stress than parents in younger families of persons with intellectual disabilities or of family caregivers of elderly persons (Seltzer and Krauss 1989).

Caregiving compensations

It is important to acknowledge that the rewards of caregiving appear to be quite pervasive and occur at all points across the lifespan (Beresford 1994; Grant *et al.* 1998). So it would be wrong to presume that they have a unique association with non-normative caregiving. In practice terms it would seem important to develop an understanding of how these rewards might mediate the experience of stressfulness in caregiving.

Personal experience suggests that some carers might not even fully acknowledge that rewards occur in their caregiving careers until a close associate or a professional worker explores the sources of these experiences with them, and how central they are in their everyday lives. We know little at present about the latent and manifest dimensions of caregiving rewards and, as Folkman (1997) has recently suggested, we need to know much more about the processes that trigger a search for positive psychological states, and the intensity and duration of such states necessary to sustain individuals in their everyday caring. Older family carers represent one group for whom exploring these connections would be very worthwhile.

Planning for the future

The 'unfinished business' described by Tobin (1996) conceals many anxieties held by older family carers about the future. Prosser (1997) recently reported that in a study of family carers of older adults only 28 per cent had made any residential care plans. In the majority of cases these carers were committed to maintaining long-term care for their relative for as long as possible. More prevalent were financial plans (63%) but in less than half of these cases guidance from solicitors had been sought, which raises the question of just how legally robust these financial arrangements were. In an earlier study Grant (1989) found that over half the family carers changed their minds over a fairly short period (two years) about the preferred long-term care arrangements for their relative.

Many factors come into play when considering the arrangements for future care (Grant 1990; Prosser 1997). Older family members may no longer be able to provide the support they once did, necessitating a change of plans. They are likely to lose valuable members of their support networks through death or incapacity. Carers continuously compare the standards of care they know they can provide against those of statutory and other services. Lack of information about different service options can leave carers uncertain as to what is best. Some carers prefer to rely on their own resources, while others turn more readily to the state for help or even 'bury their head in the sand', avoiding the issue altogether because of the pain involved. In general carers seem to be engaged in a constant 'cost-benefit' calculus of where 'best interest' might lie, or more particularly whether what is in their own best interest is necessarily in the best interest of their disabled relative.

One thing is clear amidst all this confusion – family carers need much clearer information at an earlier stage in the life cycle about the nature of realistic long-term care options, and about what part they and their relative can play in negotiating an option that meets the 'best interest' criterion. If this is neglected many older carers will struggle on until they reach breaking point when it may be too late to do anything else but deal with the immediate crisis. There are signs that this neglect persists. Heller's (1993) studies emphasize that older parents are more likely than younger parents to need help in future planning, in obtaining residential placements and in finding services.

Coping among older family carers

Coping strategies

In a recent account of the coping strategies described by families of children and adults with intellectual disabilities in their everyday caring, Grant and Whittell (2000) found that coping could be differentiated by gender, family composition (lone vs. multiple household carers) and carer age group. Compared to other carers in the sample, older family carers were more resigned to their roles, placed less emphasis on information seeking as a coping strategy, demonstrated a well-developed capacity to reframe the meaning of situations and were generally more accepting of the way things were than younger carers. They also emphazised personal and religious beliefs more than other carers, reflecting greater religiosity in older people in general.

An important qualifier to the above was that most of the older carers thought that they ought to have been more assertive than they had been in the past to get what they needed from services. This would suggest that many older carers have an awareness of their past tendency to sit back and adopt a rather passive stance with services, much to their present regret. However, it also demonstrates a reflexive capacity not always recognized in older caregivers, suggesting a preparedness to accept change in the way services operate.

These findings suggest that it does not seem to be true that as carers age their resourcefulness declines. The so-called 'wear and tear' hypothesis about ageing does not hold; on the contrary, if anything the adaptation hypothesis is more in evidence. This is quite important as it suggests that concerns arising from co-morbidity among the growing numbers of ageing family carers have perhaps been over-emphasized, and that resiliency among older family carers has been overlooked, just as some believe it has in families in general (Hawley and DeHaan 1996).

At this point it is probably true to say that neither the ingredients nor the precursors of resilience in older families are fully substantiated. We do know that many of the other coping strategies they describe as useful are held in common with younger family carers (Grant and Whittell 2000): for example having a pool of tested coping strategies from which they can choose, being able to match the appropriate coping strategy to a particular demand and, as mentioned above, being able to reframe the meaning of some challenges as non-problematic or normative so that they feel easier to deal with. However, we do not know if external factors, such as the loss of support from significant others through death or relocation, reduced income, or limited service input, compels older family carers to rely more on their own internal resources (experience, expertise, dispositions, analytic ability and so on) which they therefore become practised in using. Of course it may be that caring over the life cycle leads to the steady accumulation of expertise and competence.

There is a dearth of literature about older men as carers, probably because most of the surviving older carers are widows. However, there is reason to believe that in some cases where both parents survive into old age their coping strategies may not always be compatible with those of siblings or other close relatives, which can have negative consequences for family harmony and for the person with intellectual disabilities still living at home.

Reciprocities

Some of the compensations of caring have already been alluded to, but increasingly studies are illustrating just how important it is for carers to be able to maintain reciprocities in their relationship with their disabled relative. It has been recognized for some time that caregiving is rarely unidirectional and that some element of reciprocity is usually discernible in relationships where high intensity care is required (Grant *et al.* 1998).

Interdependencies can be expressed in different ways (Magrill 1997). Financially carers can come to depend on keeping their relative at home – the social security benefits payable to their relative can make an appreciable difference to material living standards while also acting as a disincentive for some families to relinquish caregiving when 'best interest' is at issue. Physically some older carers have come to expect their relative to do chores around the house or to assist with shopping and other practical homemaking tasks when this may be difficult or too time-consuming for themselves. But perhaps more commonly older family carers admit to emotional and psychological dependencies on their relative. Even when individuals have very limited communication capacities or personalities which are not the most expressive, carers are often able to discern signs of appreciation or acknowledgement which make their caregiving efforts all the more worthwhile. When this occurs it becomes life affirming. These carers are what has been referred to as 'other-directed', that is their desire to be nurturers is what gives meaning to their lives (Kahana and Kahana 1996). They fit profiles of altruistic orientations towards caring though there lurks a constant danger that their best intentions will, once again, not always serve 'best interest'. Perhaps the most obvious danger here is that a pursuit of emotional fulfilment by the carer might replace or subvert community inclusion for their relative.

Following the reciprocity trail, Heller, Miller and Factor (1997) used a composite measure to gauge what support was provided to older caregivers by their relative with intellectual disabilities. Included were help – with personal care, with domestic chores, with finance, and when feeling upset, combatting loneliness, sharing enjoyable activities, and giving useful advice and information. It emerged that greater support from the adult child to caregiver resulted in greater caregiving satisfaction and less perceived burden. Hence, not only was reciprocity present, it also had some important benefits. This particular study, however, only addressed whether or not the aforementioned forms of support were evident, not their intensity, regularity or perceived helpfulness.

These findings nevertheless signal an important pathway for services to help older family carers. By focusing on the person with intellectual disabilities and their social skills development linked to domestic and citizenship responsibilities it may be possible to increase their support to their ageing relatives. Another very important consideration for future research here is to explore from the perspective of the person with intellectual disabilities how they feel about assuming these responsibilities. If this is not attended to there is a danger that people with intellectual disabilities may run the risk of being exploited by their own families; their voice needs to be heard in this connection. This once again emphasizes the need for a family systems perspective in analysing family dynamics and interdependencies, typified by the work of Dunst *et al.* (1993). This at least assists the development of a more holistic view of the family.

Supporting older families

The kinds of support which family and informal carers in general might need are just as relevant to older carers, for example, information, regular respite, skills training and psychological help and counselling (Nolan and Grant 1989). However it is important for practitioners to have access to assessment frameworks and to intervention models which allow them to match resources to needs in ways which reinforce effective family care. Although evaluations of interventions aimed at assessing what works for older family carers seem to be largely missing from the literature, there is nevertheless a growing consensus about the kinds of support that families need.

Greenberg, Seltzer and Greenley's (1993) study of older family carers showed, for example, that supportive interventions such as counselling, support groups, provision of in-home services and respite may have the potential to reduce stresses and frustrations in family caregiving. However, these same interventions had little impact on rewards and gratifications experienced by family carers. The main reason for this seemed to be that gratifications were dependent upon whether or not challenging behaviour in the adult relative was problematic. It could be concluded from this that if the clinical goal is to improve the quality of the relationship as well as to reduce the burden on carers, then interventions should also strive to reduce presenting challenging behaviour. Put another way, an undue focus on stress reduction, arguably a principal concern of services to date, will ignore and frustrate other concerns and aspirations of older family carers.

The existing evidence would suggest that interventions need to be much more planned than they are at present. Carers' overriding anxieties described earlier about future care options would probably dissipate if there was a greater commitment from services to take account of the changing roles, functions, responsibilities, resources and coping strategies of families over the life course. Four dimensions are likely to be of importance here:

1. *The development/disability trajectory*: the effects of construing disability as an ongoing process with landmarks, transition points and changing demands.

2.   *The family life cycle*: the effects of shifts in intergenerational ties, in support network membership and in life stage.

3.   *The caregiving trajectory*: the effects of the 'stage' which family carers have reached in their caring in moving from 'novice' to 'expert' carers.

4.   *The service trajectory*: the effects of transitions on development and adaptation as the person with intellectual disabilities moves between health, education, social services or independent sector services.

If different developmental stages can be anticipated and planned for it is probable that more tailored interventions would follow. Predictability would seem to lie at the heart of this for family carers. Not knowing what comes next is not only incredibly disabling for families and people with intellectual disabilities themselves, but they must also find it extremely devaluing. Of course there will be circumstances that cannot be predicted: for example, if someone with Down's syndrome develops Alzheimer's disease the precise course of the disease may be difficult to anticipate though the broad stages, with their accompanying physical and psychological sequelae, could probably be described. Carers need to know so that they can be primed and helped to deal more effectively with anticipated changes in their relative's behaviour and personality. It is just this kind of specific information that many carers crave, not as an end in itself, but rather as a means to be prepared for what comes next.

   Hence the disability/development trajectory referred to above is of prime importance, changes in the health status of the individual perhaps signalling that carers have new things to learn to become experts as a new caregiving stage is reached. This therefore underlines the importance of the caregiving trajectory. An undue focus on either the person with intellectual disability or the carer by care managers and support workers may completely obscure family life cycle changes like deaths and relocations which may affect interdependencies and mutual helping in important ways. While all that is happening families will want services to be seamless regardless of who provides them. Temporal dimensions like these need to be much more centrally located in practice thinking.

The evidence reviewed earlier would suggest that services are needed which are capable of acknowledging and mapping the resilience and expertise, coping strategies, support networks and needs of families as a whole so that interventions avoid supplanting family care. Interventions which are more firmly rooted both in family systems perspectives and in competency enhancing principles (Dunst *et al.* 1993) would be one way of taking things forward, but these interventions need to be carefully evaluated for their effects on the person with intellectual disabilities, carers and the family as a whole. The evaluation studies by Dunst *et al.* with younger families offer promising indicators that interventions which work with the expertise and strengths of families not only help them to become more adept at mobilizing resources for themselves but also to play an effective and pivotal role in case management terms.

Heller *et al.* (1996) have gone some way towards this in devising a person-centred later life planning training programme for older adults with intellectual disabilities. Based on a lifespan development orientation and an ecological perspective on empowerment, the training programme had benefits in terms of increased participation for individuals and families in service planning meetings, more incorporation of the individual's desires in the written goals and increased leisure participation for those living at home. An unintended consequence was a decrease in life satisfaction ratings for people with intellectual disabilities – the product, it was surmised, of raised expectations. Empowerment strategies which enable people to speak out with greater competence will inevitably help to expose weaknesses in the service system. It is therefore important that services become even more responsive in addressing user and carer concerns resulting from better information diffusion and raised expectations.

In a not dissimilar training programme, Seltzer (1992) was able to show that the involvement of family members of older adults with intellectual disabilities in a case management system had three sets of benefits: it empowered family members by providing information to them about services and strategies for accessing resources on behalf of their relative; it also helped to reduce the workload problems of professionals who frequently hold large caseloads; and the continuity of a family member's involvement compensated for the gaps created by high turnover of case managers and service providers. Though details were not fully reported the programme was implemented among socio-economically and culturally diverse populations, suggesting that it had potentially wide applications.

Kropf and Greene (1993) describe a social work life review system as an interventive technique among older families. Illustrated by a series of case studies they showed that competence, autonomy and a sense of control over environments were crucial factors for these families. The life review process enabled them to gain a sense of control over their lives by integrating their disappointments and successes, helping to shape their perceptions about the future in more positive ways. Meanwhile O'Malley (1996) has described group work respectively with older people with intellectual disabilities and their professional carers. Findings for those with intellectual disabilities suggested that they benefited in dealing with issues related to retirement and grief, primarily through emotional ventilation, but they also became energized through the discovery of new activities which could enable them to be of service to others. Similar working methods with older family carers might prove helpful in building alliances which allow older carers to develop mutual aid strategies with one another. Quite often, because of changes in their own support networks over the years, many of them have become separated from other families who may be able to listen to their concerns and share expertise and advice.

In relation to the evidence reviewed in this chapter, it is perhaps worth suggesting some principles upon which support for older family caregivers might be based:

- use of *active and reflective listening skills* as a basis for understanding a family's needs and concerns

- forms of help which are based on *the family's own appraisal of resources and problems*

- help which reinforces the valued contributions that people with intellectual disabilities can make to family life, thereby *strengthening reciprocities*, so long as these serve the 'best interest' test

- support which recognizes and strengthens each family's *unique and effective style of coping*

- support which addresses *incompatible coping strategies used by different family members*

- support which acknowledges *how older carers can become trapped in time as 'perpetual parents'*

- support which concentrates on helping families to *realize that caregiving rewards and uplifts*

- help which is *proactive* rather than a response to crisis

- help *compatible with family culture*, that is each family's rules and norms, beliefs and cultural practices, routines and structures for coping

- support which builds on and strengthens a *family's skills, expertise and decision-making capacity*

- help which acknowledges how effective coping is embedded within *social network and social support arrangements*

- support which takes account of *lifespan factors which can disrupt the predictability of family coping efforts.*

There are still too few systematic evaluation studies of interventions designed to support older family carers of people with intellectual disabilities. Interventions which are able to operationalize and test the principles suggested above might represent one possible step forward. Yet, this still leaves open to question the issue of the preferred service model.

With growing awareness of citizenship rights and responsibilities of oppressed groups, including people with intellectual disabilities and their family carers, it is perhaps to be expected that coalitions will become a force to change society's disabling barriers (Racino and Heumann 1992). Although this is really concerned with changing the way people think about disability as well as the need to eliminate the exclusionary practices of many social institutions and organizations, it may also help to focus some welcome attention on a major unresolved issue for older family carers and adults with intellectual disabilities who are themselves approaching old age – namely the best way to plan and configure services.

At the moment there are three competing models: the 'age-integrated' model in which a cradle-to-grave commitment is given through an intellectual disability dedicated service; a 'specialist' model in which older people with intellectual disabilities are provided with services dedicated to their needs as older citizens; and finally a 'generic' model which would see older people with intellectual disabilities sharing services with older people in general. Expert opinion seems to support the idea of a generic model backed up by specialist services since this would be very much in line with a commitment to community inclusion and emancipation. As others have suggested however, further research and experimentation are required into how this is best expressed at local and national levels (Hogg *et al.* 2000).

Acknowledgements

The author would like to acknowledge the financial support from the English National Board for Nursing, Midwifery and Health Visiting towards the AGEIN Project at Sheffield University which helped to facilitate some of the database searches upon which this chapter is based.

References

Beresford, B. (1994) *Positively Parents: Caring for a Severely Disabled Child.* London: HMSO.

Department of Health (DoH) (1999) *Caring about Carers: A National Strategy for Carers.* London: The Stationery Office.

Dunst, C.J., Trivette, C.M., Starnes, A.L., Hamby, D.W. and Gordon, N.J. (1993) *Building and Evaluating Family Support Initiatives.* Baltimore: Paul H. Brookes.

Folkman, S. (1997) 'Positive psychological states and coping with severe stress.' *Social Science and Medicine 45*, 1207–1221.

Grant, G. (1989) 'Letting go: Decision-making among family carers of people with a mental handicap.' *Australia and New Zealand Journal of Developmental Disabilities 15*, 3–4, 189–200.

Grant, G. (1990) 'Elderly parents with handicapped children: anticipating the future.' *Journal of Aging Studies 4*, 4, 359–374.

Grant, G. (1993) 'Support networks and transitions over two years among adults with a mental handicap.' *Mental Handicap Research 6*, 1, 36–55.

Grant, G. and Whittell, B. (forthcoming) Differentiated coping strategies in families with children and adults with intellectual disabilities: the relevance of gender, family composition and the lifespan.' *Journal of Applied Research in Intellectual Disabilities*, forthcoming.

Grant, G., Ramcharan, P., McGrath, M., Nolan, M. and Keady, J. (1998) 'Rewards and gratifications among family caregivers: Towards a refined model of caring and coping.' *Journal of Intellectual Disability Research 42*, 1, 127–141.

Greenberg, J.S., Seltzer, M.M., and Greenley, J.R. (1993) 'Aging parents of adults with disabilities: The gratifications and frustrations of later-life caregiving.' *Gerontologist 33*, 4, 542–550.

Hawley, D. and DeHaan, L. (1996) 'Towards a definition of family resilience: Integrating lifespan and family perspectives.' *Family Process 35*, 283–298.

Hayden, M.F. and Heller, T. (1997) 'Support, problem solving/coping ability and personal burden of younger and older caregivers of adults with mental retardation.' *Mental Retardation 35*, 364–372.

Heller, T. (1993) 'Aging caregivers of persons with developmental disabilities: Changes in burden and placement desire.' In K.A. Roberto (ed) *The Elderly Caregiver: Caring for Adults with Developmental Disabilities.* Newbury Park: Sage, pp.21–38.

Heller, T., Factor, A., Sterns, H. and Sutton, E. (1996) 'Impact of person-centred later life planning training program for older adults with mental retardation.' *Journal of Rehabilitation*, Jan–Mar, 77–83.

Heller, T., Miller, A.B., and Factor, A. (1997) 'Adults and mental retardation as supports to their parents: effects on parental caregiving appraisal.' *Mental Retardation 35*, 338–346.

Hogg, J. and Lambe, L. (1998) *Older People with Learning Disabilities: A Review of the Literature on Residential Services and Family Caregiving.* London: Foundation for People with Learning Disabilities.

Hogg, J., Lucchino, R., Wang, K. and Janicki, M. (2000) *Healthy Aging – Adults with Intellectual Disabilities: Aging and Social Policy.* Geneva: World Health Organisation.

Kahana, B. and Kahana, E. (1996) 'Comments on Tobin.' In V.L. Bengston (ed) *Adulthood and Aging: Research on Continuities and Discontinuities.* New York: Springer.

Kropf, N.P. and Greene, R.R. (1993) 'Life review with families who care for developmentally disabled members: a model.' *Journal of Gerontological Social Work 21*, 1–2, 25–40.

Lazarus, R.S. and Folkman, S. (1984) *Stress, Appraisal and Coping.* New York: Springer.

McDermott, S., Tirrito, T., Valentine, D., Anderson, D., Gallup, D. and Thompson, S. (1996) 'Aging parents of adult children with mental retardation: Is age a factor in their perception of burdens or gratifications?' *Journal of Gerontological Social Work 27*, 1–2, 133–148.

McGrath, M. and Grant, G. (1993) 'The life cycle and support networks of families with a person with a learning difficulty.' *Disability, Handicap and Society 8*, 1, 25–41.

McGrother, C.W., Hauck, A., Bhaumik, S., Thorp, C. and Taub, N. (1996) 'Community care for adults with learning disability and their carers: Needs and outcomes from the Leicester register.' *Journal of Intellectual Disability Research 40*, 183–190.

Magrill, D. (1997) *Crisis Approaching: The Situation Facing Sheffield's Elderly Carers of People with Learning Disabilities.* Sheffield: Sharing Caring Project.

Nolan, M. and Grant, G. (1989) 'Addressing the needs of informal carers: A neglected area of nursing practice.' *Journal of Advanced Nursing 14*, 950–961.

O'Malley P.E. (1996) 'Group work with older people who are developmentally disabled and their caregivers.' *Journal of Gerontological Social Work 25*, 1–2, 105–119.

Oliver, M. (1996) *Understanding Disability: From Theory to Practice.* London: Macmillan.

Orr, R.R., Cameron, S.J. and Day, D.M. (1991) 'Coping with stress in families of children who have mental retardation: An evaluation of the double ABCX model.' *American Journal on Mental Retardation 95*, 444–450.

Prosser, H. (1997) 'The future care plans of older adults with intellectual disabilities living at home with family carers.' *Journal of Applied Research in Intellectual Disabilities 10*, 1, 15–32.

Prosser, H. and Moss, S. (1996) 'Informal care networks of older adults with an intellectual disability.' *Journal of Applied Research in Intellectual Disabilities 9*, 1, 17–30.

Quine, L. and Pahl, J. (1991) 'Stress and coping in mothers caring for a child with severe learning difficulties: A test of Lazarus' transactional model of coping.' *Journal of Community and Applied Social Psychology 1*, 57–70.

Racino, J.A. and Heumann, J.E. (1992) 'Independent living and community life: Building coalitions among elders, people with disabilities, and our allies.' *Generations*, winter, 43–52.

Seltzer, M.M. (1992) 'Training families to be case managers for elders with developmental disabilities.' *Generations*, winter, 65–70.

Seltzer, M.M. and Krauss, M.W. (1989) 'Aging parents with mentally retarded children: Family risk factors and sources of support.' *American Journal on Mental Retardation 94*, 303–312.

Seltzer, M.M., Krauss, M.W. and Heller, T. (1991) 'Family caregiving over the life course.' In M. Janicki and M.M. Seltzer (eds) *Proceedings of the Boston Roundtable on Research Issues and Applications in Aging and Developmental Disabilities.* Boston MA: pp.3–24.

Smith, G.C., Tobin, S.S. and Fullmer, E.M. (1995) 'Elderly mothers caring at home for offspring with mental retardation: A model of permanency planning.' *American Journal on Mental Retardation 99*, 5, 487–499.

Tobin, S.S. (1996) 'A non-normative old age contrast: Elderly parents caring for offspring with mental retardation.' In V.L. Bengston (ed) *Adulthood and Aging: Research on Continuities and Discontinuities.* New York: Springer.

Walker, C. and Walker, A. (1998) *Uncertain Futures: People with Learning Difficulties and their Ageing Family Carers.* Brighton: Pavilion and York: Joseph Rowntree Foundation.

Watson, L. and Harker, M. (1993) *Community Care Planning: A Model for Housing Need Assessment.* London: Institute of Housing and National Federation of Housing Associations.

CHAPTER 11

Stability and Change in the Later Years

The Impact of Service Provision on Older People with Intellectual Disabilities[1]

James Hogg and Loretto Lambe

Background

Throughout both the developed and developing worlds, improved health and social care have led to dramatic increases in the life expectancy of both men and women. In some western countries life expectancy has doubled during the twentieth century while those surviving to 65 years do so in better health than in the past (Kinsella and Gist 1995).

The social and medical factors leading to this improvement in longevity have also dramatically increased the lifespan of people with intellectual disabilities in the UK (Hogg, Moss and Cooke 1988) and elsewhere (Hogg *et al.* 2000). Though people with profound and multiple intellectual disabilities (Eyman, Call and White 1989), and to a lesser extent those with Down's syndrome (Eyman, Call and White 1991), tend to have a lower than average life expec-

---

1   The present chapter draws on material originally presented in Hogg, J. and Lambe, L. (1999) *Older People with Intellectual Disabilities: A Review of the Literature on Residential Services and Family Caregiving.* London: Foundation for People with Learning Disabilities. The authors wish to thank the Foundation for People with Learning Disabilities which commissioned the report for their permission to use the material in the present chapter.

tancy, a half of all of people with intellectual disabilities can now expect to live for as long as the wider population.

The impact of increased longevity on the prevalence of people with intellectual disabilities will clearly make itself felt in local administrative areas and regions, and it is this consequence which has led to a growth of interest in the subject of ageing and intellectual disability. It is important, however, to emphasize that with respect to local responses to the general demographic trend, in the next 20 years we are not dealing numerically with large increases in numbers. This may be illustrated with respect to a recent study on the epidemiology of intellectual disabilities in a single English city. Parrot *et al.* (1997) report on the increases in life expectancy of people with intellectual disabilities in the city of Sheffield. Over an 18-year period (1980–98) 64 people attained their fiftieth birthday and a further ten reached their eightieth. But when offset against deaths in the population, the number of people with intellectual disabilities aged over 60 years actually fell, both in absolute terms (from 300 to 288) and as a percentage of the total (from 12.89 per cent to 11.52 per cent). Reports from elsewhere in the UK generally show stability in the numbers of older and middle-aged people, or only modest increases (Evans *et al.* 1994). Not until the 'baby boom' generation of 1955 to 1970 reaches older age in 20 or more years are we likely to notice any appreciable increase in prevalence rates.

With respect to the proportion of people with intellectual disabilities from an ethnic minority background, this declines with age (Emerson and Hatton 1998): persons from such a background presently constitute less than 4 per cent of over-65s in the general population (Central Statistical Office 1993a, 1993b). But their numbers will undoubtedly grow over the next 20 years and the specific issues related to ageing and their own culture will have to be addressed.

The purpose of presenting these figures, however, is not to dispute that increased longevity will lead to a progressive increase during the coming years in the number of people who have intellectual disabilities over 60 years, but to note that while such an increase is to be expected, within a single locality it is gradual and does not involve dramatic surges in numbers that are inherently problematical. Taken with the data we review below on the abilities and health of older people with intellectual disabilities, we are not confronting a significant 'problem' over and above the wider need to make an increasing number of residential places available to adults with intellectual disabilities in the coming years as predicted elsewhere (Emerson *et al.* 1996; Parrott *et al.* 1997) and to ensure good quality and a wide range of choice for day opportunities.

Socially, the implication of increased longevity is that more people with intellectual disabilities than in the past will live to enjoy their later years in community settings, but will also require support comparable to that available to the wider older population. Increasing age, coupled with changing philosophies and policies will influence both the stability of their lives and sometimes profound changes in how and where they live. In order to consider such transitions, however, it is essential that we place change in the context of stability, viewing both as essentially dynamic aspects of a person's situation.

In this chapter we consider transitions that may be viewed essentially as the outcome of the person's living situation and service policies. This is not to minimize personal experiences related to change such as their own feelings about getting older, bereavement or their experience of a changing world and the possibility of personal development within it. Nor is it to imply that the family dimension, so important to all of us, is not worthy of consideration.

Here we deal with three key areas: first, with what in some ways may be viewed as the principal gateway to the later years, i.e. retirement; second, opportunities for older people with intellectual disabilities, drawing attention to their ability to benefit from services for older people generally, and the possibility of transitions to such services. We then move on to a crucial area of a person's life, where they live, and moving from one setting to another.

In contrast to a chapter on this subject in an earlier edition of this book, we here approach the subject with an age of 60 years, rather than 50 years, in mind. This decision reflects a personal view that we have tended to approach the subject of later life in people with intellectual disabilities from a perspective we would not impose on the rest of the population. True, some will show premature ageing before their sixties and age-related planning is quite legitimate. But most middle-aged people do not see themselves as being grouped in a band from 50 to 100 years – requiring something separate from 50 years onwards. We have therefore moved closer to a more conventional age for starting our consideration of later life. We would argue that at the very least people with intellectual disabilities between 50 and 60 years should be seen as adults in middle age with the same aspirations as their non-disabled peers.

Work and retirement

While employment of people with intellectual disabilities generally remains extremely limited, with respect to people over 60 years such opportunities are extremely rare. Even in a population over 50 years (Moss, Hogg and Horne 1989), no individuals in open employment were identified, and only 3.4 per cent in sheltered employment. Here, all four individuals were under the age of 60 years. Australians fare better. One study (Ashman, Suttie and Bramley 1995) reported that 8 per cent in a two-state population and 11 per cent in a national sample were fully employed. Part-time employment figures were lower, 7 per cent and 8 per cent respectively. The UK situation is perhaps unsurprising given that aggregate labour force participation by people over 55 years in the general population continues to decline in European countries (Kinsella and Gist 1995). Given the association between life satisfaction and orientation and commitment to work in people with and without intellectual disabilities reported elsewhere (Laughlin and Cotton 1994), this is a state of affairs to be regretted. Day activities for over-sixties with intellectual disabilities are therefore predominantly available in traditional day centres or increasingly realized in more dispersed, person-centred provision (Wertheimer 1996). Again, we know of no published studies focusing specifically on the development of non-centre based day activities for older people, though their involvement with this trend remains as appropriate as for younger people.

Both employment and day centre attendance have been linked to transitions from such activities with the description *'retirement'*. While in the former case this term has the same meaning as for the wider population, its meaning for someone who has attended a day service may be considered more ambiguous. Seltzer and Krauss (1987) report positively on what they refer to as *'supplemental retirement programs'* (p.85) in day service centres. In their survey they identified 30 such programmes, noting that most were clearly articulated and had the major objective of finding retirement options for individuals for whom reduction in formal programme activity was appropriate. Such options typically involved leisure pursuits, though these continued to be centre-based. Here, retirement involved the substitution of leisure activities for vocational activities within the same centre. A more radical transition considered in some UK settings (e.g. see Lambe and Hogg 1995) is for the person to leave the centre to continue life at home, a move that has been questioned (Wolfensberger 1985) and may be a threat to the elderly caregivers' ability to continue coping.

It has been reported that for a sample of older people in employment retirement presented unknown and unwanted challenges (Ashman *et al.* 1995). The factors underpinning attitudes to retirement, however, are complex and go beyond simple changes in the type of activity engaged in. Laughlin and Cotton (1994) explored attitudes to work, self and retirement in people with and without intellectual disabilities. They report marked similarities in attitudes to retirement among people with intellectual disabilities and a group of similar aged peers. Feelings of life satisfaction and preparedness for retirement were closely related, and financial preparedness, feelings about health and work attitudes all influenced attitudes to retirement. Ashman *et al.* (1995) report that older people with intellectual disabilities who had retired had not been disappointed with the change or found it unacceptable.

Preparation for retirement is a widely accepted process in the general population and Laughlin and Cotton (1994) have demonstrated its relevance to people with intellectual disabilities. Though such preparation, however, did not alter basic attitudes towards retirement or to life satisfaction. All authors concerned with this transition urge the need for pre-retirement preparation (e.g. see Ashman *et al.* 1995; Laughlin and Cotton 1994).

Projects, programmes and services

The increased interest in ageing and intellectual disability has led services to develop in two ways. On the one hand, there have been attempts to segregate people further on the basis of both age and intellectual disability, typically without reference to the individuals themselves or any attempt to explore more inclusive options. On the other, use of generic services has been undertaken, although more in the USA than the UK. Over a decade ago (Seltzer and Krauss 1987) reported 10.7 per cent of all USA community residential provision as being mixed residential programmes as well as there being appreciable access to day services for elderly people by those with intellectual disabilities. In a study undertaken within a single state, Seltzer *et al.* (1989) found that 52 per cent of services for elderly people had been accessed by people with intellectual disabilities, while in some programmes they made up at least 10 per cent of the caseload.

A distinction may be drawn between what Hogg and Moss (1993) have referred to as *'adventitious integration'* and programmatic approaches to bringing together services for people with intellectual disabilities and those for older people. The former approach is readily identifiable in the UK, while the latter has received most attention in the USA. In a study of all persons with intellectual disabilities over the age of 50 residing in or originating from one metropolitan borough in the north-west of England (Horne 1989a), 32 people unknown to providers of intellectual disabilities services were identified. Of these, 12 were living in local authority, and one other in private, accommodation for elderly people, one in social services accommodation for elderly people with physical disabilities, and three in sheltered accommodation. Thus 17 of the 32 (or 14 per cent of the total over-fifties population of people with intellectual disabilities not known to providers of learning disability services in this borough) were already residentially 'integrated'.

Horne's study did not systematically assess the quality of life of these people. Given that provision for elderly people, particularly congregate provision, can be of poor quality, integration of this sort may result in residential provision occurring adventitiously that would not be deemed acceptable by providers of intellectual disability services. Indeed, Wolfensberger (1985) was led to revise his use of the term *'normalisation'* because the poor quality of apparently 'normal' residential provision for older people did not make it acceptable for people with or without intellectual disabilities. In adopting *'social role valorisation'*, Wolfensberger was looking towards ways of life that would positively enhance the image of people with intellectual disabilities and enable them to live in a setting which would show them to be valued members of the community. Others have argued that where 'valued' services for older people are available, integration into these is feasible and desirable. The major examples of such programmatic work have been fully described (Janicki 1993; Janicki and Keefe

1992; LePore and Janicki 1990). Here successful integration of people with intellectual disabilities into generic services for elderly people, including residential provision, was demonstrated. Importantly, these publications deal in depth with the strategies for achieving successful integration and the barriers to achieving such outcomes (Janicki 1993). The attitudinal barriers to pursuing integration of both the providers of intellectual disability services and those in the ageing field, family carers' attitudes, the ageing service users' attitudes as well as those of the participants with intellectual disabilities are also described. A detailed summary appears in Moss, Lambe and Hogg (1998, pp.126–137).

A home at last?

Choice and consultation

Throughout community care plans and evolving models of service delivery, personal choice and consultation with individuals are invoked as central to planning and providing. The immediate practicalities of changing and/or improving the residential situation of people with intellectual disabilities can be at odds with these aspirations. Though there is now little doubt regarding the improved quality of life and well-being of people who have moved from institutional settings to the community, questions still exist as to how far personal choice guides providers with respect to the type of accommodation, its location and those with whom the person lives. Though most resettlement plans emphasize consultation with residents, experience of such programmes typically shows that they are in varying degrees driven by what potential providers offer, resource availability, hospital closure timetables and optimizing resources through grouping of residents. Where family care ends abruptly, similar constraints may operate even where there is proper consultation with the individual. Typically when community residential services have been put in place, investment in housing stock imposes constraints on flexible moves by the individual.

It should be added in passing that, particularly in later life, similar constraints exist for the wider population of older people where their personal financial situation precludes purchasing exactly what they wish, or where their physical and mental abilities are insufficient for them to live with the degree of independence to which they have aspired.

The limitations on individual choice in moving home are starkly captured in the words of the opening sentence of a recent report on residential transitions for older people with intellectual disabilities by the Social Services Inspectorate (1997, p.33 para. 5.39): 'Inevitably, there will be occasions when it is necessary to move people from one form of accommodation to another.' Here the essential passivity of 'being moved' is clearly signalled and this inevitably conditions the ensuing process of implementing the move which the report goes on to outline:

- clear information on why the mooted move might be appropriate
- full participation of the person and their advocates in decision making
- defining a range of options with the person and her/his advocate
- exploration of options with short stays/visits
- ensuring maintenance of existing activities and networks following the move.

While it might be unfair to suggest that these perfectly reasonable tactics involve bolting the stable door after the horse has gone, the issue which has been evaded is who makes the decision to move and under what conditions?

This extremely difficult situation of aspiring to choice for the person with intellectual disabilities and the traditional processes through which services are determined by professionals or family is a reflection of several factors. These include: the difficulty of determining the views of some people with intellectual disabilities with respect to complex decisions; the financial constraints which dictate that some preferences cannot be met within available resources; the inherent processes by which decisions are made, including the quite objective responsibilities that service providers have for the person for whom they provide; and finally, the nature of the service and type of model about which deliberations are to be made.

Choice constrained

Various influences may limit or curtail choice for older people with intellectual disabilities. Some individuals will receive their services through continuing

NHS provision, often in settings more restrictive than would be the case in the community. Though challenging and criminal behaviour decline with age (Moss 1991), we would still anticipate a few individuals over 60 years being in contact with the criminal justice system or a danger to themselves or others. Clearly comprehensive planning of services for the whole population of older people with intellectual disabilities will have to take into consideration the needs of these people.

Research into residential provision for older people with intellectual disabilities
CHANGE AND STABILITY IN THE LIVES OF PEOPLE WITH INTELLECTUAL DISABILITIES
The situation of older people with intellectual disabilities is paradoxically characterized by both extreme stability and instability, often within the lifetime of a single person, and typically influenced by policy decisions far beyond their control. Many people with intellectual disabilities will have lived in a single residential setting for many years, and it is far from unknown for them to have spent 50 years or more with their family or in a long-stay institution. This stability, however, has been seriously disturbed by two trends: the decline in the availability of family care with increasing age and the progressive reduction of places in long-stay institutions. Hogg and Moss (1993) reported that during the previous five years 37 per cent of their population of over-fifties with intellectual disabilities had moved home at least once. Similarly, May and Hogg (1997) report that 86 per cent of their community population had moved during the past 10 years and 75 per cent during the past 5 years. Of those who had moved to a community residence in the past 10 years, the largest category of such moves was within the community to residences offering increased independence (41 per cent), followed by moves from the family home (30 per cent) and from a long-stay hospital (17 per cent).

However, it has been noted (May and Hogg 1997), and the same point may be applied to Hogg and Moss's data, that this residential instability reflects 'a response to a particular, and largely time-specific, set of circumstances that is unlikely to be repeated, and as such offers little guide to future developments'. Though this is undoubtedly the case, the degree of disruption experienced does hold lessons for future planning. The majority of these transitions have been initiated either by service providers in response to policy objectives or as a result of family caregiving no longer being tenable. Though consultation with individuals may have taken place and change been in the best interest of the person, the overall picture is not one of people with intellectual disabilities being empowered to make personal choices regarding where they live in future. This aspect of choice must be central to any consideration of respect for individuality, choice and decision making.

The changing situation with respect to where people live may be illustrated by two studies that have explored the residential situation of older people with intellectual disabilities. May and Hogg (1997) found in a longitudinal study of adults with intellectual disabilities, the percentage of those living at home declined from 60 per cent in their early twenties, to 37 per cent in their forties. In the same study, a comparison was made between three cross-sectional cohorts in the age ranges: 18–23 years; 38–43 years; and 58–63 years. Overall, of 38 per cent (67/178) of individuals who lived at home with their families, all but three lived with one or both parents. As would be expected, there was a decline with age in the numbers living at home: 66 per cent at 18–23 years; 31 per cent at 38–43 years and only 6 per cent at 58–63 years. By far the best predictor of whether a person remains at home is the presence of both parents, though the survival of one parent, usually the mother, is almost as good a predictor. We will return to this point in our discussion of family care, below.

McGrother *et al.* (1996) report very similar findings: 43.5 per cent of adults with intellectual disabilities still living at home with family carers, their numbers again declining sharply with age. In their study of 2117 adults, they found only 18 over the age of 60 years still in the family home, i.e. just 0.85 per cent of the total population of adults with intellectual disabilities.

The concomitant of these figures is, of course, that with increasing age the number of people moving into residential provision accelerates. Indeed the majority of transitions from the family home will have taken place before the person with intellectual disabilities reaches 60 years.

There is a further aspect to the issue of stability that also has an important bearing on how we view the life of the person with intellectual disabilities as she or he gets older. The lives of the majority of people in society are characterized by periods of stability punctuated by highly significant transitions. While the advent of education for people with intellectual disabilities in the UK during the 1970s means that school leaving is now as much a part of their lives as other young people, the hoped for progression into employment, career development and retirement is lacking from the lives of all but a few people with intellectual disabilities. Similarly, relationships leading to marriage or a long-term partnership, having children and their growth to adulthood and their own careers and families, is typically very restricted (Seltzer 1992).

RESIDENTIAL MODELS AND OLDER PEOPLE WITH INTELLECTUAL DISABILITIES

Two distinct categories of research question with respect to residential provision for older people with intellectual disabilities can be formulated. The first category is concerned with where people live and the relation between age, the characteristics of individuals and different types of residential model. There is a sense in which such a consideration is value-free and describes the situation at a particular point in time. In contrast to such descriptive work, the second category of questions is far more complex and indeed contentious. Here subgroups of older people with intellectual disabilities are defined and the effectiveness of different types of residential model with respect to these subgroups are then investigated. Seltzer and Krauss (1987) have clearly articulated such an agenda:

> The person-environment fit concept is particularly important in light of the heterogeneity of the population of elders with mental retardation. Comparative studies of the effects of the various program types on specific subgroups of elderly mentally retarded persons are needed. This information will further our understanding of the best methods of meeting the different service needs of this heterogeneous and vulnerable population. (Seltzer and Krauss 1987, p.169)

With respect to available research studies it is evident that the first of these categories has received considerably more attention than the latter and we will shortly review them. With respect to the latter, however, there is an absence of information and indeed good reasons why the pursuit of matching subgroups of people to types of residential service is quite inappropriate. The first reason is essentially philosophical as such an approach cannot be regarded as individualized and needs-led. The second has an empirical basis in that research has now shown that it is not the category of residential provision that determines the quality of the service, but a wide range of variables related to management and operational polices. In the present review, therefore, we will consider studies identifying where older people with intellectual disabilities live, and whether there is any evidence to suggest that particular models are inherently unsuitable for them as they get older. We will then comment further on the research agenda proposed (Seltzer and Krauss 1987) in order to elaborate on the inappropriateness of such a pursuit.

The first major study on the distribution of residential provision with respect to the age of people with intellectual disabilities was Seltzer and Krauss' national (USA) survey of programmes for this population. The typology developed for this work identified: foster homes (adult placement); group homes; group homes with nurses; intermediate care facilities; apartment programmes and mixed residential programmes. We will not here define these categories (see Seltzer and Krauss 1987, pp.59–70), except to note that apartment programmes are also referred to as semi-independent living programmes and do not have 24-hour staffing, while mixed residential programmes also serve generic elderly people and people with other forms of difficulty than intellectual disability. Differences in the distribution of older people in these settings were reported, with the highest percentage in mixed programmes and the lowest in apartment houses. The latter also had the most able people in contrast to the intermediate care facilities where people with the greatest intellectual disabilities were found.

Distinct differences in programmatic aspects and correlates of contrasted types of residential provision were also reported. Thus, the mixed residential programmes approximated least to conventional intellectual disability services as they had the highest percentage of residents at home during the day without formal programmes. In contrast, intermediate care facilities offered structured programmatic activities supporting residents, including those with highly significant needs. Group houses, both with and without nursing staff, occupied an intermediate position with respect to structured programmes. Apartment programmes which approximate most closely to supported living models enabled greater access to generic elderly services, supported individuals with milder intellectual disabilities, and adopted a supportive rather than pro-gramme-orientated model of provision.

There is no comparable national UK survey of community residential provision for older people with intellectual disabilities. However, Moss *et al.* (1989) and Hogg and Moss (1993) provide a detailed picture of one metropolitan borough in which special care was taken to identify all residents with intellectual disabilities of 50 years and over, even those not known to intellectual disability services. In this population, 14 per cent lived at home with families while 24 per cent remained in long-stay hospitals. Of the remainder living in the community, 21 per cent lived in group houses or other forms of supported accommodation, 35 per cent in hostels and 6 per cent in some form of sheltered accommodation. In the decade since this study was undertaken, it may be anticipated that the balance of institutional to community provision will have moved decisively in favour of the latter, as will the reduced proportion of people in hostels relative to small community accommodation. As in the US study noted above, intellectual differences were reported with respect to residents, with those in group houses and independent settings, and those in sheltered accommodation, most able. Adaptive behaviour assessment of community competence showed a similar pattern, though with respect to personal competence (e.g. self-help abilities) hostel and family residents were the most able.

McGrother *et al.* (1996) suggest a somewhat different typology for classifying residences, consisting of: (a) NHS; (b) local authority; (c) private; (d) voluntary; (e) other residential; (f) family home; (g) at home without family. Re-analysis of the original data from this study enables some points of comparison to the findings of Moss *et al.* In the 50 years plus group, McGrother *et al.*'s data indicates that 12.6 per cent of individuals lived in the family home compared with Moss *et al.*'s 14 per cent, a remarkably similar figure. If we consider the over-sixties, the former figure is 8.3 per cent of people with intellectual disabilities. McGrother *et al.*'s figure for NHS provision of 31.5 per cent for the 50-plus group is slightly lower than Moss *et al.*'s institutional figure of 34 per cent. With respect to the former's other categories, the figures for the 50 years plus and 60 years plus groups respectively are: local authority 9.0 per cent and 5.1 per cent; private 31.2 per cent and 41.7 per cent; voluntary 6.7 per cent and 5.6 per cent; at home with no carer 8.8 and 10.2 per cent.

Both the US and UK studies cited above must be viewed as snapshots at a particular point in time, and indeed in specific locations. Against a background of progressive long-stay hospital closure (see Emerson and Hatton 1994), the balance towards community care provision has been and is continuing to shift to the latter. Though some earlier studies indicated that older people with intellectual disabilities in long-stay hospitals tended not to be selected for discharge to the community before younger residents (e.g. Hogg *et al.* 1988b), as numbers reduce an increasing number of older people has been discharged. In a study undertaken in 1997, for example, Hogg *et al.* (1997) report highly successful adjustment to living in group houses by recently discharged residents ranging in age from 26 to 81 years (mean 53 years).

It is important to acknowledge, however, that some studies have expressed concern regarding the impact on older people of relocation. In a recent review of studies on the consequences of relocation from hospital, concern has been expressed regarding the general dearth of information on its impact on physical and mental health and the lack of reference to the effect of age with respect to health (Hatton and Emerson 1996). Similarly an important US study (Strauss *et al.* 1998), while showing increased probability of mortality following relocation to the community, particularly in the immediate period following discharge, does not relate this specifically to the age of the individuals. These authors consider their findings not in terms of any argument for the continuation of institutional provision, but with respect to the development of high quality medical input in community settings – an issue that has received increasing attention in the UK (Hogg, 2000). Given the increased medical vulnerability of older people, this observation has particular relevance.

We will now return to the second proposal of the research agenda noted above: the match between specific subgroups of older people with intellectual disabilities and types of residential provision (Seltzer and Krauss 1987). We have noted that such a match is hardly reflective of a needs-led approach, but there are further arguments that may be advanced. First, research into specific models of residential provision, particularly staffed group houses, has shown that the functional aspects of the residence, e.g. management practice and staff activities, influence the quality of residents' lives, not the specific model itself. Second, the movement to community provision has been accompanied by the development and extension of a variety of models generated by differing philo-sophical responses to the strengths and weaknesses of existing models. Thus, in addition to staffed group houses, we have the supported living movement, con-tinued life in the family home following the death of family carers, adult place-ment, sheltered and very sheltered accommodation and the re-emergence of ad-vocates of village communities. Any comprehensive consideration of residential provision for older people needs to be placed within this complex framework (Emerson *et al.* 1999a, 1999b).

Staffed group houses have constituted the principal model of community residential provision for people for nearly two decades, and providers report that this is still the principal form of accommodation for older people with intel-lectual disabilities. Most studies of such provision indicate that they are no less effective settings for older people with intellectual disabilities than for their younger peers (e.g. Hogg *et al.* 1997). Indeed, in their extensive review of the lit-erature on this subject Hatton and Emerson (1996) do not allude to age as a pre-dictor of quality of life in staffed group homes. On the contrary Felce (1996) has emphasized the potential benefits arising from properly managed group houses; an outcome equally applicable to many older people if we adopt a third age perspective and what it should mean to get older in a fulfilling way.

We have not identified any studies dealing specifically with the issue of age and supported living arrangements. It is, however, in the very nature of the com-munity living philosophy that there has been no need to focus specifically on the fact of people's ages in making provision for them. Since the development of support begins with the individual's needs, then age-related needs will be taken into account as part of the needs assessment, and changing functions or abilities will be responded to accordingly. The option of remaining in a home owned by the family as home owner when family carers die or move on, as well as oppor-tunities for personal tenancies or home ownership, are natural outcomes for older people with intellectual disabilities and completely consistent with the paths followed by older people generally. Clearly an individualized life in one's own home is viewed as desirable for all older people, though as Scottish Human Services (1995) notes: 'For older people, the situation is worse, with a rapid growth in provision of nursing homes and private residential care homes and very little attention to developing flexible personal assistance services' (p.11).

Clearly for older people with intellectual disabilities the range of needs to be met will be wide and will change as an individual gets older. Given the relatively high level of competence and general absence of difficult behaviours among older people with intellectual disabilities, it may be anticipated that many will live with only the need for very limited support, and in circumstances to which they themselves aspire.

Similarly, both the philosophical and practical conditions involved in home ownership indicate that there is nothing in the arrangements described that precludes home ownership as an option for people with intellectual disabilities who are 60 years plus (King 1996). Examples of home ownership reported by King, however, do not involve people older than their mid-fifties. For some older people, home ownership will present itself as the option most likely to attain the objectives of supported living.

Research evidence with respect to adult placement is increasing, especially in the USA (Dagnan 1997; Bothwick-Duffy *et al.* 1992). Though the general findings from such research will inevitably be relevant to older people with intellectual disabilities, specific age-related issues have received little attention. Newman, Sherman and Frenkel (1985) provide one important study of people between 45 to 92 years, with a similarly broad range of intellectual disability, including profound intellectual disability. Within the family, interactions with the person with intellectual disabilities was high and the quality of relationships family-like. A number of measures of acceptance by neighbours and community participation were taken, viewed in relation to activities involving the carers as well as independent activities. In general, acceptance by neighbours was high though the level of acquaintance was relatively casual. Use of community resources was also high, including doctors' visits, shopping, going out to restaurants, churches and entertainment. Of particular importance were the characteristics of the carers as it was their own level of socializing and involvement in outside activities which predicted the person's engagement in these. With respect to the person's characteristics, it was the younger and more able who showed greater independent activity than those who were older or less able. However, age *per se* was not related to engaging in activities with carers. These authors conclude:

Family care not only provides the residents with encouragement to use the community but that the care providers actually serve as facilitators of the participation. This is particularly important for elderly residents who tend not to participate as much in activities without the providers. (Newman *et al.* 1985, p.375)

Adult placement schemes have also been widely developed in the UK, though to a lesser extent than in North America. Such schemes have typically embraced a wide age range. Figures provided by Hampshire County Council Social Services Department indicate that both older women and men have participated with 30 per cent of the total receiving this service being 60 years plus. Robinson and Simons (1996) reviewed 168 adult placement schemes interviewing a total of 42 people with intellectual disabilities ranging from 18 years of age through to their early seventies, nine of whom were 60-plus years old. As there is no specific comment on the influence of age on the success of these placement, it must be assumed that the overall conclusion drawn by these authors is equally applicable across the age range: that such placements were valued by people with intellectual disabilities. However, a minority wished to live elsewhere and little was being done to assist them in this aspiration. In addition, in some situations the values that we have discussed with respect to choice and individuality were not realized and controls inappropriate for adults were employed. Carers themselves emphasized the value of family life, the personal nature of the care, the homeliness of the environment and the lack of expense relative to residential environments. However, Robinson and Simons (1996) note that these criteria were not invariably met and in some cases there was confusion as to the caregiver's role. They also give detailed consideration to the issue of registration.

Older people with intellectual disabilities do live in various forms of sheltered and very sheltered accommodation. Horne (1989) identified three people with intellectual disabilities unknown to providers of intellectual disability services living in sheltered accommodation. Lambe and Hogg (1995) present a case study of a 59-year-old woman who was a tenant in her own self-contained flat in a very sheltered housing complex living with people with a wide range of disabilities and supported by a home carer. This woman reported a high level of satisfaction with her living situation. Despite the relatively scarce nature of such accommodation, it is an option which is consistent with the aspirations and criteria of supported living and one which brings together services for people with intellectual disabilities and those for older individuals.

With respect to village communities, and significantly for the present review, Cox and Pearson (1995) implicate the increasing population of older and ageing people with intellectual disabilities in their argument: 'Life expectancy for mentally handicapped people is increasing. This is generating greater need for care for those who would not previously have survived for so long' (p.5). In raising this issue the language employed is extraordinarily emotive to the point of hyperbole:

> Demographic trends indicate a time bomb which will explode in the near future, causing widespread suffering for many mentally handicapped people and their families. This time bomb, now ticking away, has been created by a mismatch between need and provision. (Cox and Pearson 1995, p.5)

It is of interest to note that similar language has been applied to the wider ageing population. We commented above on the gap between such rhetoric and the relatively small numbers in any given administrative area. A fuller appraisal of the advantages and disadvantages of village communities and NHS campus provision in relation to community care has recently been published (Emerson *et al.* 1999a, 1999b).

The extent to which age plays a part in the advantages or disadvantages offered by these different models has been almost entirely neglected in past studies. Nevertheless, it can reasonably be assumed that older people with intellectual disabilities are as likely to be subjected to these negative trends as they are to have benefited from the positive gains in quality of life that the move towards small group living has enabled. Good practice at policy development, management and practice levels are therefore of critical importance to the well-being of older people and underpin all small-scale models.

THE WIDER SPECTRUM

The residential models described above, together with provision in the family home, will serve the majority of older people with intellectual disabilities. Though there is no research specifically in relation to older people with intellectual disabilities, attention must also be drawn to other minorities within this minority, specifically homeless people and those who may have come into contact with the criminal justice system or viewed as 'mentally disordered'.

Technically, the 'homeless' refers to people who find themselves on the street, in a squat, in a hostel, in bed and breakfast accommodation, or in prison or hospital awaiting discharge without a home of their own to go to, whether alone or with family friends. More typically, 'homeless' is used to refer to 'rough sleepers'. Reed (1992, p.85), cites the Governmental Statistical Service as stating that of 38,460 households officially accepted as homeless in the first quarter of 1992, 4 per cent belonged to the priority need category of those 'vulnerable as a result of mental illness or mental handicap'. It is also noted that among these are 'mentally disordered offenders'. No breakdown of homeless people with mental illness as opposed to intellectual disabilities is available and the possibility of the co-occurrence of both conditions (i.e. 'dual diagnosis') is probably high. In focusing in this report on the more visible individuals who spend their lives well within the ambit of social and health services, it is important not to lose sight of this small but particularly vulnerable group of disadvantaged people, though there is no information on the age of homeless people with intellectual disabilities or the proportion of them over the age of 60 years.

In addition, a small number of older people with intellectual disabilities will be held in secure accommodation or in prison, following contact with the criminal justice system. The prevalence of people with intellectual disabilities in prison, however, is known to be low (Kiernan and Alborz 1989). It has been estimated that there are about 400 prisoners with intellectual disabilities in England, a figure that would suggest about 40 such people in Scottish prisons (Gunn, Maden and Swinton 1991). There are no age breakdowns in these studies, though the decline in problematical behaviour from middle age (Moss 1991) would indicate numbers are low. With respect to gender, Gunn *et al.*'s study shows that women with intellectual disabilities outnumber men in prison by 2: 1. Though again the number of women with intellectual disabilities in prison will not be high, it has been commented on in relation to female offenders: 'Small numbers don't mean small problems' (Chesney-Lind 1997, p.87), an observation that is highly applicable in the present context. Certainly the issue of gender, intellectual disability and imprisonment merits further exploration.

Conclusions

In the past, concern has been expressed that people with intellectual disabilities as they get older are in danger of being disadvantaged twice over, not only because of their disabilities, but also because of their age. Because those in receipt of services in their middle years tend to continue receiving support into their later life, this view is generally incorrect. However, in responding to the dimension of age, social workers and other service providers are in danger of imposing inappropriate age-related concepts on those they provide for. Following the research, providers have tended to view 50 years of age as the point at which ageing becomes an issue. From 50 we are supposed to want a quieter life, Radio 2 rather than Radio 1, older companions, and so on. However, this choice of age is a very non-normative one. Even taking a conventional retirement age would move this on by 15 years, while at the time of writing British Telecom are seriously contemplating a retirement age of 70 years in order to make best use of experience and the human resources it has at its disposal. On a number of occasions this threshold has been used to set up intellectual disability services for the over-fifties.

At issue, however, is the need to determine and meet need in a way that is sensitive to the consequences of ageing, but does not impose a service based on possibly inaccurate assumptions about the implications of age on an individual. Service providers should listen and offer choice and take their direction for facilitating opportunities in the community in the same way that they would for much younger or middle-aged people. This applies equally to residential provision and day opportunities where exactly the same principles apply across the age range. When age-related change does necessitate a move to a different form of accommodation or an alteration to day provision, it is equally important that individual need and choice are the primary guides. The automatic move to a nursing home when someone becomes frail or develops dementia (really or apparently) has to be challenged unless this can be shown to be in the person's best interests.

As with those of us in the general population, the person's health needs to be monitored and where necessary illness treated. There is now a considerable literature on the subject of intellectual disability and health status in the later years, and all staff need to be aware of how to respond to signs of ill health.

Getting older, and perhaps living into extreme old age, are realities for all of us. Despite the pervasive negative imagery and attitudes to older people in western societies – and increasingly elsewhere – older age may be viewed as an opportunity to enjoy life and develop further. Such a view should underpin our approach to older people with intellectual disabilities. Though the course of their life is very likely to have been atypical (few have married and have children to support them in later life, networks of friends are often impoverished, and they will rarely have had a career comparable to that enjoyed by many), their later years offer them similar opportunities and challenges as those presented to the rest of us.

References

Ashman, A.F., Suttie, J.N. and Bramley, J. (1995) 'Employment, retirement and elderly persons with an intellectual disability.' *Journal of Intellectual Disability Research 39*, 107–115.

Bothwick-Duffy, S.A., Widaman, K.F., Little, T.D. and Eyman, R. (1992) 'Foster family care for persons with mental retardation.' *Monographs of the American Association on Mental Retardation, 17.*

Central Statistical Office (1993a) *Monthly Digest of Statistics (Annual Supplement)*. Vol. 565, January. London: HMSO.

Central Statistical Office (1993b) *Regional Trends*. Vol. 28. London: HMSO.

Chesney-Lind, M. (1997) *The Female Offender: Girls, Women and Crime*. London: Sage.

Cox, C. and Pearson, M. (1995) *Made to Care: The Case for Residential and Village Communities for People with a Mental Handicap*. London: Rannoch Trust.

Dagnan, D. (1997) 'Family placement schemes offering long-term care for adults with learning disabilities: A review of the evaluation literature.' *Disability and Society 12*, 593–604.

Emerson, E. and Hatton, C. (1994) *Moving Out: The Impact of Relocation from Hospital to Community on the Quality of Life of People with Learning Disabilities*. London: HMSO.

Emerson, E. and Hatton, C. (1998) 'Residential provision for people with intellectual disabilities in England, Wales and Scotland.' *Journal of Applied Research in Intellectual Disability 10*, 250–253.

Emerson, E., Cullen, C., Hatton, C. and Cross, B. (1996) *Residential Provision for People with Learning Disabilities: Summary report*. Manchester: Hester Adrian Research Centre, University of Manchester.

Emerson, E., Robertson, J., Gregory, N., Hatton, C., Kessissoglou, S., Hallam, A., Knapp, M., Järbrink, K., Netten, A. Walsh, P.N. (1999a) *A Comparative Analysis of Quality and Costs in Village Communities, Residential Campuses and Dispersed Housing Schemes*. Manchester: Hester Adrian Research Centre, University of Manchester.

Emerson, E., Robertson, J., Gregory, N., Kessissoglou, S., Hatton, C., Hallam, A., Knapp, M., Järbrink, K. and Netten, A. (1999b) *An Observational Study of Supports Provided to People with Severe and Complex Learning Disabilities in Residential Campuses and Dispersed Housing Schemes.* Manchester: Hester Adrian Research Centre, University of Manchester.

Evans, G., Todd, S., Beyer, S., Felce, D. and Perry, J. (1994) 'Assessing the impact of the All-Wales Mental Handicap Strategy: A survey of four districts.' *Journal of Intellectual Disability Research 38,* 109–133.

Eyman, R.K., Call, T.L. and White, J.F. (1989) 'Mortality of elderly mentally retarded persons in California.' *Journal of Applied Gerontology 8,* 203–215.

Eyman, R.K., Call, T. and White, J.F. (1991) 'Life expectancy of persons with Down syndrome.' *American Journal of Mental Retardation 95,* 603–612.

Felce, D. (1996) 'Quality of support for ordinary living.' In J. Mansell and K. Ericcson (eds) *Deinstitutionalization and Community Living: Intellectual Disability Services in Britain, Scandinavia and the USA.* London: Chapman & Hall, pp.117–133.

Gunn, M., Maden, A. and Swinton, M. (1991) *Mentally Disordered Prisoners.* London: HMSO.

Hatton, C. and Emerson, E. (1996) Residential Provision for People with Learning Disabilities: A Research Review. Manchester: Hester Adrian Research Centre, University of Manchester.

Hogg, J. (2000) *Improving Essential Healthcare for People with Learning Disabilities: Strategies for Success.* Dundee: White Top Research Unit, University of Dundee.

Hogg, J. and Moss, S. (1993) 'Characteristics of older people with intellectual disabilities in England.' In N.W. Bray (ed) *International Review of Research in Mental Retardation.* Vol. 19. London: Academic Press, pp.71–96

Hogg, J., Lucchino, R., Wang, L. and Janicki, M. (2000) *Health Issues and Practices Relative to Ageing Persons with Intellectual and Developmental Disabilities: Social Policy.* Geneva: World Health Organisation (WHO) and International Association for the Scientific Study of Intellectual Disabilities.

Hogg, J., Malek, M., Gillies, B. and Busby, S. (1997) *Final Report: Part 1 The Lennox Castle Hospital Discharge Programme, Expectations and Outcomes.* Glasgow: Greater Glasgow Health Board Learning Disability Strategy.

Hogg, J., Moss, S. and Cooke, D. (1988) *Ageing and Mental Handicap.* London: Croom Helm.

Horne, M. (1989) *Identifying a 'Hidden' Population of Older Adults with Mental Handicap: The Outreach Study in Oldham: A Demographic Study of Older People with Mental Handicap in Oldham Metropolitan Borough – Part 4.* Manchester: Hester Adrian Research Centre, University of Manchester.

Janicki, M.P. (1993) *Building the Future: Planning and Community Development in Aging and Developmental Disabilities,* 2nd edn. Albany NY: New York State Office of Mental Retardation and Developmental Disabilities.

Janicki, M.P. and Keefe, R.M. (1992) *Integration Experiences Casebook: Program Ideas in Aging and Developmental Disabilities.* Albany NY: New York State Office of Mental Retardation and Developmental Disabilities.

Kiernan, C.C. and Alborz, A. (1989) *People with Mental Handicap who Offend.* Manchester: Hester Adrian Research Centre, University of Manchester.

King, N. (1996) *Ownership Options: A Guide to Home Ownership Options for People with Learning Disabilities.* London: National Federation of Housing Associations.

Kinsella, K. and Gist, Y.J. (1995) *Older Workers, Retirement and Pensions: A Comparative International Chartbook.* Washington DC: Bureau of the Census.

Lambe, L. and Hogg, J. (1995) *Their Face to the Wind: Service Developments for Older People with Learning Disabilities in Grampian Region.* Glasgow: Enable.

Laughlin, C. and Cotton, P.D. (1994) 'Efficacy of a pre-retirement planning intervention for ageing individuals with mental retardation.' *Journal of Intellectual Disability Research 38,* 317–328.

LePore, P. and Janicki, M. (1990) *The Wit to Win: How to Integrate Older Persons with Developmental Disabilities into Community Aging Programs.* Albany NY: New York State Office of Mental Retardation and Developmental Disabilities.

McGrother, C.W., Hauck, A., Bhaumik, S., Thorp, C. and Taub, N. (1996) 'Community care for adults with learning disability and their carers: Needs and outcomes from the Leicester register.' *Journal of Intellectual Disability Research 40,* 183–190.

May, D. and Hogg, J. (1997) *Experiencing Adulthood: Age-related Needs and Quality of Life of People with Learning Disabilities and their .* Final Report Project to the Scottish Office Grant no. K/OP/2/2D105. Dundee: University of Dundee.

Moss, S.C. (1991) 'Age and functional abilities of people with a mental handicap: Evidence from the Wessex mental handicap register.' *Journal of Mental Deficiency Research 35,* 430–445.

Moss, S., Hogg, J. and Horne, M. (1989) *Residential Provision and Service Patterns in a Population of People over the Age of 50 Years and with Severe Intellectual Impairment: A Demographic Study of Older People with Mental Handicap in Oldham Metropolitan Borough – Part 2.* Manchester: Hester Adrian Research Centre, University of Manchester.

Moss, S., Lambe, L. and Hogg, J. (1998) *Ageing Matters: Pathways for Older People with Learning Disabilities: Managers' Readers.* Kidderminster: BILD Publications.

Newman, E.S., Sherman, S.R. and Frenkel, E.R. (1985) 'Foster family care: A residential alternative for mentally retarded older persons.' In M.P. Janicki and H.M. Wisniewski (eds) *Ageing and Developmental Disabilities: Issues and Approaches.* Baltimore MD: Paul H. Brookes, pp.367–377.

Parrott, R., Emerson, E., Hatton, C. and Wolstenholme, J. (1997) *Future Demand for Residential Provision for People with Learning Disabilities.* Manchester: Hester Adrian Research Centre, University of Manchester.

Reed, J. (1992) *Review of Health and Social Services for Mentally Disordered Offenders and Others Requiring Similar Services: Final Summary Report.* London: HMSO.

Robinson, C. and Simons, K. (1996) *In Safe Hands: Quality and Regulation in Adult Placements Services for People with Learning Disabilities.* Sheffield: University of Sheffield Joint Unit for Social Services Research Monographs.

Scottish Human Services (1995) *Community Living: Implications for People and Agencies.* Edinburgh: Scottish Human Services.

Seltzer, M.M. (1992) 'Aging in persons with developmental disabilities.' In J.E. Birren, R.B. Sloane and G.D. Cohen (eds) *Handbook of Mental Health and Aging*, 2nd edn. London: Academic Press, pp.583–599.

Seltzer, M.M. and Krauss, M.W. (1987) *Aging and Mental Retardation: Extending the Continuum.* Washington DC: American Association on Mental Retardation.

Seltzer, M.M., Krauss, M.W., Litchfield, L.C. and Modlish, N.J. (1989) 'Utilization of aging network services by elderly persons with mental retardation.' *Gerontologist 29*, 234–238.

Social Services Inspectorate (1997) *Services for Older People with Learning Disabilities.* London: Department of Health.

Strauss, D., Shavelle, R., Baumeister, A. and Anderson, T.W. (1998) 'Mortality in persons with developmental disabilities after transfer into community care.' *American Journal on Mental Retardation 102*, 569–581.

Wertheimer, A. (1996) *Changing Days: Developing New Day Opportunities with People who have Learning Difficulties.* London: King's Fund.

Wolfensberger, W. (1985) 'An overview of social role valorisation and some reflections on elderly mentally retarded persons.' In M. Janicki and H.M. Wisniewski (eds) *Ageing and Developmental Disabilities: Issues and Approaches.* Baltimore MD: Paul H. Brookes, pp.61–76.

The Contributors

Dorothy Atkinson is a senior lecturer in the School of Health and Social Welfare at the Open University. Her background in social work includes several years' experience working with people with intellectual disabilities. She is co-editor of the *British Journal of Learning Disabilites*. Her research interests include the use of oral and life history work with people with intellectual disabilities.

Gordon Grant is Professor of Cognitive Disability at the School of Nursing and Midwifery, University of Sheffield, and Doncaster and South Humber Healthcare NHS Trust. His main research interests concern family caregiving across the life course, participatory and emancipatory research with people with intellectual disabilities, and social inclusion.

James Hogg is Professor of Profound Disabilities and Director of the White Top Research Unit in the Department of Social Work at the University of Dundee. For the past 15 years he has undertaken research and service development in the field of ageing and intellectual disability, recently completing a major report on social policy in this area for the World Health Organisation.

Loretto Lambe is the co-founder and Director of PAMIS (Profound and Multiple Impairment Service). She has worked in the voluntary sector for the past 25 years, developing services for family carers and undertaking research into ageing and intellectual disability.

David May is a senior lecturer in Sociology iat the University of Dundee, where he teaches both medical and social work students. He has in the past carried out research in delinquency, the organization of juvenile justice, nursing and mental illness, but in recent years he has focused on intellectual disability, with special reference to adolescence and emerging adulthood. He was co-editor, with the late Gordon Horobin, of an earlier volume in the series: *Living with Mental Handicap*.

Carol Robinson is Reader in Social Policy at the Norah Fry Research Centre, University of Bristol. Her main research interests are the rights of disabled children to effective support services. She has conducted numerous research projects in this field and has written books and articles on the subject. Carol was a social worker with Essex County Council before joining the University of Bristol in 1980.

Billie Shepperdson is a Research Fellow at the Nuffield Community Care Studies Unit, University of Leicester. She has recently carried out work on health and social care for older people, and is currently following up one of the cohorts of people with Down's syndrome in South Wales discussed in Chapter 4 of this book, to compare with the progress of people in an earlier cohort.

Murray K. Simpson is a lecturer in the Department of Social Work at the University of Dundee. Research interests include the study of discourse and power in intellectual disability. Publications have covered historical and theoretical aspects of intellectual disability, as well as offending and alcohol use among people with intellectual disabilities.

George O.B. Thomson is Professor of Educational Psychology at the University of Edinburgh. His research interests include assessment practices in identifying educational support needs. Professor Thomson has just completed a longitudinal study of individuals with such needs in transition to the post-school world of work, the labour market and adulthood.

Patricia Noonan Walsh lectures in the Clinical Psychology doctoral programme at the National University of Ireland, Dublin, where she is Director of the Centre for the Study of Developmental Disabilities. Her research interests include ageing, gender issues, quality of life and inclusive employment. She contributed to the reports on 'Ageing and Intellectual Disabilities – Improving Longevity and promoting Healthy Ageing' published by the World Health Organization and IASSIS – International Association for the Scientific Study of Intellectual Disability (2000).

Subject Index

Author Index